Collectors' Coins - Decimal Issues of the United Kingdom

(Formerly Check Your Change)

By C H Perkins.

AF166729

10th Edition © October 2024

ISBN: 978-0-901170-43-9

This title is available as an eBook edition and some of its price data is also part of the 'Check Your Change' app.

A comprehensive UK decimal coin catalogue with values, descriptions and photographs

Special thanks to Lee Holt for his tireless research, Candice Clews, Peter Joseph Halford, Sarah Grant and others.

Dedicated to Kelly Christine Bishop, 1978 - 2024.

COIN PUBLICATIONS

coinpublications.com

020 308 69996

TABLE OF CONTENTS

INTRODUCTION

OBVERSES

LISTINGS

INTRODUCTION

Welcome to the "Collectors' Coins - Decimal Issues of the UK" 2024 edition. This inexpensive book, with listings and colour pictures of every circulated decimal coin type (and a lot more) should provide an excellent guide to modern coinage and as such, should aid existing collectors and hopefully stimulate new ones.

Decimal coinage first appeared fifty-six years ago and has become increasingly popular over the last few years. People want authoritative information without the urban myths, rumours and influence of media hype. This book has evolved over more than fifty years to provide that information.

NEW IN 2024

The new King and more specifically the glut of commemorative (and various franchise tie-in) coins continue to pose a problem within these cramped pages. To provide more space, the obverse types for all of the lowest denominations (half penny to ten pence) and the old round pound coins are now shown only once, instead of repeating them at the beginning of each denomination. This saves a little space, but this book is still 16 pages larger than the previous edition.

There has been a longer-than-normal wait for this new edition to be published, the reason is that I felt publication towards the end of a calendar year makes more sense than at the beginning of the year.

Non-commemorative coins bearing King Charles III are slowly making their way into circulation, in fact the mintage numbers for 2023 have just been made available in early October 2024. For the 8th consecutive year there have been no £2 coins struck for circulation and many of the 2023 dated definitives have been produced in fairly low numbers, especially the Salmon 50p which will probably go silly on online selling websites - in fact it already has, before I'd even finished this sentence! When and if it settles down to a realistic level will probably depend on how many tabloids and click-bait websites pick up on the 'low' mintage number!

For our large Facebook group: Search there for 'Check Your Change'. Info on the Check Your Change app is detailed on the inside front cover. Thank-you to each and every book owner, group member and app user for your support!

Christopher Henry Perkins, October 2024.
checkyourchange.co.uk

USING THIS BOOK

The values listed in this catalogue are the result of many hours of compiling and comparing sale prices from a few sources. For some items, there is such a limited number of transactions on which to base the values that they may seem conservative. Others may seem to high - remember, all coins are essentially worth what someone else is willing to pay for them, and that worth can change fairly quickly.

For coins that have consistent extra value in used condition, a 'Used' value is shown. Sometimes other coins can sell for more than face value in 'Used' condition, it all depends on how badly someone needs it and how much they are willing to pay for the convenience of not having to go through their own change to find one.

MINTAGES

The numbers given as mintages are based on information available from many sources, including other reference works, online sources, and the Royal Mint. The accuracy of these numbers is by no means guaranteed, and modifications may be made as better information becomes available. It should also be noted that for some of the most recent special issues, the mintages given are the "maximum mintages", and the actual number of pieces struck may be currently unknown. Again, updates will be made when new information is available.

COIN GRADES

The listings in this catalogue contain three or four values, where applicable. These are as follows:

Used - A coin from circulation with normal wear and the usual bumps and scrapes from use. Most coins are just worth face value in used condition but for those that consistently sell for more than face value a 'Used' value is shown.

Uncirculated (UNC) - Sometimes referenced within the text - A coin that appears as it did when it left the Mint. There will be no signs of wear or handling. It may show minimal "bag marks", as is common for mass-produced coins. It should be free of other major faults and in an ideal world you'd also expect the dies that were used to strike the coin to have been in good condition and free from signs of excessive use.

As-New (formerly 'BU') - A coin in as-new condition with full or virtually full mint-lustre, i.e. brilliance. For older decimal coins, pre approx 2002-ish it is possible (but quite difficult) to find very well kept circulation issue coins that are practically flawless and what I would deem 'as-new' - with excellent surfaces and full mint lustre. In fact some older circulation coins seem to be of higher quality than modern coins in BU packaging (manufacturing standards were considerably higher then it would seem)! More recent coins struck to the Royal Mint 'Brilliant Uncirculated' standard (without any damage or signs of use) can also be considered 'as-new' in most cases.

Proof - A coin struck from specially prepared coin dies on a specially prepared metal blank. Because of this extra care, Proofs usually exhibit much sharper detail and have mirror-like blank flat areas (technically called the 'fields'). Some proof coins show frosted design details and such coins with contrasting raised design elements and mirror-like fields are sometimes called 'cameo', a term that originated in the USA.

PRECIOUS METAL VALUES

The price of gold influences the gold coin prices quoted in this book. The prices quoted here are based on a gold value of about £2,020.00 per ounce or £65,000.00 per kilogramme. The value of silver is currently £24.40 per ounce or £780.00 per kilogramme.

This two-page spread shows the obverse types used for the lower denomination coins - half penny to ten pence and also the round one pound coins. The images are larger than actual size for better clarity.

OBVERSES

OBVERSE 1
(used 1971 - 1984)
D•G•REG•F•D•(date) || ELIZABETH II
Elizabeth II, Dei Gratia Regina, Fidei Defensor
(Elizabeth II, By the Grace of God Queen and Defender of the Faith)
Portrait by: Arnold Machin

OBVERSE 2
(used 1985 - 1997)
ELIZABETH II || D•G•REG•F•D•(date)
Elizabeth II, Dei Gratia Regina, Fidei Defensor
(Elizabeth II, By the Grace of God Queen and Defender of the Faith)
Portrait by: Raphael Maklouf

OBVERSE 2B

Similar to previous but smaller in size and used to differentiate the reduced size 5p (introduced 1990) and 10p (introduced 1992).

OBVERSE 3
(used 1998 - 2008)
ELIZABETH•II•D•G || REG•F•D•(date)
Elizabeth II, Dei Gratia Regina, Fidei Defensor
(Elizabeth II, By the Grace of God Queen and Defender of the Faith)
Portrait by: Ian Rank-Broadley

OBVERSE 4 (similar to last, with no rim beading. Used with the new-style shield section reverses)
(used 2008 - 2015)
ELIZABETH•II•D•G || REG•F•D•(date)
Elizabeth II, Dei Gratia Regina, Fidei Defensor
(Elizabeth II, By the Grace of God Queen and Defender of the Faith)
Portrait by: Ian Rank-Broadley

OBVERSES - continued

OBVERSE 5
(used 2015 - 2022)
ELIZABETH II•DEI•GRA•REG•FID•DEF•(date)
Elizabeth II, Dei Gratia Regina, Fidei Defensor
(Elizabeth II, By the Grace of God Queen and Defender of the Faith)
Portrait by: Jody Clark

OBVERSE 6
(used 2023 onwards)
CHARLES III•DEI•GRA•REX•FID•DEF•(date)
Charles III, Dei Gratia Rex, Fidei Defensor
(Charles III, By the Grace of God King and Defender of the Faith)
Portrait by: Martin Jennings

What's currently legal tender?

No half pennies are legal tender. They were demonetised on the 31st December 1984. Banks do theoretically accept them, but some require a minimum total amount of £5 and some refuse them outright.

Which are hard to find?

The 1972 coin was made as a proof only and was only included in proof sets, so is harder to find. The last coin, dated 1984 was also made for proof and BU sets only.

REVERSES

REVERSE 1
(used 1971 - 1981)
Regal Crown
½ NEW PENNY
Design by: Christopher Ironside

REVERSE 2
(used 1982 - 1984)
Regal Crown
½ HALF PENNY
Design by: Christopher Ironside

TYPE 1 (obverse 1, reverse 1)

			Used	As-New	Proof
1971	1,394,188,250		FV	£0.20	£2.00
1972	107,807	Proof Only	£1.00		£5.00
1973	365,680,000		FV	£0.20	£2.00
1974	365,448,000		FV	£0.20	£2.00
1975	197,600,000		FV	£0.20	£2.00
1976	412,172,000		FV	£0.20	£2.00
1977	66,368,000		FV	£0.20	£2.00
1978	59,532,000		FV	£0.20	£2.00
1979	219,132,000		FV	£0.20	£2.00
1980	202,788,000		FV	£0.20	£2.00
1981	46,748,000		FV	£0.20	£2.00

TYPE 2 (obverse 1, reverse 2)

			Used	As-New	Proof
1982	190,752,000		FV	£0.20	£2.00
1983	7,600,000		FV	£0.20	£2.00
1984	265,340	Proof/ BU sets only	£1.00	£5.00	£5.00

What's currently legal tender?

All 1p coins are legal tender. Merchants are allowed by law to refuse payments made in 1p or 2p coins if the combined total value of the 'coppers' is more than 20p in any one transaction.

Which are hard to find?

1972 coins were made as proofs only and were only included in proof sets, so are not likely to be found in circulation. 2018 and 2019 coins were made for BU and proof sets only, so are also unlikely to appear in circulation. 1992 and 1999 dated coins made of bronze (non magnetic) were also never circulated and are not usually found in circulation. See the end of this penny section for details on portcullis reverse varieties.

REVERSES

REVERSE 1
(used 1971 - 1981)
Crowned portcullis
[A portcullis with chains royally crowned]
NEW PENNY 1
Design by: Christopher Ironside

REVERSE 2
(used 1982 - 2008 and for 2018 silver pennies)
Crowned portcullis
[A portcullis with chains royally crowned]
ONE PENNY 1
Design by: Christopher Ironside

REVERSE 3
(used 2008 - 2022)
Lower left section of the Royal coat of Arms of the
United Kingdom.
ONE PENNY
Design by: Matthew Dent

REVERSE 4
(used 2023 onwards)
Dormouse laying on two leaves
1 PENNY
Design by: Royal Mint in-house

20.32 mm • 3.56 grammes • bronze • plain edge

TYPE 1 (obverse 1, reverse 1)

			Used	As-New	Proof
1971	1,521,666,250		FV	£0.20	£2.00
1972	107,807	Proof Only (from sets)	£1.00		£6.00
1973	280,196,000		FV	£1.00	£4.00
1974	330,892,000		FV	£1.00	£3.00
1975	221,604,000		FV	£1.00	£3.00
1976	300,160,000		FV	£1.00	£3.00
1977	285,430,000		FV	£1.50	£3.00
1978	292,770,000		FV	£1.00	£3.00
1979	459,000,000		FV	£1.50	£3.00
1980	416,304,000		FV	£1.50	£3.00
1981	301,800,000		FV	£1.50	£3.00

TYPE 2 (obverse 1, reverse 2)

		Used	As-New	Proof
1982	100,292,000	FV	£1.50	£4.00
1983	243,002,000	FV	£1.00	£4.00
1984	154,759,625	FV	£1.50	£3.00

TYPE 3 (obverse 2, reverse 2)

			Used	As-New	Proof
1985	200,605,245		FV	£1.50	£3.00
1986	369,989,130		FV	£1.50	£3.00
1987	499,946,000		FV	£1.50	£3.00
1988	793,492,000		FV	£1.50	£3.00
1989	658,142,000		FV	£1.50	£3.00
1990	529,047,500		FV	£1.50	£3.00
1991	206,457,600		FV	£1.50	£3.00
1992	155,426 ‡	Bronze	FV	£5.00	£7.00

TYPE 4 (obverse 2, reverse 2)
From now on, made of copper-plated steel (which is slightly magnetic)

		Used	As-New	Proof
1992	253,867,000	FV	£1.500	-
1993	602,590,000	FV	£2.00	£3.00
1994	843,834,000	FV	£1.50	£3.00
1995	303,314,000	FV	£1.50	£3.00
1996	723,840,060	FV	£1.50	£3.00
1997	396,874,000	FV	£2.00	£3.00

TYPE 5 (obverse 3, reverse 2)

			Used	As-New	Proof
1998	739,770,000		FV	£1.50	£3.00
1999	891,392,000	(‡¹ also in bronze)	FV	£1.50	£3.00
2000	1,060,420,000		FV	£1.50	£3.00
2001	928,698,000		FV	£1.50	£3.00
2002	601,446,000		FV	£2.00	£3.00
2003	539,436,000		FV	£1.50	£3.00
2004	739,764,000		FV	£1.50	£3.00
2005	536,318,000		FV	£1.50	£3.00
2006	524,605,000		FV	£1.50	£3.00
2007	548,002,000		FV	£1.50	£3.00
2008	180,600,000		FV	£1.50	£3.00

TYPE 6 (obverse 4, reverse 3)

		Used	As-New	Proof
2008 ‡²	507,952,000	FV	£1.50	£3.00
2009	556,412,800	FV	£1.50	£3.00
2010	609,603,000	FV	£1.50	£3.00
2011	431,004,000	FV	£1.50	£3.00
2012	227,201,000	FV	£1.50	£3.00
2013	260,800,000	FV	£1.50	£3.00
2014	464,801,520	FV	£1.50	£4.00
2015	154,600,000	FV	£2.00	£4.00

TYPE 7 (obverse 5, reverse 3)

		Used	As-New	Proof
2015	418,201,016	FV	£3.00	£5.00
2016	368,482,000	FV	£1.50	£5.00
2017	240,990,600	FV	£1.50	£4.00
2018	29,909	Available in sets only	£9.00	£10.00
2019	30,098	Available in sets only	£9.00	£10.00
2020	88,071,910	FV	£1.50	£4.00
2021	56,000,000	FV	£3.00	£5.00
2022	30,000,000	FV	£3.00	£4.00

TYPE 8 (obverse 6, reverse 4, Charles III)

			As-New	Proof
2023	600,000		£3.00	£5.00
2023	Crown privy mark*	Available in sets only	£3.00	£5.00
2024	Not yet known	Currently available in sets only	£3.00	£5.00

* 2023 coins made available in annual sets all feature a crown 'privy mark' behind the King's head. See page 37.

Special Sterling Silver Coins (Type 6 to 2015)

Sterling Silver pennies struck by the Royal Mint, marketed as gifts for new born babies from 2009 onwards. Originally they were identical to Type 6 on the previous page. From 2018 the reverse was changed to feature the date under an earlier style portcullis design (in place of the '1') and not on the obverse. Changes to the design of the regular circulation penny are not reflected on their silver counterparts. Different styles of packaging have been offered over the years.

			BU
1996	Unknown	Silver coin, originally part of a set	£20.00
2009	8,467	All below prices inc. original packaging	£15.00
2010	9,701		£15.00
2011			£15.00
2012	5,548		£15.00
2013	8,920	Plus 1,679 definitive silver pennies?	£14.00
2014 & 2015		Royal Mint, price new	£30.00
2016	Type 7	Royal Mint, price new	£30.00
2017	Type 7	Royal Mint, price new	£30.00
2018	Reverse 2	Royal Mint, price new (2 pack types)	£15/£30
2019	Reverse 2, date below	Royal Mint, price new	£15/£30
2020	?	Royal Mint, price new	exists?
2021	799	Royal Mint, price new	£30.00
2022	1,715	Royal Mint, price new	£30.00
2023	CIII	Royal Mint, price new	£30.00
2024	CIII	Royal Mint, price new	£22.00

NOTES

‡1   In 1992, a change in alloy was made from bronze to copper-plated steel. In 1992 the original bronze planchets were only used for the BU Mint folders and Proof sets. The copper-plated steel planchets were used for circulation strikes only. The same thing happened in 1999 when bronze blanks were used in proof and BU sets.

‡2   The Dent reverse 2008 1p has been reported to exist with 180 degree (inverted) die alignment.

There are varieties of 1p coins that concern the rivets on the portcullis. It seems that for some years the coins in the BU sets (and proofs) were struck using different dies, resulting in two different types. Both types of rivets (either circles as shown in the right image or dots as seen in the left image) occur for the following portcullis reverse coins: '86, '88, '89, '90, '92, '93, '07, '08.

What's currently legal tender?

All 2p coins are legal tender. Merchants are allowed by law to refuse payments made in 1p or 2p coins if the combined total value of the 'coppers' is more than 20p in any one transaction.

Which are hard to find?

The change from using bronze to using copper-plated steel led to a couple of scarcer types - The 1992 coin made of bronze (i.e. non magnetic) is much scarcer than the 1992 coin made of copper-plated steel due to the former only being used for coins in BU and proof sets. Both bronze and copper-plated steel were also used in 1998, although both types seem fairly common. 2018 to 2020 coins were only issued in sets, i.e. none were circulated.

By far the rarest and most expensive 2p is the 1983 error coin, which has 'NEW PENCE' on the reverse, instead of 'TWO PENCE'. This mistake just affects the 1983 2p; no other dates are affected. The error coins went into some BU sets and were not generally circulated.

REVERSES

REVERSE 1
(used 1971 - 1981 and for the error 1983 coin)
Plumes in Coronet
[OFFICIALLY: The Badge of the Prince of Wales, with his motto ICH DIEN]
NEW PENCE 2
Design by: Christopher Ironside

REVERSE 2
(used 1982 - 2008)
Plumes in Coronet
[OFFICIALLY: The Badge of the Prince of Wales, with his motto ICH DIEN]
TWO PENCE 2
Design by: Christopher Ironside

REVERSE 3
(used 2008 - 2022)
Upper right section of the Royal coat of Arms of the United Kingdom.
TWO PENCE
Design by: Matthew Dent

REVERSE 4
(used 2023 onwards)
Red Squirrel.
2 PENCE
Design by: Royal Mint in-house

TYPE 1 (obverse 1, reverse 1)

			Used	As-New	Proof
1971	1,454,856,250		FV	£0.30	£2.00
1972	107,807	Proof Only (from sets)	Used: £2.00		£4.50
1973	75,424	Proof Only (from sets)	Used: £2.00		£8.00
1974	72,355	Proof Only (from sets)	Used: £2.00		£5.00
1975	145,545,000		FV	£1.00	£2.00
1976	181,379,000		FV	£1.00	£3.00
1977	109,281,000		FV	£1.00	£2.00
1978	189,658,000		FV	£1.00	£2.00
1979	260,200,000		FV	£1.00	£2.00
1980	408,527,000		FV	£1.00	£2.00
1981	353,191,000		FV	£1.00	£3.00

TYPE 2 (obverse 1, reverse 2)

			Used	As-New	Proof
1982	323,630	BU/Proof sets only	£1.00	£5.00	£8.00
1983	614,655	BU/Proof sets only	£1.00	£5.00	£8.00
1983	Error, 'NEW PENCE' reverse	Used: £500 - £600	£1k - £1.2k		
1984	265,340	BU/Proof sets only	£1.00	£5.00	£6.00

TYPE 3 (obverse 2, reverse 2)

			Used	As-New	Proof
1985	107,113,000		FV	£2.00	£3.00
1986	168,967,500		FV	£1.50	£3.00
1987	218,100,750		FV	£1.50	£3.00
1988	419,889,000		FV	£2.00	£3.00
1989	359,226,000		FV	£2.00	£3.00
1990	204,499,700		FV	£1.50	£3.00
1991	86,625,250		FV	£1.50	£3.00
1992	155,426	#2 Bronze	£1.00	£5.00	£3.00

TYPE 4 (obverse 2, reverse 2) From now on, made of copper-plated steel (slightly magnetic)

			Used	As-New	Proof
1992	102,247,000		FV	£2.00	-
1993	235,674,000		FV	£2.00	£2.00
1994	531,628,000		FV	£2.00	£3.00
1995	124,482,000		FV	£2.00	£3.00
1996	296,278,000	Silver proof exists	FV	£2.00	£3.00
1997	496,116,000		FV	£1.50	£3.00

NOTES

There are some very subtle 2p 'micro varieties'.

TYPE 5 (obverse 3, reverse 2)

			Used	As-New	Proof
1998	115,154,000 [3]	Copper/Steel	FV	£2.00	£3.00
1998	98,676,000 [3]	Bronze	FV	£2.00	
1999	353,816,000	Copper/Steel	FV	£2.00	£3.00
1999	259,962 [4]	Bronze, from sets	£0.50	£4.00	£4.00
2000	536,659,000		FV	£1.50	£3.00
2001	551,880,000		FV	£1.50	£3.00
2002	168,556,000		FV	£1.50	£3.00
2003	260,225,000		FV	£1.50	£3.00
2004	356,396,000		FV	£1.50	£3.00
2005	280,396,000		FV	£1.50	£3.00
2006	170,637,000		FV	£1.50	£3.00
2007	254,500,000		FV	£1.50	£4.00
2008	10,600,000		FV	£3.00	£4.00

TYPE 6 (obverse 4, reverse 3)

		Used	As-New	Proof
2008	241,679,000	FV	£2.00	£4.00
2009	150,500,500	FV	£1.50	£3.00
2010	99,600,000	FV	£1.50	£3.00
2011	114,300,000	FV	£2.00	£3.00
2012	67,800,000	FV	£2.00	£4.00
2013	40,600,000	FV	£2.00	£4.00
2014	247,600,020	FV	£2.00	£4.00
2015	85,900,000	FV	£2.00	£4.00

TYPE 7 (obverse 5, reverse 3)

		Used	As-New	Proof
2015	139,200,000	FV	£2.00	£4.00
2016	185,600,000	FV	£2.00	£4.00
2017	16,600,000	FV	£3.00	£5.00
2018	29,909	Available in sets only	£9.00	£9.00
2019	30,098	Available in sets only	£8.00	£10.00
2020	47,830	Available in sets only	£1.50	£4.00
2021	117,700,000	FV	£2.50	£4.00
2022	67,029	Available in sets only	£3.00	£4.00

TYPE 7 (obverse 6, reverse 4, Charles III)

		Used	As-New	Proof
2023	Not yet known	Available in sets only*	£2.00	£4.00
2024	Not yet known	FV	£2.00	£4.00

* 2023 coins were only made available in annual sets and all feature a crown 'privy mark' behind the King's head. See page 37.

What's currently legal tender?

Only the smaller post-1990 5p coins are legal tender. The older large coins can be paid into UK bank accounts at face value. The predecessor of the five pence, the shilling, should also be accepted at most UK banks as five pence. Check any shillings have no collectable worth using the Coin Publications book "Collectors' Coins GB 1760 - 1970" before redeeming them at five pence face value.

Which are hard to find?

The old large 5p coins are no longer found in change (unless someone has managed to pass one off as a 10p, which sometimes happens). The scarcest are those that were made just to go into sets, or as proofs only: notably 1972 to 1974, 1976, a few of the early and mid 1980s coins and the last large 5p struck in 1990. The 2018 coin is also one that can only be found in sets. From 2012 onwards the 5p is made of nickel-plated steel and is magnetic.

REVERSES

REVERSE 1
(used 1968 - 1981)
Crowned Thistle
[OFFICIALLY: The Badge of Scotland, a thistle royally crowned]
5 NEW PENCE
Design by: Christopher Ironside

REVERSE 2
(used 1982 - 1990)
Crowned Thistle
[OFFICIALLY: The Badge of Scotland, a thistle royally crowned]
5 FIVE PENCE
Design by: Christopher Ironside

REVERSE 3
(used 1990 - 2008)
Crowned Thistle, as above. Size reduced.
5 FIVE PENCE
Design by: Christopher Ironside

REVERSE 4
(used 2008 - 2022)
Middle part of the Royal coat of Arms of the United Kingdom.
FIVE PENCE
Design by: Matthew Dent

REVERSE 5
(used 2023 onwards)
Oak sprig.
5 PENCE
Design by: Royal Mint in-house

TYPE 1 (obverse 1, reverse 1)

			Used	As-New	Proof
1968	98,868,250		FV	£1.00	
1969	120,270,000		FV	£2.00	
1970	225,948,525		FV	£2.00	
1971	81,783,475		FV	£1.50	£3.00
1972	107,807	Proof only	£0.50		£3.00
1973	75,424	Proof only	£0.50		£6.00
1974	72,355	Proof only	£0.50		£3.00
1975	141,539,000		FV	£1.50	£3.00
1976	75,000	Proof only	£0.50		£8.00
1977	24,308,000		FV	£2.00	£3.00
1978	61,094,000		FV	£2.00	£3.00
1979	155,456,000		FV	£2.00	£3.00
1980	220,566,000		FV	£1.50	£3.00
1981	98,500	Proof only	£1.00		£6.00

TYPE 2 (obverse 1, reverse 2)

			Used	As-New	Proof
1982	323,630	Available in sets only	£2.00	£4.00	£5.00
1983	614,655	Available in sets only	£1.00	£3.00	£5.00
1984	265,340	Available in sets only	£1.00	£2.00	£4.00

TYPE 3 (obverse 2, reverse 2)

			Used	As-New	Proof
1985	280,390	Available in sets only	£1.00	£3.00	£5.00
1986	167,000	Available in sets only	£1.00	£2.00	£5.00
1987	48,220,000		FV	£2.00	£3.00
1988	120,744,610		FV	£1.50	£3.00
1989	101,406,000		FV	£2.00	£3.00
1990	181,658	Available in sets only	£2.00	£3.00	£4.00

The large five pence coins were demonetised on the 31st December 1990

TYPE 4 - Reduced in size from 23.59mm to 18mm (obverse 2B, reverse 3)

			Used	As-New	Proof
1990	1,634,976,005	Edge varieties	FV	£2.00	£3.00
		1990 silver proof pair, Type 3 and Type 4			£22.00
1991	724,979,000		FV	£1.00	£3.00
1992	453,173,500		FV	£1.00	£3.00
1993	137,729	Available in sets only	£1.00	£4.00	£6.00
1994	93,602,000		FV	£2.00	£3.00
1995	183,384,000		FV	£1.00	£3.00
1996	302,902,000	(exists in silver)	FV	£1.50	£3.00
1997	236,596,000		FV	£1.00	£3.00

18.00 mm • 3.25 grammes • cu-ni / ni plated • milled edge

TYPE 5 (obverse 3, reverse 3)

		Used	As-New	Proof
1998	217,376,000	FV	£1.00	£3.00
1999	195,490,000	FV	£1.00	£3.00
2000	388,512,000	FV	£1.50	£3.00
2001	337,930,000	FV	£1.00	£3.00
2002	219,258,000	FV	£1.50	£3.00
2003	333,230,000	FV	£1.50	£3.00
2004	271,810,000	FV	£1.00	£3.00
2005	236,212,000	FV	£1.00	£3.00
2006	317,697,000	FV	£1.00	£3.00
2007	246,720,000	FV	£1.00	£3.00
2008	92,880,000	FV	£1.00	£3.00

TYPE 6 (obverse 4, reverse 4, Nickel plated steel from 2012 onwards)

		Used	As-New	Proof
2008	165,172,000	FV	£1.50	£4.00
2009	132,960,300	FV	£2.00	£4.00
2010	396,245,500	FV	£1.50	£4.00
2011	50,400,000	FV	£3.00	£4.00
2012	339,802,350	FV	£2.50	£4.00
2013	378,800,750	FV	£2.00	£4.00
2014	885,004,520	FV	£2.00	£4.00
2015	163,000,000	FV	£3.00	£4.00

TYPE 7 (obverse 5, reverse 4)

		Used	As-New	Proof
2015	536,600,000	FV	£3.00	£4.00
2016	305,740,000	FV	£2.00	£4.00
2017	220,515,000	FV	£1.50	£4.00
2018	29,909	Available in sets only	£10.00	£12.00
2019	92,800,000	FV	£2.00	£4.00
2020	49,200,000	FV	£1.50	£4.00
2021	28,000,000	FV	£1.50	£4.00
2022	42,800,000	FV	£1.50	£4.00

TYPE 8 (obverse 6, reverse 5, Charles III)

			As-New	Proof
2023	32,400,000		£2.00	£4.00
2023	Crown privy mark*	Available in sets only	£2.00	£4.00
2024	Not yet known	Currently available in sets only	£2.00	£4.00

* 2023 coins made available in annual sets all feature a crown 'privy mark' behind the King's head. See page 37.

What's currently legal tender?

Only the smaller post-1992 10p coins are legal tender. The older large coins can be paid into UK bank accounts. The predecessor of the ten pence, the florin or two-shillings, should also be accepted at most UK banks. Check any florins have no collectable worth using the Coin Publications book "Collectors' Coins GB 1760 - 1970 " before redeeming them at ten pence face value.

Which are hard to find?

The rarest 10p is the 2009 coin with the wrong (previous type) reverse! Only two or three of these are known so far and it is thought that they were included erroneously in some baby gift sets - it's certainly one that can easily be overlooked. The old large 10p coins are no longer found in change. The scarcest of those were made just to go into sets, or as proofs: notably 1972, 1978 and all of the large type coins from 1982 onwards. The alphabet 10p coins are in circulation but are all hard to find. 2018 and 2019 standard 10p coins were not made for circulation and can be found in sets only. There are lots of known varieties for the Ten Pence, both larger size and current size. Search online for the relevant predecimal.com forum topics. From 2012 onwards the 10p is made of nickel-plated steel and is magnetic.

REVERSES

REVERSE 1

(used 1968 - 1981)
Lion Passant Guardant
[Part of the crest of England, a lion passant guardant royally crowned]
10 NEW PENCE
Design by: Christopher Ironside

REVERSE 2

(used 1982 - 1992)
Lion Passant Guardant
[Part of the crest of England, a lion passant guardant royally crowned]
10 TEN PENCE
Design by: Christopher Ironside

REVERSE 3

(used 1992 - 2008)
Lion Passant Guardant
[Part of the crest of England, a lion passant guardant royally crowned]
10 TEN PENCE
Design by: Christopher Ironside

28.50 mm • 11.31 grammes • cupro-nickel • milled edge

REVERSE 4
(used 2008 to 2022)
Upper left section of the Royal coat of Arms of the
United Kingdom.
TEN PENCE
Design by: Matthew Dent

REVERSE 5
(used 2023 onwards)
Capercaillie (a Woodland Grouse)
10 PENCE
Design by: Royal Mint in-house

TYPE 1 (obverse 1, reverse 1)

			Used	As-New	Proof
1968	336,143,250		FV	£1.00	
1969	314,008,000		FV	£2.00	
1970	133,571,000		£0.50	£2.00	
1971	63,205,000		FV	£1.50	£3.00
1972	107,807	Proof Only (from sets)	£1.00		£5.00
1973	152,174,000		FV	£1.50	£3.00
1974	92,741,000		FV	£1.50	£3.00
1975	181,559,000		FV	£2.00	£3.00
1976	228,220,000		FV	£2.00	£3.00
1977	59,323,000		FV	£2.00	£3.00
1978	88,100	Proof Only (from sets)	£1.00		£10.00
1979	115,457,000		FV	£2.00	£3.00
1980	88,650,000		FV	£2.00	£3.00
1981	3,487,000		£2.00	£8.00	£8.00

TYPE 2 (obverse 1, reverse 2)

			Used	As-New	Proof
1982	323,630	Available in sets only	£2.00	£5.00	£6.00
1983	614,655	Available in sets only	£2.00	£2.50	£6.00
1984	265,340	Available in sets only	£1.50	£2.50	£6.00

TYPE 3 (obverse 2, reverse 2)

			Used	As-New	Proof
1985	280,390	Available in sets only	£1.50	£2.50	£5.00
1986	167,000	Available in sets only	£1.00	£1.50	£5.00
1987	261,084	Available in sets only	£1.50	£2.50	£5.00
1988	213,381	Available in sets only	£1.50	£3.00	£5.00
1989	162,643	Available in sets only	£2.00	£3.00	£5.00
1990	181,658	Available in sets only	£2.00	£3.00	£5.00
1991	130,119	Available in sets only	£2.00	£5.00	£5.00
1992	155,426	Available in sets only	£2.00	£3.00	£5.00

The large ten pence coins were demonetised on the 30th June 1993

TYPE 4 - Reduced in size from 28.5mm to 24.5mm (obverse 2B, reverse 3)

1992	1,413,455,170 [‡1]		FV	£2.00	£3.00
1993	137,729	Available in sets only	£0.50	£6.00	£6.00
1994	259,359	Available in sets only	£0.50	£4.00	£6.00
1995	43,259,000		FV	£1.50	£3.00
1996	118,738,000 [‡2]		FV	£1.50	£3.00
1997	99,196,000		FV	£1.00	£3.00

TYPE 5 (obverse 3, reverse 3)

1998	196,203	Available in sets only	£0.50	£5.00	£6.00
1999	259,962	Available in sets only	£0.50	£4.00	£6.00
2000	134,733,000		FV	£1.00	£3.00
2001	129,281,000		FV	£1.00	£3.00
2002	80,934,000		FV	£1.00	£3.00
2003	88,118,000		FV	£1.50	£3.00
2004	99,602,000		FV	£1.50	£3.00
2005	69,604,000 [‡1]	'I' of '10' to bead or to space	FV	£2.00	£3.00
2006	118,803,000 [‡1]		FV	£1.50	£3.00
2007	72,720,000		FV	£1.00	£3.00
2008	9,720,000		FV	£1.50	£3.00

[*]   A mismatch of dies known as a mule has resulted in three (so far) 2009 coins with the incorrect previous reverse (Ironside's "lion passant guardant").

[‡1]   Varieties exist for the 1992 issue and have also been noted for 2005 and possibly for 2006 dated coins. The best source of info is the predecimal.com forum.

[‡2]   Exists as a silver proof, originally part of a set

24.50 mm • 6.5 grammes • cu-ni / ni plated • milled edge

TYPE 6 (obverse 4, reverse 4. Nickel plated steel from 2012 onwards)

			Used	As-New	Proof
2008	71,447,000		FV	£2.00	£4.00
2009	84,360,000		FV	£1.50	£4.00
2009	2 or 3 known*	Mule, rev. 3		no data	
2010	96,600,500		FV	£2.00	£3.00
2011	59,603,850		FV	£3.00	£3.00
2012	11,600,030		FV	£2.00	£5.00
2013	320,200,750		FV	£3.00	£5.00
2014	490,202,020		FV	£4.00	£5.00
2015	119,000,000		FV	£4.00	£5.00

TYPE 7 (obverse 5 reverse 4)

			Used	As-New	Proof
2015	91,900,000		FV	£4.00	£5.00
2016	135,380,000		FV	£4.00	£5.00
2017	33,300,000		FV	£2.00	£5.00
2018	29,909	Available in sets only		£6.00	£6.00
2019	30,098	Available in sets only		£4.00	£6.00
2020	45,347,846		FV	£1.50	
2021	71,200,000		FV	£1.50	£5.00
2022	38,000,000		FV	£3.00	£5.00

TYPE 8 (obverse 6, reverse 5, Charles III)

				As-New	
2023	600,000			£2.00	
2023	Crown privy mark*	Available in sets only		£2.00	
2024	Not yet known	Currently available in sets only		£2.00	

* 2023 coins made available in annual sets all feature a crown 'privy mark' behind the King's head. See page 37.

Check the Check Your Change App!

The Alphabet Ten Pence coins - 2018 and 2019

Introduced in March 2018, the twenty-six A-Z 10p coins were sold by the Royal Mint, designated as 'early strike' for £2 each. Post offices also sold individual coins for £4 each. They did enter circulation but don't seem to have been widely distributed and I am not aware of anyone who has actually managed to get all twenty-six letters from change.

The same alphabet themed coins were also struck again, dated 2019, which meant that more entered circulation, but they were and remain very difficult to find in change. 2019 dated coins were made in lower numbers than 2018. The easiest way to obtain a full set is probably to buy a ready-assembled set and just pay the one postage charge, instead of buying them all individually.

Silver proof versions of the 2018 alphabet 10p's were offered. They were priced £35, supplied in just a capsule, or for an extra £10 you got a box to go with it! I don't think they were massively popular.

| Angel of the North | Bond | Cricket | Double-Decker | English Breakfast |

| Fish and Chips | Greenwich Meridian | Houses of Parliament | Ice Cream | Jubilee (coach) |

| King Arthur | Loch Ness Monster | Mackintosh | NHS | Oak |

| Postbox | Queuing | Robin | Stonehenge | Tea |

Union Flag   Village   World Wide Web   X marks the spot   Yeoman Warder

Zebra Crossing   Obverse type - common to all

TYPE 8 (obverse 7 with alphabet letter reverse)

2019 Used As-New
Circulation Mintage: (figs for each letter) 84,000 for "A" to "P", "S" to "V" and "X" | 83,000 for "Q" | 64,000 for "R" | 63,000 for "W", "Y" and "Z".

Additionally, approx. 10-14k of each coin were minted and sold as 'Uncirculated'.

2018 Used As-New
Circulation Mintage: 220k per coin

	Used	As-New
2018 "A"	£15.00	£23.00
2018 "B"	£7.00	£9.00
2018 "C"	£2.30	£2.80
2018 "D"	£2.30	£2.80
2018 "E"	£2.30	£2.80
2018 "F"	£2.30	£2.80
2018 "G"	£2.30	£2.80
2018 "H"	£2.30	£2.80
2018 "I"	£2.30	£4.00
2018 "J"	£2.30	£2.80
2018 "K"	£2.30	£2.80
2018 "L"	£2.30	£2.80
2018 "M"	£2.30	£2.80
2018 "N"	£3.00	£4.00
2018 "O"	£2.30	£2.80
2018 "P"	£2.30	£2.80
2018 "Q"	£2.30	£2.80
2018 "R"	£3.00	£8.00
2018 "S"	£2.30	£2.80
2018 "T"	£2.30	£5.00
2018 "U"	£2.30	£2.80
2018 "V"	£2.30	£2.80
2018 "W"	£2.30	£2.80
2018 "X"	£2.30	£2.80
2018 "Y"	£2.30	£4.00
2018 "Z"	£2.30	£2.80

	Used	As-New
2019 "A"	£18.00	£22.00
2019 "B"	£8.00	£12.00
2019 "C"	£5.00	£6.00
2019 "D"	£4.00	£5.00
2019 "E"	£4.00	£6.00
2019 "F"	£4.00	£5.00
2019 "G"	£3.00	£5.00
2019 "H"	£4.00	£5.00
2019 "I"	£3.00	£5.00
2019 "J"	£4.00	£5.00
2019 "K"	£3.00	£5.00
2019 "L"	£4.00	£5.00
2019 "M"	£4.00	£5.00
2019 "N"	£4.00	£5.00
2019 "O"	£4.00	£5.00
2019 "P"	£4.00	£5.00
2019 "Q"	£3.00	£5.00
2019 "R"	£8.00	£12.00
2019 "S"	£4.00	£5.00
2019 "T"	£4.00	£5.00
2019 "U"	£4.00	£5.00
2019 "V"	£4.00	£5.00
2019 "W"	£6.00	£7.00
2019 "X"	£3.00	£5.00
2019 "Y"	£7.00	£10.00
2019 "Z"	£8.00	£12.00

What's currently legal tender?

All 20p coins are legal tender. Victorian Double Florins also appear to be legal tender for 20p (4 shillings) as the author is unable to find any evidence that they were demonetised in 1971 with the rest of the old denominations. To spend one would be quite silly though, as the value of the silver contained within a double florin is far higher than 20p.

Which are hard to find?

The 1986, 2017 and 2018 were issued in sets only and are therefore incredibly hard to find in change.

The new (2008) design 20p with no date is scarce. This coin is technically known as a mule and occurred because the Royal Mint used the old obverse die (OBVERSE 3) combined with the new reverse die (REVERSE 2) in error, resulting in a coin with no date on it. All the errors coins were struck in 2008. The error was noticed after somewhere between 100,000 to 250,000 coins were struck.

OBVERSES

OBVERSE 1
(used 1982 - 1984)
ELIZABETH II || D•G•REG•F•D
Elizabeth II, Dei Gratia Regina, Fidei Defensor
(Elizabeth II, By the Grace of God Queen and Defender of the Faith)
Portrait by: Arnold Machin

OBVERSE 2
(used 1985 - 1997. Altered and made slightly larger (right image) from 1992 onwards)
ELIZABETH II || D•G•REG•F•D
Elizabeth II, Dei Gratia Regina, Fidei Defensor
(Elizabeth II, By the Grace of God Queen and Defender of the Faith)
Portrait by: Raphael Maklouf

OBVERSE 3
(used 1998 - 2008)
ELIZABETH II || D•G•REG•F•D
Elizabeth II, Dei Gratia Regina, Fidei Defensor
(Elizabeth II, By the Grace of God Queen and Defender of the Faith)
Portrait by: Ian Rank-Broadley

OBVERSE 4
(used 2008 - 2015)
ELIZABETH•II•D•G•REG•F•D•(date)
Elizabeth II, Dei Gratia Regina, Fidei Defensor
(Elizabeth II, By the Grace of God Queen and Defender of the Faith)
Portrait by: Ian Rank-Broadley

OBVERSES - continued

OBVERSE 5
(used 2015 -2022)
ELIZABETH II•DEI•GRA•REG•FID•DEF•(date)
Elizabeth II, Dei Gratia Regina, Fidei Defensor
(Elizabeth II, By the Grace of God Queen and Defender of the Faith)
Portrait by: Jody Clark

OBVERSE 6
(used 2023 onwards)
CHARLES III•DEI•GRA•REX•FID•DEF•(date)
Charles III, Dei Gratia Rex, Fidei Defensor
(Charles III, By the Grace of God King and Defender of the Faith)
Portrait by: Martin Jennings

REVERSES

REVERSE 1
(used 1982 - 2008)
Crowned Tudor Rose
[The Badge of England, a royally crowned double rose]
20 TWENTY PENCE (date)
Design by: William Gardner

REVERSE 2
(used 2008 - 2022)
Lower right section of the Royal coat of Arms of the
United Kingdom.
TWENTY PENCE
Design by: Matthew Dent

REVERSE 3
(used 2023 onwards)
Puffin
20 PENCE
Design by: Royal Mint in-house

21.40 mm • 5.00 grammes • cupro-nickel • plain edge

TYPE 1 (obverse 1, reverse 1)

			Used	As-New	Proof
1982	740,815,000		FV	£2.00	£4.00
	Silver piedfort proof				£25.00
1983	158,463,000		FV	£2.00	£4.00
1984	65,350,965		FV	£2.00	£4.00

TYPE 2 (obverse 2, reverse 1)

				Used	As-New	Proof
1985	74,273,699			FV	£2.00	£4.00
1986	167,000	Available in sets only			£8.00	£10.00
1987	137,450,000			FV	£1.50	£4.00
1988	38,038,344			FV	£2.00	£4.00
1989	132,013,890			FV	£2.00	£4.00
1990	88,097,500			FV	£1.50	£4.00
1991	35,901,250			FV	£1.50	£4.00
1992	31,205,000 (both)	Small head*		FV	£3.00	£5.00
1992		Large head*	£0.50	£5.00		exists?
1993	123,123,750			FV	£2.00	£4.00
1994	67,131,250			FV	£1.50	£4.00
1995	102,005,000			FV	£1.50	£4.00
1996	83,163,750	*		FV	£2.00	£4.00
1997	89,518,750			FV	£1.50	£4.00

TYPE 3 (obverse 3, reverse 1)

			Used	As-New	Proof
1998	76,965,000		FV	£1.50	£4.00
1999	73,478,750		FV	£1.50	£4.00
2000	136,428,750		FV	£2.00	£4.00
2001	148,122,500		FV	£2.00	£4.00
2002	93,360,000		FV	£3.00	£4.00
2003	153,383,750		FV	£2.00	£4.00
2004	120,212,500		FV	£2.00	£4.00
2005	124,488,750		FV	£1.00	£4.00
2006	114,800,000		FV	£2.00	£4.00
2007	117,075,000		FV	£1.00	£4.00
2008	11,900,000		FV	£3.00	£5.00

* The 1992 small head coin was thought to be scarcer than the large head, but new information would seem to imply that the large head coins are the coins that were circulated in large numbers and are now hardest to find (especially in top condition as most have seen normal usage). It is now thought that the proof version only exists with the small head. The easiest way to tell the difference is that the small head bust has a much sharper point where the neck ends at the bottom.

1996 also exists as a silver proof, originally part of a set.

MULE ERROR (mismatching obverse 3 and reverse 2)

		Used	As-New	Proof
(2008) Also known as the 'dateless' 20p		£40	£80	-

Chinese made fakes exist. They have a dirty matt appearance, thinner lettering and a lack of detail.

TYPE 4 (obverse 4, reverse 2)

Year		Used	As-New	Proof
2008 [+3]	115,022,000	FV	£4.00	£5.00
2009	121,625,300	FV	£3.00	£5.00
2010	112,875,500	FV	£2.00	£5.00
2011	191,625,000	FV	£3.00	£5.00
2012	69,650,030	FV	£3.00	£5.00
2013	66,325,000	FV	£4.00	£5.00
2014	173,775,000	FV	£4.00	£5.00
2015	63,175,000	FV	£4.00	£5.00

TYPE 5 (obverse 5, reverse 2)

Year		Used	As-New	Proof
2015	131,250,000	FV	£4.00	£5.00
2016	212,625,000	FV	£4.00	£5.00
2017	47,626	Available in sets only	£15.00	£15.00
2018	29,909	Available in sets only	£13.00	£13.00
2019	125,125,000	FV	£1.00	£4.00
2020	32,725,000	FV	£2.00	£4.00
2021	19,600,000	FV	£3.00	£4.00
2022	42,875,000	FV	£3.00	£4.00
2022	40th Anniversary*	Available in sets only, £35.00 price new		

TYPE 6 (obverse 6, reverse 2, Charles III)

Year		Used	As-New	Proof
2023	525,000		£4.00	£5.00
2023	Crown privy mark*	Available in sets only	£4.00	£5.00
2024	Not yet known	Currently available in sets only	£3.00	£5.00

NOTES

* 2002 40th anniversary coin, issued with 3 used coins (one for each portrait). The 2022 BU coin included has a small 20p shaped '40' mintmark on the obverse, to the left of the JC initials (below).

* 2023 coins made available in annual sets all feature a crown 'privy mark' behind the King's head. See page 37.

2022 20p with '40' mintmark.

Historically the Crown was five shillings (one quarter of a 20 shilling pound). For that reason, the new decimal crowns initially had a face value of 25p. These four commemorative crown coins are legal tender for 25p, but they are rarely used by the public, probably because they are too big to be convenient, and to collectors they are usually worth a little more than face value. Members of the public often assume incorrectly that they have a face value of £5. The crown was re-valued as £5 in 1990, although the size and weight of the coin remained the same.

For later Crowns, see the FIVE POUNDS sections.

These four coins were issued to mark the following occasions: 1972 – The 25th Wedding Anniversary of the Queen and Prince Philip. 1977 - The Silver Jubilee of the Queen. 1980 - The 80th Birthday of the Queen Mother. 1981 - The Royal Wedding of Charles and Diana.

COMMEMORATIVE TYPE 1
Obverse: Standard portrait of QE II
Design by: Arnold Machin

Reverse: Elizabeth and Philip,
20 November 1947-1972
Design by: Arnold Machin

		Used	As-New	Proof
1972	7,452,100	£0.30	£1.50	£4.00
	100,000	.925 sterling silver proof		£20.00

COMMEMORATIVE TYPE 2
Obverse: Equestrian portrait of QE II
Design by: Arnold Machin

Reverse: Ampulla and anointing spoon, items used during the Coronation
Design by: Arnold Machin

		Used	As-New	Proof
1977	37,061,160	£0.30	£1.00	£4.00
	Specimen in folder		£1.00	
	377,000	.925 sterling silver proof		£15.00

COMMEMORATIVE TYPE 3
Obverse: Standard portrait of QE II
Design by: Arnold Machin

Reverse: Portrait of Queen Mother, surrounded by bows and lions
Design by: Richard Guyatt

1980	9,306,000	£0.30	£1.50	-
	Specimen in folder		£2.00	
	83,672	.925 sterling silver proof		£20.00

COMMEMORATIVE TYPE 4
Obverse: Standard portrait of QE II
Design by: Arnold Machin

Reverse: Conjoined busts of Charles & Diana
Design by: Philip Nathan

1981	26,773,600	£0.30	£1.50	-
	Specimen in folder		£2.00	
	218,000	.925 sterling silver proof		£20.00

Set of 4 (72, 77, 80 and 81) Crowns as silver proofs in large case. 5,000 sets issued   £65.00

31

30 mm • 13.5 grammes • cupro-nickel • plain edge

What's currently legal tender?
Only the smaller (post-1997) 50p coins are legal tender now. Most banks will allow you to pay in the pre-1997 larger 30mm coins.

Which are hard to find?
The most valuable 50p that could potentially be found in change is the withdrawn Olympic Aquatics coin with the lines on the swimmers' face. See Commemorative Type 17. The prices for the Kew Gardens 2009 50p remain high. The 1992-1993 EU coin is also higher priced after it was hyped up as being the older larger-size 50p with the lowest mintage. 2009 dated Blue Peter high-jump 50p coins are also in demand. Some recent shield reverse coins can only be found in sets and were not circulated - these can also be expensive to source.

Special proof sets of 50p coins were made in 2009 and proof/BU sets were made in 2019. All of the coins are the newer 27.3mm size and all feature the portrait of the Queen current in 2009 and 2019 respectively. See info after commemorative type 5 for the 2009 set and info after commemorative types 69 and 75 for the 2019 sets.

OBVERSES

OBVERSE 1
(used 1969 - 1972, 1974 - 1984)
D•G•REG•F•D•(date) || ELIZABETH II
Elizabeth II, Dei Gratia Regina, Fidei Defensor
(Elizabeth II, By the Grace of God Queen and Defender of the Faith)
Portrait by: Arnold Machin

OBVERSE 2
(used 1985 - 1997)
ELIZABETH II || D•G•REG•F•D•(date)
Elizabeth II, Dei Gratia Regina, Fidei Defensor
(Elizabeth II, By the Grace of God Queen and Defender of the Faith)
Portrait by: Raphael Maklouf

REVERSES

REVERSE 1 (left)
(used 1969 - 1972, 1974 - 1981 and for 2019 commemoratives)
Britannia
[The seated figure of Britannia]
50 NEW PENCE
Design by: Christopher Ironside

REVERSE 2 (right)
(used 1982 - 93, 1995 - 1997)
Britannia
[The seated figure of Britannia]
50 FIFTY PENCE
Design by: Christopher Ironside

DEFINITIVE TYPE I (obverse I, reverse I)

			As-New	Proof
1969	188,400,000	Used: £1.50	£5.00	
1970	19,461,500	Used: £4.00	£10.00	
1971	229,819 Proof Only (from the sets)	Used: £2.00		£12.00
1972	107,807 Proof Only (from the sets)	Used: £2.00		£12.00
1974	72,355 Proof Only (from the sets)	Used: £2.00		£10.00
1975	72,323 Proof Only (from the sets)	Used: £2.00		£8.00
1976	43,746,500	Used: £1.50	£5.00	£5.00
1977	49,536,000	Used: £1.50	£5.00	£5.00
1978	72,005,500	Used: £1.50	£3.00	£4.00
1979	58,680,000	Used: £1.50	£4.00	£4.00
1980	89,086,000	Used: £1.50	£4.00	£4.00
1981	74,002,000	Used: £1.50	£3.00	£4.00

DEFINITIVE TYPE 2 (obverse I, reverse 2)

			As-New	Proof
1982	51,312,000	Used: £1.50	£3.00	£4.00
1983	62,824,904	Used: £1.50	£3.00	£4.00
1984	265,340 ‡I	Used: £4.00	£8.00	£8.00

DEFINITIVE TYPE 3 (obverse 2, reverse 2)

			As-New	Proof
1985	682,103	Used: £5.00	£9.00	£9.00
1986	167,000 ‡I	Used: £4.00	£5.00	£8.00
1987	261,084 ‡I	Used: £4.00	£7.00	£8.00
1988	213,381 ‡I	Used: £4.00	£8.00	£8.00
1989	162,643 ‡I	Used: £4.00	£7.00	£8.00
1990	181,658 ‡I	Used: £4.00	£8.00	£8.00
1991	130,119 ‡I	Used: £4.00	£12.00	£12.00
1992	155,426 ‡I	Used: £4.00	£7.00	£8.00
1993	137,729 ‡I	Used: £4.00	£7.00	£8.00
1994	Smaller type. Marked 'ROYAL MINT TRIAL'	Used: no data (see below)		
1995	186,330 ‡I	Used: £4.00	£10.00	£10.00
1996	176,034 ‡I	Used: £4.00	£8.00	£8.00
1997	215,653 ‡I	Used: £4.00	£8.00	£8.00

‡I These years were not issued for circulation, and the "business strikes" were made for BU mint folders, only.

Below: Rare 1994 50p trial coins, one round, one conventionally shaped.

OBVERSES

A new smaller sized 50p was introduced in 1997. Its size (diameter and thickness) was reduced and the resultant coin has a diameter of 27.3mm and a weight of 8g. These smaller coins, shown on the following four pages, are the current circulation 50p type. Current commemorative 50p coins start on page 39. The vast majority of recent commemorative 50p coins are sold in packages, rather than actually circulated for use.

OBVERSE 3
(used 1997)
ELIZABETH II || D•G•REG•F•D• (date)
Portrait by: Raphael Maklouf

OBVERSE 4
(used 1998 - 2008 and for most commemorative coins dated 1998 - 2015, except where shown)
ELIZABETH II || D•G•REG•F•D• (date)
Portrait by: Ian Rank-Broadley

OBVERSE 5 (similar to last, with different alignment)
(used 2008 - 2015, with Reverse 4)
ELIZABETH II || D•G•REG•F•D• (date)
Portrait by: Ian Rank-Broadley

OBVERSE 6
(used 2015 - 2022, with variations for commemorative coins)
ELIZABETH II•DEI•GRA•REG•FID•DEF• (date)
Portrait by: Jody Clark

OBVERSE 7
(used 2022 - date, with variations for commemorative coins)
CHARLES III•DEI•GRA•REX•FID•DEF• (date)
Portrait by: Martin Jennings

REVERSES

REVERSE 3
(used 1997 - 2008)
Often referred to as the 'Britannia issue' to distinguish it from the commemorative issues.
[The seated figure of Britannia]
FIFTY PENCE 50
Design by: Christopher Ironside

REVERSE 4
(used 2008 to 2022)
Bottom section of the Royal coat of Arms of the United Kingdom.
FIFTY PENCE
Design by: Matthew Dent

REVERSE 5
(used 2022 to date)
Atlantic Salmon, repeating pattern of three interlocked C's .
50 PENCE
Design by: Royal Mint in-house

This logo depicted towards the lower-right of the current commemorative coin images (page 39 onwards) indicates a coin which actually entered circulation - most recent ones do not:

DEFINITIVE TYPE 4 - Reduced size from 30mm to 27.3mm (obverse 3, reverse 3)

			As-New	Proof
1997	456,364,100		£3.50	£5.00

DEFINITIVE TYPE 5 (obverse 4, reverse 3)

			As-New	Proof
1998	64,306,500		£5.00	
1999	24,905,000		£4.00	£5.00
2000	27,915,500		£4.00	£5.00
2001	84,998,500		£4.00	£5.00
2002	23,907,500		£5.00	£5.00
2003	23,583,000		£5.00	£5.00
2004	35,315,500		£5.00	£5.00
2005	25,363,500		£4.00	£5.00
2006	24,567,000	(not in BU sets)	£5.00	£5.00
2007	11,200,000	(not in BU sets)	£5.00	£5.00
2008	3,500,000	Used: £1.00	£6.00	£7.00

DEFINITIVE TYPE 6 (obverse 5, reverse 4)

			As-New	Proof
2008	22,747,000		£10.00	£12.00
2009	None for circulation	(108,816 in BU sets) up to	£50.00	no data
2010	None for circulation	(69,167 in BU sets) up to	£30.00	no data
2011	None for circulation	(57,467 in BU sets) up to	£40.00	no data
2012	32,300,030		£10.00	£10.00
2013	10,301,000		£10.00	£10.00
2014	49,001,000		£8.00	£10.00
2015	20,101,000		£8.00	£10.00

DEFINITIVE TYPE 7 (obverse 6, reverse 4)

			As-New	Proof
2015	39,300,000		£8.00	£9.00
2016	None for circulation (39,502 in BU sets)	Used: £60	£70.00	no data
2017	1,800,000	Used: £1.00	£7.00	£8.00
2018	None for circulation (29,909 in BU sets)		£40.00	no data
2019	122,000,000		£3.00	£5.00
2020	46,540,375		£4.00	£6.00
2021	50,267	Available in sets only	£18.00	£20.00
2022	9,500,000		£12.00	£14.00

DEFINITIVE TYPE 8 (obverse 7, reverse 4)

			As-New	Proof
2023	With crown privy mark	Available in sets only*	£10.00	£10.00
2023	200,000**	Used: £100.00		
2024	Not yet known	Currently available in sets only	£9.00	£10.00

* At the time of writing, the 2023 dated set containing the Salmon 50p with crown privy mark was still available to purchase new, for £34.

**During 2024 there was speculation and some conflicting information about the mintage figure of the circulation 2023 Atlantic Salmon 50p - the final figure is quite low and as a result, prices are expected to be volatile until it finds its natural level (which I suspect will, as ever, depend on the amount of media hype and actual demand).

Close-up of the Crown Privy Mark featured on the 2023 coins that were sold in sets.

COMMEMORATIVE TYPE 1
1973 || 50 || pence (centre)
Nine clasped hands forming a circle
(Britain's entry into the European
Economic Community)
Reverse design by: David Wynne
(also exists dated 2009, see page 39)

		Used	As-New	Proof
1973	89,775,000	£1.00	£3.00	£3.00
	Proof in leatherette case			£4.00
	Thicker planchet but not recorded as Piedfort			Extremely Rare

COMMEMORATIVE TYPE 2
1992-1993 (upper) || 50 pence (lower)
Conference table with seats and stars
(completion of the EC single market and
the British Presidency)
Reverse design by: Mary Milner Dickens
(also exists dated 2009, see page 39)

		Used	As-New	Proof
1992-1993	109,000	£35.00	£40.00	£50.00
	23,262 Specimen in folder (inc. 1993 Britannia issue)		£60.00	
	26,890 .925 sterling silver proof			£60.00
	15,000 .925 sterling silver piedfort proof			£80.00
	1,864 .917 gold proof			£1,400.00

COMMEMORATIVE TYPE 3
50 pence (lower right)
**Ships and planes taking part in the
D-Day landings**
(50th Anniversary of the D-Day Invasion)
Reverse design by: John Mills
(also exists dated 2009 and 2019,
see pages 39 and 64)

		Used	As-New	Proof
1994	6,705,520	£3.00	£5.00	£8.00
	Specimen in folder		£7.00	
	40,500 .925 sterling silver proof			£25.00
	10,000 .925 sterling silver piedfort proof			£45.00
	1,877 .917 gold proof			£1,100.00

COMMEMORATIVE TYPE 4
1973 EU 1998 || 50 pence (lower)
Fireworks pattern of 12 stars
(25th Anniversary - UK entry into EEC)
Design by: John Mills
(also exists dated 2009, see below)

		Used	As-New	Proof
1998	5,043,000	£1.00	£7.00	£15.00
15,370	Specimen in folder (including Britannia issue)		£30.00	
8,859	.925 sterling silver proof			£25.00
5,117	.925 sterling silver piedfort proof			£35.00
1,177	.917 gold proof			£900.00

COMMEMORATIVE TYPE 5
FIFTIETH ANNIVERSARY (upper) || 50 pence (lower)
Caring Hands, holding sun's rays
(50th Anniversary - National Health Service)
Design by: David Cornell
(also exists dated 2009, see below)

		Used	As-New	Proof
1998	5,001,000	£1.50	£10.00	
	Specimen in folder		£25.00	
9,032	.925 sterling silver proof			£20.00
5,117	.925 sterling silver piedfort proof			£25.00
651	.917 gold proof			£900.00

The 2009 retrospective 40th Anniversary set of sixteen fifty pence coins.

From the introduction of the 50p in 1969 up to and including the 2009 Kew Gardens coin there were a total of 16 different 50p reverses used. These large types:

Standard Britannia with 'NEW PENCE' (REVERSE 1)
EEC Hands (commemorative TYPE 1)
Standard Britannia with 'FIFTY PENCE' (REVERSE 2)
EC 1992-1993 (commemorative TYPE 2)
D-Day (commemorative TYPE 3)

And also the smaller commemorative types 4 to 13 and the REVERSE 4 of the normal 50p.

All of these designs were sold in sets of 16, all featuring OBVERSE 4 and all being of the newer 27.3mm diameter, even the five listed above that were originally larger. Just over 1,000 of each cupro-nickel or silver sets were made and they are both hard to find. Value: £700+.

Very rare: There were also 70 gold proof sets and 40 gold proof piedfort sets sold!

27.3 mm • 8.0 grammes • cupro-nickel • plain edge

COMMEMORATIVE TYPE 6
1850-2000 (upper) || PUBLIC LIBRARIES (lower)
Open book upon pillared building
(150th Anniversary - British Libraries)
Design by: **Mary Milner Dickens**
(also exists dated 2009, see page 39)

			As-New	Proof
2000	11,263,000		£7.00	£12.00
		Specimen in folder	£45.00	
	7,634	.925 sterling silver proof		£25.00
	5,721	.925 sterling silver piedfort proof		£30.00
	710	.917 gold proof		£900.00

COMMEMORATIVE TYPE 7
50 pence (left) || 1903-2003 (lower right)
Suffragette with WSPU banner
(100th Anniversary - Women's Social and Political Union)
Design by: **Mary Milner Dickens**
(also exists dated 2009, see page 39)

			Used	As-New	Proof
2003	3,124,030	(43,513 proofs in sets)	£2.00	£12.00	£20.00
	9,582	Specimen in folder		£40.00	
	6,267 of 15k	.925 sterling silver proof			£30.00
	6,795 of 7.5k	.925 sterling silver piedfort proof			£40.00
	942 of 1000	.917 gold proof			£900.00

* Increased value recently due to someone 'discovering' 13 years later that 3.1m mintage is on the low side compared to most other 50p coins!

COMMEMORATIVE TYPE 8
50 pence (lower)
Runner's legs and stopwatch
(50th Anniversary - Roger Bannister's 4-minute mile run)
Design by: **James Butler**
(also exists dated 2009 and 2019, see pages 39 and 61)

			As-New	Proof
2004	9,032,500	(35,020 proofs in sets)	£8.00	£15.00
	10,371	Specimen in folder	£15.00	
	4,924 of 15k	.925 sterling silver proof		£30.00
	4,054 of 7.5k	.925 sterling silver piedfort proof		£40.00
	644 of 1,250	.917 gold proof		£900.00

COMMEMORATIVE TYPE 9
50 (upper) || JOHNSON'S DICTIONARY 1755 (lower)
Dictionary entries for Fifty and Pence
(250th Anniversary - Samuel Johnson's English Dictionary)
Design by: Tom Phillips
(also exists dated 2009, see page 39)

			As-New	Proof
2005	17,649,000	(40,563 proofs in sets)	£7.00	£12.00
	4,029 of 7,500	.925 sterling silver proof		£25.00
	3,808 of 5,000	.925 sterling silver piedfort proof		£30.00
	579	.917 gold proof		£900.00

Also, 10,822 BU coins sold in packs with the 2005 £2 (Gunpowder plot) and 2005 £1 (Menai bridge). Value: £20

COMMEMORATIVE TYPE 10
FIFTY PENCE (lower)
Representation of the heroic acts performed by VC recipients
(150th Anniversary - Institution of the Victoria Cross)
Design by: Clive Duncan
(also exists dated 2009 and 2019, see pages 39 and 64)

			As-New	Proof
2006	10,000,500*	(37,689 proofs in sets)	£6.00	£12.00
	37,176	Specimen in folder	£15.00	
	6,872 of 7,500	.925 sterling silver proof		£30.00
	3,415 of 5,000	.925 sterling silver piedfort proof		£40.00
	816 of 1000**	.917 gold proof		£900.00

COMMEMORATIVE TYPE 11
VC || FIFTY PENCE
The obverse and reverse of the Victoria Cross
(150th Anniversary - Institution of the Victoria Cross)
Design by: Claire Aldridge
(also exists dated 2009 and 2019, see pages 39 and 64)

			As-New	Proof
2006	12,087,000*	(37,689 proofs in sets)	£6.00	£12.00
	37,176	Specimen in folder	£15.00	
	6,310 of 7,500	.925 sterling silver proof		£30.00
	3,532 of 5,000	.925 sterling silver piedfort proof		£30.00
	881 of 1000**	.917 gold proof		£900.00

* Pair of Type 10 and Type 11 coins in folder: £9.00

** 58 single coins of Type 10, 123 single coins of Type 11 and 758 pairs of Type 10 and Type 11.

27.3 mm • 8.0 grammes • cupro-nickel • plain edge

COMMEMORATIVE TYPE 12
FIFTY PENCE | 1907 | BE PREPARED | 2007
The scouting badge
(100th Anniversary - The Scout Movement)
Design by: Kerry Jones
(also exists dated 2009 and 2019, see pages 39 and 61)

			As-New	Proof
2007	7,710,750	(38,215 proofs in sets)	£7.00	£10.00
	28,942	Specimen in folder	£30.00	
	10,895 of 12,500	.925 sterling silver proof		£30.00
	1,555 of 5,000	.925 sterling silver piedfort proof		£35.00
	1,250 of 1,250	.917 gold proof		£900.00

COMMEMORATIVE TYPE 13
1759 2009 | KEW
Chinese Pagoda
(250th Anniversary - Kew Gardens)
Design by: Christopher Le Brun
(also exists dated 2019, see page 61)

			Used	As-New	Proof
2009	210,000	(34,438 proofs in sets)	£145.00	£250.00	£250.00
	11,281	Specimen in folder		£350.00	
	2,340 of 20k	.925 sterling silver proof			£380.00
	2,967	.925 sterling silver piedfort proof			£440.00
	629 of 1,000	.917 gold proof			£1,500-£2,000

Beware of Chinese made Kew Gardens 50p fakes. Some are marked as 'COPY' but many are not! The quality of the Queen's portrait tends to be poor, especially around the eye.

The Kew Gardens 50p remains the most expensive circulation type 50p and is still very much in demand. Many simply cannot bear the thought of having a gap in their 50p collection and finding one in change these days is a rare occurrence. There are speculators involved too, and prices fluctuate. Originally there was very low demand for them and they could be purchased for a couple of pounds before the mintage number was published - I still believe that far too much emphasis is put on mintage numbers these days.

A total of 210,000 (it's actually over 400k if the single packaged coins and those in the BU year-sets are included) is pretty low compared to the other fifty-pences that are currently in circulation, but there are theoretically plenty to go round, as there simply aren't anywhere near 400k people in the world that really want one to keep, and not just to turn a profit on.

COMMEMORATIVE TYPE 14
50 PENCE
An Olympic High Jumper - Obverse dated 2009
(The young viewers of Blue Peter were invited to submit
entries for the design - This was the winner)
Design by: Florence Jackson (aged 9)
Obverse: 4

As-New

2009	Initially 100k were planned, it appears to have been reduced to a max. limit of 50k. Only 19,722 were sold.		
	Specimen on card only (this coin was not circulated) **Used:£180.00**		£220.00

The mintage number of this coin wasn't made available until any years later. Few were sold and even though they were just a few pounds a few years ago, more people want one now. The increased demand has driven the value up.

COMMEMORATIVE TYPE 15
CELEBRATING ONE HUNDRED YEARS OF GIRLGUIDING UK| 50 | PENCE
Girl Guide emblems
(100th Anniversary - The Girl Guides)
Design by: Jonathan Evans and Donna Hainan
(also exists dated 2019, see page 61)

			As-New	Proof
2010	7,410,090		£5.50	£10.00
	36,693	Specimen in folder	£10.00	
	5,271 of 20k	.925 sterling silver proof		£30.00
	2,879	.925 sterling silver piedfort proof		£50.00
	355 of 1,000	.917 gold proof		no data

COMMEMORATIVE TYPE 16
WWF / 2011
Animal and plant shapes
(50th Anniversary - Word Wildlife Fund)
Design by: Matthew Dent

		Used	As-New	Proof
2011	3,400,000	£1.50	£11.00	£15.00
	11,983	Specimen in folder	£35.00	
	24,870 of 40k	.925 sterling silver proof		£50.00
	2,244	.925 sterling silver piedfort proof		£100.00
	243 of 1,500	.917 gold proof		no data

43

27.3 mm • 8.0 grammes • cupro-nickel • plain edge

COMMEMORATIVE TYPE 17 (Olympic 1)
50 PENCE
Swimmer
(London 2012 Olympics - Aquatics)
Design by: Jonathan Olliffe
Obverse: 4

		Used	As-New
2011	2,179,000	£1.50	£5.00
157,990	Specimen sealed on card		£16.00
	Withdrawn coin. Error - lines on face etc, right image £2,200.00*		
6,600	.925 Silver BU, card pack inc. specification card		around £20

* Manipulated normal coins with extra scratched lines on the face exist. Chinese made fakes are also plentiful (sometimes even in fake packaging) and continue to plague eBay and other online selling platforms.

COMMEMORATIVE TYPE 18 (Olympic 2)
50 PENCE
Hand Pulling an Arrow
(London 2012 Olympics - Archery)
Design by: Piotr Powaga
Obverse: 4

		Used	As-New
2011	3,345,500	£1.00	£4.00
140,195	Specimen sealed on card		£8.00
5,205	.925 Silver BU, card pack inc. specification card		around £20

COMMEMORATIVE TYPE 19 (Olympic 3)
50 PENCE
An Olympic High Jumper - Obverse dated 2011
(London 2012 Olympics - Athletics, see also Commemorative type 14)
Design by: Florence Jackson (aged 9)
Obverse: 4

		Used	As-New
2011	2,224,000	£1.50	£4.00
168,498	Specimen sealed on card		£8.00
7,640	.925 Silver BU, card pack inc. specification card		around £20

COMMEMORATIVE TYPE 20 (Olympic 4)

50 PENCE

Shuttlecock

(London 2012 Olympics - Badminton)

Design by: Emma Kelly

Obverse: 4

		Used	As-New
2011	2,133,500	£1.50	£5.00
124,237	Specimen sealed on card		£8.00
5,257	.925 Silver BU, card pack inc. specification card		around £20

COMMEMORATIVE TYPE 21 (Olympic 5)

50 PENCE

Players on Ball-Textured Background

(London 2012 Olympics - Basketball)

Design by: Sarah Payne

Obverse: 4

		Used	As-New
2011	1,748,000	£2.00	£5.00
137,157	Specimen sealed on card in undamaged plastic		£30.00
11,445	.925 Silver BU, card pack inc. specification card		around £30

COMMEMORATIVE TYPE 22 (Olympic 6)

50 PENCE

Player

(London 2012 Olympics - Boccia)

Design by: Justin Chung

Obverse: 4

		Used	As-New
2011	2,166,000	£1.50	£5.50
126,662	Specimen sealed on card		£8.00
5,229	.925 Silver BU, card pack inc. specification card		around £20

COMMEMORATIVE TYPE 23 (Olympic 7)

50 PENCE

Boxing Gloves with Ring Ropes

(London 2012 Olympics - Boxing)

Design by: Shane Abery

Obverse: 4

		Used	As-New
2011	2,148,500	£1.50	£5.00
142,151	Specimen sealed on card		£8.00
5,872	.925 Silver BU, card pack inc. specification card		around £20

 27.3 mm • 8.0 grammes • cupro-nickel • plain edge

COMMEMORATIVE TYPE 24 (Olympic 8)
50 PENCE
Canoeist in Choppy Waters
(London 2012 Olympics - Canoeing)
Design by: Timothy Lees
Obverse: 4

		Used	As-New
2011	2,166,500	£1.50	£5.00
116,114	Specimen sealed on card		£8.00
8,498	.925 Silver BU, card pack inc. specification card		around £20

COMMEMORATIVE TYPE 25 (Olympic 9)
50 PENCE
Cyclist
(London 2012 Olympics - Cycling)
Design by: Theo Crutchley-Mack
Obverse: 4

		Used	As-New
2011	2,090,500	£1.50	£5.00
156,872	Specimen sealed on card		£8.00
16,379	.925 Silver BU, card pack inc. specification card		around £20

COMMEMORATIVE TYPE 26 (Olympic 10)
50 PENCE
Horse, Jumping
(London 2012 Olympics - Equestrian)
Design by: Thomas Babbage
Obverse: 4

		Used	As-New
2011	2,142,500	£1.50	£5.00
145,122	Specimen sealed on card		£9.00
5,382	.925 Silver BU, card pack inc. specification card		around £20

COMMEMORATIVE TYPE 27 (Olympic 11)
50 PENCE
Fencing
(London 2012 Olympics - Fencing)
Design by: Ruth Summerfield
Obverse: 4

		Used	As-New
2011	2,115,500	£1.50	£4.50
130,815	Specimen sealed on card		£9.00
7,183	.925 Silver BU, card pack inc. specification card		around £20

COMMEMORATIVE TYPE 28 (Olympic 12)
OFFSIDE EXPLAINED / 50 PENCE
Diagram of the Offside Rule
(London 2012 Olympics - Football)
Design by: Neil Wolfson
Obverse: 4

		Used	As-New
2011	1,125,500	£14.00	£23.00
188,262	Specimen sealed on card		£25.00
6,688	.925 Silver BU, card pack inc. specification card		around £20

COMMEMORATIVE TYPE 29 (Olympic 13)
50 PENCE
Player with Ball
(London 2012 Olympics - Goalball)
Design by: Jonathan Wren
Obverse: 4

		Used	As-New
2011	1,615,500	£2.50	£5.00
114,334	Specimen sealed on card		£9.00
5,131	.925 Silver BU, card pack inc. specification card		around £20

COMMEMORATIVE TYPE 30 (Olympic 14)
50 PENCE
Gymnast
(London 2012 Olympics - Gymnastics)
Design by: Jonathan Olliffe
Obverse: 4

		Used	As-New
2011	1,720,813	£2.00	£5.00
145,895	Specimen sealed on card		£9.00
7,083	.925 Silver BU, card pack inc. specification card		around £20

COMMEMORATIVE TYPE 31 (Olympic 15)
50 PENCE
Player with Ball
(London 2012 Olympics - Handball)
Design by: Natasha Ratcliffe
Obverse: 4

		Used	As-New
2011	1,676,500	£1.50	£5.50
117,566	Specimen sealed on card		£9.00
5,593	.925 Silver BU, card pack inc. specification card		around £20

27.3 mm • 8.0 grammes • cupro-nickel • plain edge

COMMEMORATIVE TYPE 32 (Olympic 16)
50 PENCE
Two Hockey Players
(London 2012 Olympics - Hockey)
Design by: Robert Evans
Obverse: 4

		Used	As-New
2011	1,773,500	£2.50	£5.50
130,813	Specimen sealed on card		£9.00
5,642	.925 Silver BU, card pack inc. specification card		around £20

COMMEMORATIVE TYPE 33 (Olympic 17)
50 PENCE
Judo Throw
(London 2012 Olympics - Judo)
Design by: David Cornell
Obverse: 4

		Used	As-New
2011	1,161,500	£10.00	£15.00
128,442	Specimen sealed on card		£20.00
5,624	.925 Silver BU, card pack inc. specification card		around £20

COMMEMORATIVE TYPE 34 (Olympic 18)
50 PENCE
Swimmer and four Silhouettes
(London 2012 Olympics - Modern Pentathlon)
Design by: Daniel Brittain
Obverse: 4

		Used	As-New
2011	1,689,500	£2.00	£6.00
123,357	Specimen sealed on card		£9.00
5,889	.925 Silver BU, card pack inc. specification card		around £20

COMMEMORATIVE TYPE 35 (Olympic 19)
50 PENCE
Slogans and Two Rowers
(London 2012 Olympics - Rowing)
Design by: Davey Podmore
Obverse: 4

		Used	As-New
2011	1,717,300	£2.00	£5.50
140,997	Specimen sealed on card		£9.00
9,042	.925 Silver BU, card pack inc. specification card		around £20

COMMEMORATIVE TYPE 36 (Olympic 20)
50 PENCE
Sailing Boats on the Sea
(London 2012 Olympics - Sailing)
Design by: Bruce Rushin
Obverse: 4

		Used	As-New
2011	1,749,500	£2.00	£5.50
138,535	Specimen sealed on card		£9.00
7,267	.925 Silver BU, card pack inc. specification card		around £20

COMMEMORATIVE TYPE 37 (Olympic 21)
50 PENCE
Figure, Shooting
(London 2012 Olympics - Shooting)
Design by: Pravin Dewdhory
Obverse: 4

		Used	As-New
2011	1,656,500	£2.50	£5.50
125,398	Specimen sealed on card		£9.00
5,358	.925 Silver BU, card pack inc. specification card		around £20

COMMEMORATIVE TYPE 38 (Olympic 22)
50 PENCE
Table Tennis Bats, Ball etc
(London 2012 Olympics - Table Tennis)
Design by: Alan Linsdell
Obverse: 4

		Used	As-New
2011	1,737,500	£2.00	£5.50
123,195	Specimen sealed on card		£9.00
5,797	.925 Silver BU, card pack inc. specification card		around £20

COMMEMORATIVE TYPE 39 (Olympic 23)
50 PENCE
Two Figures Participating in Taekwando
(London 2012 Olympics - Taekwando)
Design by: David Gibbons
Obverse: 4

		Used	As-New
2011	1,664,000	£2.00	£6.00
120,210	Specimen sealed on card		£9.00
5,305	.925 Silver BU, card pack inc. specification card		around £20

27.3 mm • 8.0 grammes • cupro-nickel • plain edge

COMMEMORATIVE TYPE 40 (Olympic 24)
50 PENCE
Tennis Ball and Net
(London 2012 Olympics - Tennis)
Design by: Tracy Baines
Obverse: 4

		Used	As-New	Proof
2011	1,454,000	£3.00	£5.50	
144,535	Specimen sealed on card		£9.00	
6,137	.925 Silver BU, card pack inc. specification card		around £20	

COMMEMORATIVE TYPE 41 (Olympic 25)
50 PENCE
Silhouettes of Runner, Cyclist and Swimmer
(London 2012 Olympics - Triathlon)
Design by: Sarah Harvey
Obverse: 4

		Used	As-New
2011	1,163,500	£10.00	£14.00
146,354	Specimen sealed on card		£20.00
7,247	.925 Silver BU, card pack inc. specification card		around £20

COMMEMORATIVE TYPE 42 (Olympic 26)
50 PENCE
Three Players and Central Net
(London 2012 Olympics - Volleyball)
Design by: Daniela Boothman
Obverse: 4

		Used	As-New
2011	2,133,500	£1.50	£5.50
124,115	Specimen sealed on card		£9.00
5,870	.925 Silver BU, card pack inc. specification card		around £20

COMMEMORATIVE TYPE 43 (Olympic 27)
50 PENCE
Basic Outline of a Weightlifter
(London 2012 Olympics - Weightlifting)
Design by: Rob Shakespeare
Obverse: 4

		Used	As-New
2011	1,879,500	£2.00	£5.00
121,778	Specimen sealed on card		£10.00
5,500	.925 Silver BU, card pack inc. specification card		around £20

COMMEMORATIVE TYPE 44 (Olympic 28)
50 PENCE
Man Playing, Ball in Lap
(London 2012 Olympics - Wheelchair Rugby)
Design by: Natasha Ratcliffe
Obverse: 4

		Used	As-New
2011	1,765,500	£2.00	£5.00
121,175	Specimen sealed on card		£10.00
5,956	.925 Silver BU, card pack inc. specification card		around £20

COMMEMORATIVE TYPE 45 (Olympic 29)
50 PENCE
Wrestlers
(London 2012 Olympics - Wrestling)
Design by: Roderick Enriquez
Obverse: 4

		Used	As-New
2011	1,129,500	£8.00	£10.00
127,279	Specimen sealed on card		£15.00
5,727	.925 Silver BU, card pack inc. specification card		around £20

Olympic 30
Medallion Only (309,013 were sold.)
The Royal Mint issued a medallion with the 29x 50p coins. It's not
a coin, but is mentioned here for completeness. Values are around
£30 - £40.
Similar 'completer' medals were issued later with a different non
Olympic design and are usually cheaper.

Gold Versions:

Gold proofs were struck by the Royal Mint and given to the designers of the coins. They are
therefore extremely rare.

Gold piedfort proofs were struck for eleven sports that Great Britain won medals for. Seventeen
complete sets of eleven coins were sold, plus some singles. Total coins: Athletics - 12, Boxing - 3, Canoeing - 2, Cycling - 11, Equestrian - 7, Rowing - 11, Sailing - 2, Taekwondo - 1, Tennis - 10 and Triathlon
- 7. The higher numbers shown in previous editions are assumed to have been maximum mintages.

51

27.3 mm • 8.0 grammes • cupro-nickel • plain edge

COMMEMORATIVE TYPE 46
FIFTY PENCE / 50
Ironside's rejected design for the original 1969 50p
(This is what the original first 50p might have looked like)
Design by: Christopher Ironside
Obverse: 4

		As-New	Proof
2013	7,000,000	£40.00	£40.00
4,403	Specimen in folder	£80.00	
1,823 of 6,513	.925 sterling silver proof		£60.00
816 of 1,500	.925 sterling silver piedfort proof		£90.00
198 of 340	.917 gold proof, price new		£800.00

COMMEMORATIVE TYPE 47
BENJAMIN / COMPOSER BORN 1913 / BRITTEN
His name in a double stave,
'Blow Bugle blow' and 'Set the
wild echoes flying'.
(To mark the centenary of the birth
of Benjamin Britten)
Design by: Tom Phillips

		Used	As-New	Proof
2013	5,300,000	£1.00	£45.00	
5,098	Specimen in folder		£60.00	
717 of 2k	.925 sterling silver proof*			£200.00
515 of 1,000	.925 sterling silver piedfort proof			£280.00
70 of 150	.917 gold proof, price new			£1,000.00

*The relatively low silver proof mintage combined with some tabloid hype caused this one to rise in value during 2016. People were also asking silly prices for the normal circulation coin as a result!

COMMEMORATIVE TYPE 48
XX / COMMONWEALTH GAMES GLASGOW / 2014
Male cyclist and female runner
(To commemorate the
20th Commonwealth Games)
Design by: Alex Loudon and Dan Flashman

		As-New	Proof
2014	6,500,000	£9.00	£12.00
14,581*	Specimen in folder	£12.00	
2,159 of 6,014	.925 sterling silver proof		£45.00
992 of 1,000	.925 sterling silver piedfort proof		£70.00
233 of 385	.917 gold proof		£1,000.00
	*plus 7,918 sold with stamps.		

COMMEMORATIVE TYPE 49a
THE BATTLE OF BRITAIN 1940
WITHOUT DENOMINATION
(Pilots scrambling, planes in flight above)
Design by: Gary Breeze & Lee Breeze
Obverse: 4
(Ian Rank-Broadley portrait, as shown)

Note that the denomination is omitted on all coins with the Ian Rank-Broadley portrait (from the 2015 sets), shown here. Apparently deliberate, but I'm sure this was actually an oversight! Confusingly, silver proof and silver piedfort proofs also exist, originally only as part of sets made early in 2015.

		Used	As-New	Proof
2015	(4th portrait, originally in sets only)	£5.00	£10.00	£30.00
35,199	Specimen in folder		£20.00	
1,500 max.	.925 sterling silver proof, only available in sets			£75.00?
1,500 max.	.925 sterling silver piedfort proof, only available in sets			£100.00?
233	.917 gold proof, from annual set			no data

COMMEMORATIVE TYPE 49b
THE BATTLE OF BRITAIN 1940
ALSO WITHOUT DENOMINATION
Precious metal proofs only, reverse as 49a
(Jody Clark portrait, no denomination, as shown)

Bizarrely the main issue precious metal proof coins have the new portrait, but are also missing the denomination.

    Proof

		Proof
2015	(5th portrait, precious metal proofs only)	
4,200 max.	.925 sterling silver proof	£80.00
1,940 max.	.925 sterling silver piedfort proof	£100.00
520 max.	.917 gold proof	£1,200.00

COMMEMORATIVE TYPE 49c
THE BATTLE OF BRITAIN 1940
WITH DENOMINATION
Circulation issue, reverse as 49a
(Jody Clark portrait, with '50 PENCE', as shown)
(also dated 2019, see page 64)

For circulation issues the Royal Mint released these coins, which not only have the new Jody Clark 5th portrait of the Queen, they also have the denomination written as '50 PENCE' on the obverse.

	Used	As-New
2015 5,900,000 (5th portrait with '50 PENCE')	FV	£5.00

53

27.3 mm • 8.0 grammes • cupro-nickel • plain edge

COMMEMORATIVE TYPE 50
BATTLE OF HASTINGS / 1066 / 2016
(Representation of a soldier inspired by the Bayeux Tapestry)
Design by: John Bergdahl
(also dated 2019, see page 64)

		As-New	Proof
2016	6,700,000	£8.00	£18.00
21,718*	Specimen in folder	£12.00	
2,338 of 6k	.925 sterling silver proof		£50.00
1,469 of 1,500	.925 sterling silver piedfort proof		£120.00
237 of 500	.917 gold proof		no data

* Plus 7,877 in packs with stamps and 5,139 BU coins in tubes (to other retailers).

COMMEMORATIVE TYPE 51
BEATRIX POTTER SERIES No.1, BEATRIX POTTER
(Silhouette of Beatrix Potter, name, dates and Peter Rabbit character)
Design by: Emma Noble

		As-New	Proof
2016	6,900,000	£8.00	
61,658*	Specimen in pack	£12.00	
7,471 of 7,750	.925 sterling silver proof		£180.00
2,486	.925 sterling silver piedfort proof		£230.00
732 of 750	.917 gold proof		no data

* Plus 14,777 in sets of five Potter coins and 48,650 BU coins in tubes (to other retailers).

COMMEMORATIVE TYPE 52
BEATRIX POTTER SERIES, No.2, PETER RABBIT
(The character Peter Rabbit, his name either side)
Design by: Emma Noble
Obverse: As Type 51

		As-New	Proof
2016	9,700,000 Standard, non-coloured coin	£6.00	
	Standard, non-coloured coin. Extra left whisker, (die damage). Used: £3.00		
93,851	Standard, non-coloured coin in pack (+42,384 in tubes) £10.00		
14,995	.925 coloured sterling silver proof in clear Perspex box		£350.00
500	.925 coloured sterling silver proof in First Day Cover envelope		£250.00
250	.925 coloured sterling silver proof in black box (from Potter shops)		£300.00
250	.925 coloured sterling silver proof in cherry box + extras		no data

Despite the coins all being the same, the type of packaging and even the serial number (some people prefer very low numbers) can play a role with values! There are some variations to the values, which seem to be down to the mood of buyers and the number on offer.

54

COMMEMORATIVE TYPE 53
BEATRIX POTTER SERIES, No. 3,
JEMIMA PUDDLE-DUCK
(The character Jemina Puddle-Duck, her name either side**)
Design by: Emma Noble
Obverse: As Type 51

		Used	As-New	Proof
2016	2,100,000 Standard, non-coloured coin	£8.00	£15.00	
54,929*	Standard, non-coloured coin in pack		£16.00	
14,921	.925 sterling silver proof in clear Perspex box			£100.00
250**	.925 sterling silver proof in black box			£120.00

* Plus 69,231 sold in tubes. ** Plus 750 in Royal Mail boxes.
The Puddle-Duck 50p is often seen with signs of 'die-clash', which results in outlines of the duck and/or the Queen appearing on the opposing side.

COMMEMORATIVE TYPE 54
BEATRIX POTTER SERIES, No. 4,
SQUIRREL NUTKIN
(The character Squirrel Nutkin, his name either side**)
Design by: Emma Noble
Obverse: As Type 51

		As-New	Proof
2016	5,000,000 Standard, non-coloured coin	£7.00	
45,884*	Standard, non-coloured coin in pack	£12.00	
14,893	.925 sterling silver proof in clear Perspex box		£60.00
250**	.925 sterling silver proof in black box		£80.00

* Plus 53,660 sold in tubes. ** Plus 750 in Royal Mail boxes.

COMMEMORATIVE TYPE 55
BEATRIX POTTER SERIES, No.5,
MRS TIGGY-WINKLE
(The character Mrs Tiggy-Winkle, her name either side**)
Design by: Emma Noble
Obverse: As Type 51

		As-New	Proof
2016	8,800,000 Standard, non-coloured coin	£6.00	
47,597*	Standard, non-coloured coin in pack (+52,937 in tubes)	£12.00	
14,993	.925 sterling silver proof in clear Perspex box		£60.00
250**	.925 sterling silver proof in black box		£80.00

* Plus 52,937 sold in tubes. * Plus 750 in Royal Mail boxes.

COMMEMORATIVE TYPE 56
TEAM GB
(Swimmer, Team GB logo and Olympic rings)
Design by: Tim Sharp
Obverse: As Type 51

		As-New	Proof
2016	6,400,000	£5.00	
34,162*	Specimen in folder	£8.00	
3,956 of 5k*	.925 sterling silver proof		£30.00
1,296 of 2,016	.925 sterling silver piedfort proof		£55.00
302 of 306	.917 gold proof		£900.00

* Plus 500 silver proof in capsules and 8,484 'BU' coins in tubes for other retailers.

COMMEMORATIVE TYPE 57
SIR ISAAC NEWTON
(Rings and ellipses around the sun/
SIR ISAAC NEWTON above,
FIFTY PENCE below)
Design by: Aaron West

		Used	As-New	Proof
2017 (57A)	1,801,500 (many exist with die-clash)	£3.00	£6.00	
64,859	Specimen in folder		£15.00	
3,926 of 7k	.925 sterling silver proof			£55.00
1,985 of 3k	.925 sterling silver piedfort proof			£75.00
287 of 634	.917 gold proof			£900.00
2018 (57B)	Dated 2018, 'Strike Your Own' in card package.	See SYO section		

706 base metal proof versions were also sold.

COMMEMORATIVE TYPE 58
THE TALE OF PETER RABBIT
BEATRIX POTTER SERIES, No.6
(Peter Rabbit walking right with the title text
surrounding him)
Design by: Emma Noble
Obverse: As Type 51, dated 2017

		As-New	Proof
2017	19,900,000	£4.00	
223,661	Specimen in folder, price new	£10.00	
29,885	.925 coloured sterling silver proof in clear Perspex box		£30.00
3,150 max.*	.925 coloured sterling silver proof in black box (various)		£30.00
3,500 max.*	.925 coloured sterling silver proof in large box with book		£60.00
377	.917 gold proof, 15.5g in large box with book		£1,200.00

The Specimen in folders figures for all 2017 Beatrix Potter coins also include coins sold to retailers in tubes.

*A max. figure of 40k for the total silver proofs was quoted on the Royal Mint website.

COMMEMORATIVE TYPE 59
MR JEREMY FISHER
BEATRIX POTTER SERIES, No.7
(The character Mr Jeremy Fisher, his name to the left)
Design by: Emma Noble
Obverse: As Type 51, dated 2017

			As-New	Proof
2017	9,900,000		£4.00	
167,160	Specimen in folder		£9.00	
27,955*	.925 coloured sterling silver proof in clear Perspex box			£25.00
*?	.925 coloured sterling silver proof in black box (various)			£25.00
1,427 of 3.5k	.925 coloured sterling silver proof in large box with book			£60.00

* A max. figure of 40k quoted, see notes for coin type 58.

COMMEMORATIVE TYPE 60
TOM KITTEN
BEATRIX POTTER SERIES, No.8
(The character Tom Kitten facing, his name flanking him)
Design by: Emma Noble
Obverse: As Type 51, dated 2017

			As-New	Proof
2017	9,500,000		£4.00	
160,497	Specimen in folder		£9.00	
27,955*	.925 coloured sterling silver proof in clear Perspex box			£28.00
?*	.925 coloured sterling silver proof in black box (various)			£28.00
1,427 of 3.5k	.925 coloured sterling silver proof in large box with book			£50.00

* A max. figure of 40k quoted, see notes for coin type 58.

COMMEMORATIVE TYPE 61
BENJAMIN BUNNY
BEATRIX POTTER SERIES, No.9
(The character Benjamin Bunny, facing his name flanking him)
Design by: Emma Noble
Obverse: As Type 51, dated 2017

			As-New	Proof
2017	25,000,000		£4.00	
106,040	Specimen in folder		£7.00	
29,801*	.925 coloured sterling silver proof in clear Perspex box			£32.00
?*	.925 coloured sterling silver proof in black box (various)			£32.00
1,607 of 3.5k	.925 coloured sterling silver proof in large box with book			£50.00

* A max. figure of 40k quoted, see notes for coin type 58.

27.3 mm • 8.0 grammes • cupro-nickel • plain edge

COMMEMORATIVE TYPE 62
REPRESENTATION OF THE PEOPLE ACT
(Group of people with '1918 REPRESENTATION OF THE PEOPLE ACT' above them)
Design by: Stephen Taylor
Obverse: As Type 51, dated 2018

		As-New	Proof
2018	9,000,000 circ + 50,925 total BU	£4.00	£12.00
	Specimen in folder (12,311)	£10.00	
1,773 of 6.5k	.925 sterling silver proof		£40.00
1,918 max.	.925 sterling silver piedfort proof		£60.00
139 of 300	.917 gold proof		£1,000.00

See also coin 57, for the 2018 dated Isaac Newton 50p.

COMMEMORATIVE TYPE 63
PETER RABBIT
BEATRIX POTTER SERIES, No.10
(Peter Rabbit eating radishes)
Design by: Emma Noble
Obverse: As Type 51, dated 2018

		Used	As-New	Proof
2018	1,400,000 circ + 163,403 total BU	£4.00	£6.00	
	Specimen in folder (48,229)		£9.00	
34,681 of 45k*	.925 coloured sterling silver proof			£30.00
2,700 of 3.5k	As above, in box with book			£60.00
262 of 450	.917 gold proof, in box with book, price new			£1,000.00

COMMEMORATIVE TYPE 64
FLOPSY BUNNY
BEATRIX POTTER SERIES, No.11
(Flopsy Bunny looking right)
Design by: Emma Noble
Obverse: As Type 51, dated 2018

		Used	As-new	Proof
2018	1,400,000 circ + 132,759 total BU	£5.00	£7.00	
	Specimen in folder (29,929)		£10.00	
32,692 of 45k*	.925 coloured sterling silver proof			£30.00
1,729 of 3.5k	As above, in box with book			£60.00

* Various other silver proof presentations were sold.

COMMEMORATIVE TYPE 65
THE TAILOR OF GLOUCESTER
BEATRIX POTTER SERIES, No.11
(Helpful little mouse reading a newspaper)
Design by: Emma Noble
Obverse: As Type 51, dated 2018

		Used	As-New	Proof
2018	3,900,000 circ + 136,357 total BU	£1.50	£5.00	
	Specimen in folder (27,079)		£7.00	
26,955 of 40k	.925 coloured sterling silver proof, price new			£32.00
970 of 3.5k	As above, in box with book			£60.00

COMMEMORATIVE TYPE 66
MRS TITTLEMOUSE
BEATRIX POTTER SERIES, No.12
(Mrs Tittlemouse facing left)
Design by: Emma Noble
Obverse: As Type 51, dated 2018

		Used	As-New	Proof
2018	1,700,000 circ + 130,385 total BU	£3.00	£5.00	
	Specimen in folder (27,497)		£10.00	
27,081 of 40k	.925 coloured sterling silver proof			£30.00
885 of 3.5k	As above, in box with book			£60.00

COMMEMORATIVE TYPE 67
PADDINGTON BEAR 60th ANNIVERSARY (1 of 4)
(Paddington bear sitting at Paddington Station)
Design by: David Knapton
Obverse: As Type 51, dated 2018

		As-New	Proof
2018	5,001,000 circ + 174,546 total BU	£4.00	£5.00
	Specimen in folder (57,206)	£10.00	
39,482 of 75k	.925 coloured sterling silver proof		£26.00
599 of 1,250	.917 gold proof		£900.00

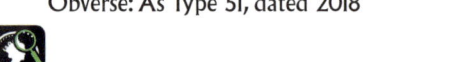

27.3 mm • 8.0 grammes • cupro-nickel • plain edge

COMMEMORATIVE TYPE 68
PADDINGTON BEAR 60th ANNIVERSARY (2 of 4)
(Paddington bear waving flag, Buckingham palace in background)
Design by: David Knapton
Obverse: As Type 51, dated 2018

		As-New	Proof
2018	5,901,000 circ + 149,842 total BU	£4.00	
	Specimen in folder (45,544), price new	£10.00	
33,370 of 75k	.925 coloured sterling silver proof		£24.00
597 of 1,250	.917 gold proof		£900.00

COMMEMORATIVE TYPE 69
RAYMOND BRIGGS' 'SNOWMAN' 40th ANNIVERSARY
(Snowman and boy flying)
Design by: Natasha Ratcliffe
Obverse: As Type 51, dated 2018

		As-New	Proof
2018	170,705 total BU	£15.00	
	Specimen in folder (67,644)	£25.00	
14,968 of 20k*	.925 coloured sterling silver proof		£45.00
400	.917 gold proof		£1,000.00

* Plus another 5,863 in other packaging/presentations.

The 2019 retrospective 50th Anniversary set, part one (British Culture).

In a similar fashion to 2009 for the 40th anniversary of the 50p coin, the Royal Mint released sets of 50p coins for the 50th anniversary. This time around the reverse types seem to have been chosen fairly randomly.

Despite it being made clear from the outset that both sets of five coins would only be available to buy in proof form, they were also sold as BU sets a few weeks later - this no doubt facilitated a hefty wedge of extra profit for the Royal Mint and there were quite a few disappointed people who had bought the proof sets, only to find out later on that their coins were less exclusive.

The first set of five different coins included the following:

The obverses are shown first, matched to the five different reverses. The original reverse designs for three of the coins (right) already include the face value, and for that reason an obverse type with just the date and no '50 PENCE' has been used.

Set of 5 'British Culture' themed fifty pence coins, comprising:

NEW PENCE Britannia* (original REVERSE 1), Kew Gardens (TYPE 13), the Four Minute Mile (TYPE 8), Scouting (TYPE 12) and Girlguiding (TYPE 15).

		As-New	Proof
31,250*	Base metal 'Uncirculated' set	£90.00	
3,500	Base metal proof set		£110.00
1,933 of 1,969	Silver proof set		£200.00
569 of 1,220	Silver piedfort proof set		£350.00
71	Gold proof set, price new		£3,825.00
50	Gold piedfort proof set, price new		£9,370.00

* Plus around 53,000 of each coin, sold to trade customers.

All of the above proof set versions sold out very quickly (before people knew they would also appear in non-proof form) and a lot appeared - instantly - on eBay and other online sales platforms. Many sets have been split for the Kew Gardens coin, as it's a cheaper way of filling the gap, instead of sourcing an original 2009 coin - for this reason the Kew on its own tends to be more expensive than the others (approx £70 at the moment). Another set of five different coins appeared later in 2019, see page 64.

*The coin with the Britannia 'NEW PENCE' type reverse was also made available as a 'Strike Your Own' at the beginning of 2019 (see next page and the Strike Your Own section).

COMMEMORATIVE TYPE 70
SIR ARTHUR CONAN DOYLE
(Silhouette of Sherlock Holmes, book titles flanking him)
Design by: Stephen Raw
Obverse: As Type 57, dated 2019

		As-New	Proof
2019	8,602,000 circ + 80,094 total BU	£4.00	£7.00
	Specimen in folder (30,349) (also an SYO)£10.00		
5,805 of 7.5k	.925 sterling silver proof		£30.00
2,485 of 2.5k	.925 sterling silver piedfort proof		£50.00
398 of 600	.917 gold proof		£900.00

STRIKE YOUR OWN (TYPE 71)
NEW PENCE BRITANNIA REVERSE
(The original 50p reverse, used 1969 - 1981)
Design by: Christopher Ironside

See page 192 for more info on the 'Strike Your Own' coins.

COMMEMORATIVE TYPE 72
THE GRUFFALO (1 of 2)
(The Gruffalo facing right, his name above)
Design by: Magic Light Pictures Ltd
Obverse: As Type 71

		As-New	Proof
2019	236,552 total BU	£8.00	
	Specimen in folder (108,014), price new	£10.00	
24,614*	.925 coloured sterling silver proof		£45.00
599	.917 gold proof		£900.00

* Plus another 1,806 sold for use in other presentations.

COMMEMORATIVE TYPE 73
STEPHEN HAWKING
(Innovation in Science series no. 1)
(Representation of a black hole with an equation and his name)
Design by: Edwina Ellis
Obverse: As Type 71

		As-New	Proof
2019	212,209 total BU	£8.00	
	Specimen in folder (107,209), price new	£10.00	
5,465 of 7k	.925 sterling silver proof		£60.00
2,481	.925 sterling silver piedfort proof		£110.00
396	.917 gold proof		£1,100.00

COMMEMORATIVE TYPE 74
PETER RABBIT
Design by: Emma Noble
(Peter Rabbit again)
Obverse: As Type 71

		As-New	Proof
2019	125,660 total BU	£14.00	
	Specimen in folder (47,527), price new	£20.00	
27,703 of 35k*	.925 sterling silver proof (with colour)		£40.00
497 of 500	.917 gold proof, price new		£980.00

* Plus 250 sold via the Post Office

COMMEMORATIVE TYPE 75
PADDINGTON BEAR 60th ANNIVERSARY? (3 of 4)
(Paddington bear wearing coat, Tower of London in back-
ground)
Design by: David Knapton
Obverse: As Type 71

		Used	As-New	Proof
2019	9,001,000 circ + 87,965 total BU	FV	£5.00	
	Specimen in folder (32,465), price new		£10.00	
16,887 of 32.5k	.925 sterling silver proof (with colour)			£65.00
596	.917 gold proof, price new			£1,020.00

The 2019 retrospective 50th Anniversary set, part two (British Military).

This is the second set of five different loosely themed coins. It includes the following:

The obverses are shown first, matched to the five different reverses. The original reverse designs for three of the coins (right) already include the face value, and for that reason an obverse type with just the date and no '50 PENCE' has been used.

Set of 5 'British Military' themed fifty pence coins, comprising: D-Day (TYPE 3), Victoria Cross award and acts (TYPES 10 & 11), Battle of Britain (TYPE 49) and the Battle of Hastings (TYPE 50).

		As-New	Proof
9,902*	Base metal 'Uncirculated' set	£40.00	
3,144 of 3,500	Base metal proof set		£50.00
1,934 of 1,969	Silver proof set		£120.00
333 of 1,220	Silver piedfort proof set		£400.00
75	Gold proof set, price new		£3,825.00
44 of 50	Gold piedfort proof set, price new		£9,370.00

* Plus 22,500 of each coin, sold to trade customers.

COMMEMORATIVE TYPE 76
PADDINGTON BEAR 60th ANNIVERSARY? (4 of 4)
(Paddington doffing hat, St. Paul's Cathedral in background)
Design by: David Knapton
Obverse: As Type 71

		Used	As-New	Proof
2019	9,001,000 circ + 83,718 total BU	FV	£5.00	
	Specimen in folder (28,219), price new		£10.00	
13,877 of 32.5k	.925 sterling silver proof (with colour), price new*			£65.00
556	.917 gold proof			£900.00

* Plus a further 140 sold to trade customers.

COMMEMORATIVE TYPE 77
GRUFFALO & MOUSE (2 of 2)
(The second Gruffalo commemorative)
Design by: Magic Light Pictures
Obverse: As Type 71

		As-New	Proof
2019	98,244 total BU	£12.00	
	Specimen in folder (37,994)	£16.00	
12,435 of 30k	.925 sterling silver proof (with colour), price new		£65.00
443	.917 gold proof, price new		£1,020.00

COMMEMORATIVE TYPE 78
BRITANNIA with mint mark and lettered angles
(Re-issue of the original 50p design, 50 years after its first use)
Design by: Christopher Ironside (in the 1960s)
Obverse: As Type 71

		As-New	Proof
2019	84,688 total BU	£7.00	
	Specimen in folder (10,990), price new	£10.00	
3,479	.925 sterling silver proof		£55.00
1,962	.925 sterling silver piedfort proof		£110.00
299	.917 gold proof, price new		£945.00
69	.925 gold piedfort proof, price new		?

27.3 mm • 8.0 grammes • cupro-nickel • plain edge

COMMEMORATIVE TYPE 79
SNOWMAN 2 (2019)
Design by: Snowman Enterprises
(Another Snowman coin, issued about a
year after the first - Type 69)
Obverse: As Type 71

		As-New	Proof
2019	118,250 total BU	£7.00	
	Specimen in folder(41,959) price new	£10.00	
12,452 of 27.5k	.925 sterling silver proof (with colour), price new*		£65.00
315 of 600	.917 gold proof, price new		£1,020.00

* Plus another 200 sold to trade customers.

COMMEMORATIVE TYPE 80
WALLACE & GROMIT
Design by: Nick Park
(To mark the 30th anniversary of Wallace & Gromit)
Obverse: As Type 71

		As-New	Proof
2019	102,750 total BU	£20.00	
	Specimen in folder (42,251)	£25.00	
15,085 of 27.5k	.925 sterling silver proof (with colour), price new		£65.00
624 of 630	.917 gold proof, price new		£1,020.00

COMMEMORATIVE TYPE 81
TEAM GB
Design by: David Knapton
(In support of Team GB at the
2020 Tokyo Olympics)
Obverses: as shown, right

			As-New	Proof
2020		64,816*	£9.00	£14.00
2021	84,559	(2021) Specimen in folder (22,362), price new	£10.00	
11,865		(2021) As above, with added colour, price new	£20.00	
5,485		(2021) .925 sterling silver proof (with colour), price new		£67.50
1,495		(2021) .925 sterling silver piedfort proof (with colour), price new		£105.00
250		(2021) .917 gold proof, price new		£1,005.00

*Due to the pandemic, the Tokyo 2020 Olympic games was re-scheduled and took place in 2021. 2020 dated
Team GB coins were originally included in the 2020 BU/Proof sets and BU coins were also sold to trade customers. In June 2021 the Royal Mint introduced individual BU packs and precious metal proof versions of the
coin, all dated 2021.

COMMEMORATIVE TYPE 82
BREXIT (Withdrawal from the EU)
Design by: Royal Mint in-house
(Withdrawal from the European Union, 31st January 2020)
Obverse: As Type 81

		Used	As-New	Proof
2020	10,001,000 circ + 303,373 total BU	FV	£4.00	
	Escapee with incorrect 31st October 2019 date		one known	
	Specimen in folder (206,671), price new		£10.00	
4,989	Specimen in folder with a 1973 EEC entry 50p*		£60.00	
46,903	.925 sterling silver proof, price new			£60.00
1,494	.917 gold proof			£950.00

* The 1973 coins have been sourced second hand and many I've seen have been in unremarkable condition, despite them being described as 'Brilliant Uncirculated' on the back of the packs.

COMMEMORATIVE TYPE 83
DINOSAURIA (1 of 3 in 2020)
Design by: Robert Nicholls
(Megalosaurus - one of three Dinosauria themed coins)
Obverse: As Type 81

		As-New	Proof
2020	106,506 total BU	£5.00	
	Specimen in folder (29,037), price new	£10.00	
27,830 of 50k	Specimen in folder with added colour, price new	£20.00	
2,999	.925 sterling silver proof, price new		£60.00
7,001	.925 sterling silver proof with added colour, price new		£65.00
342	.917 gold proof, price new		£1,020.00

COMMEMORATIVE TYPE 84
DINOSAURIA (2 of 3 in 2020)
Design by: Robert Nicholls
(Iguanodon - one of three Dinosauria themed coins)
Obverse: As Type 81

		As-New	Proof
2020	92,266 total BU	£6.00	
	Specimen in folder (25,277), price new	£10.00	
25,671 of 50k	Specimen in folder with added colour, price new	£20.00	
2,427 of 3,010	.925 sterling silver proof, price new		£60.00
6,339 of 7,710	.925 sterling silver proof with added colour, price new		£65.00
218 of 360	.917 gold proof, price new		£1,020.00

COMMEMORATIVE TYPE 85
PETER RABBIT
Design by: Emma Noble
(Peter Rabbit, again. Squeezing under a gate)
Obverse: As Type 81

		As-New	Proof
2020	109,987 total BU	£20.00	
	Specimen in folder (34,647)	£25.00	
14,478	.925 sterling silver proof (with colour), price new		£60.00
278 of 500	.917 gold proof, price new		£1,020.00

COMMEMORATIVE TYPE 86
DINOSAURIA (3 of 3 in 2020)
Design by: Robert Nicholls
(Hylaeosaurus - one of three Dinosauria themed coins)
Obverse: As Type 81

		As-New	Proof
2020	91,086 total BU	£6.00	
	Specimen in folder (23,048), price new	£10.00	
23,048 of 50k	Specimen in folder with added colour, price new	£20.00	
2,188 of 3,010	.925 sterling silver proof, price new		£62.50
5,973 of 7k	.925 sterling silver proof with added colour, price new		£67.50
190 of 360	.917 gold proof, price new		£1,005.00

COMMEMORATIVE TYPE 87
ROSALIND FRANKLIN
(Innovation in Science series no. 2)
Design by: David Knapton
(Rosalind Franklin DNA helix discovery)
Obverse: As Type 81

		As-New	Proof
2020	69,277 total BU	£7.00	
	Specimen in folder (17,527), price new	£10.00	
3,469	.925 sterling silver proof, price new		£57.50
1,500	.925 sterling silver piedfort proof, price new		£100.00
240	.917 gold proof, price new		£1,005.00

COMMEMORATIVE TYPE 88
WINNIE-THE-POOH
Design by: © Disney
(The first of 9 Winnie-the-Pooh themed coins)
Obverse: As Type 81

		As-New	Proof
2020	100,731 total BU	£6.00	
	Specimen in folder (31,735), price new	£10.00	
27,217 of 45k	Specimen in folder with added colour, price new	£20.00	
17,150	.925 sterling silver proof with added colour, price new		£67.50
520	.917 gold proof, price new		£1,005.00
96	.917 gold piedfort proof		no data

COMMEMORATIVE TYPE 89
WINNIE-THE-POOH - Christopher Robin
Design by: © Disney
(The second of 9 Winnie-the-Pooh themed coins)
Obverse: As Type 81

		As-New	Proof
2020	82,939 total BU	£6.00	
	Specimen in folder (19,178), price new	£10.00	
22,440 of 45k	Specimen in folder with added colour, price new	£20.00	
10,840 / 18,010	.925 sterling silver proof with added colour, price new		£67.50
287 of 535	.917 gold proof, price new		£1,005.00

COMMEMORATIVE TYPE 90
DIVERSITY
Design by: Dominique Evans
(A British Diversity themed coin)
Obverse: As Type 81

		As-New	Proof
2020	10,300,000 circ + 65,517 total BU	£3.00	
	Specimen in folder (39,522), price new	£10.00	
1,415 of 25,010	.925 sterling silver proof, price new		£57.50
609 of 2.5k	.925 sterling silver piedfort proof, price new		£100.00
73 of 960	.917 gold proof, price new		£1,005.00
78 of 200	.917 gold piedfort proof, price new		£2,015.00

69

27.3 mm • 8.0 grammes • cupro-nickel • plain edge

COMMEMORATIVE TYPE 91
WINNIE-THE-POOH - Piglet
Design by: © Disney
(The third of 9 Winnie-the-Pooh themed coins)
Obverse: As Type 81

		As-New	Proof
2020	83,213 total BU	£5.00	
	Specimen in folder (22,714), price new	£10.00	
19,069 of 45k	Specimen in folder with added colour, price new	£20.00	
10,660 / 18,010	.925 sterling silver proof with added colour, price new		£67.50
258 of 535	.917 gold proof, price new		£1,005.00

COMMEMORATIVE TYPE 92
SNOWMAN 3 (2020)
Design by: Robin Shaw
(Another Snowman coin, issued two years after the
actual Snowman commemorative - Type 69)
Obverse: As Type 81

		As-New	Proof
2020	84,318 total BU	£6.00	
	Specimen in folder (18,337), price new	£10.00	
8,513 of 15k	Specimen in folder with added colour, price new	£20.00	
6,973	.925 sterling silver proof with added colour, price new		£67.50
259	.917 gold proof, price new		£1,125.00

COMMEMORATIVE TYPE 93
JOHN LOGIE BAIRD
(Innovation in Science series no. 3)
Design by: Osborne Ross
(To mark 75 years since the death of J Logie Baird)
Obverse: as shown, right

		As-New	Proof
2021	61,559 total BU	£6.00	
	Specimen in folder (11,361), price new	£10.00	
1,665 of 5,010	.925 sterling silver proof, price new		£57.50
946 of 1.9k	.925 sterling silver piedfort proof, price new		£100.00
96 of 300	.917 gold proof, price new		£1,005.00

COMMEMORATIVE TYPE 94A / 94B
DECIMALISATION DAY
Design by: Dominique Evans
(To mark 50 years since decimalisation)
Obverses: A - the Arnold Machin portrait, shown right or obverse B - the Jody Clark portrait, for some coins sold individually (same obverse as Type 93).

		As-New	Proof
2021	(not put into general circulation)		
49,411 BU	Sold to trade, also within annual sets (Obverse A)	£12.00	
84,086 BU	Specimen in folder (25,388) (Obverse B), price new	£10.00	
5,721 of 6,710	.925 sterling silver proof (Obverse B), price new		£57.50
2,494	.925 sterling silver piedfort proof (Obverse B), price new		£100.00
474 max	.917 gold proof (Obverse B), price new*		£1,005.00
199	.917 gold piedfort proof, (Obverse B) price new		£2,015.00

* A maximum of 700 (464 sold) were also available as 'Strike on the Day' (15th Feb 2021), priced £1,225.00.

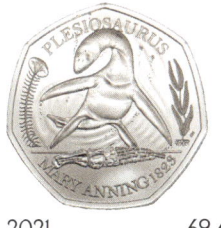

COMMEMORATIVE TYPE 95
MARY ANNING (1 of 3)
Design by: Robert Nicholls
(Temnodontosaurus - one of three Mary Anning dinosaur themed coins)
Obverse: As Type 93

		As-New	Proof
2021	71,581 total BU	£8.00	
	Specimen in folder (13,173), price new	£10.00	
10,694 of 50k	Specimen in folder with added colour, price new	£20.00	
1,108 of 3,010	.925 sterling silver proof, price new		£62.50
3,884 of 7,410	.925 sterling silver proof with added colour, price new		£67.50
130 of 260	.917 gold proof, price new		£1,005.00

COMMEMORATIVE TYPE 96
MARY ANNING (2 of 3)
Design by: Robert Nicholls
(Plesiosaurus - one of three Mary Anning dinosaur themed coins)
Obverse: As Type 93

		As-New	Proof
2021	69,621 total BU	£8.00	
	Specimen in folder (12,594), price new	£10.00	
10,364 of 50k	Specimen in folder with added colour, price new	£20.00	
901 of 3,010	.925 sterling silver proof, price new		£62.50
3,685 of 7,410	.925 sterling silver proof with added colour, price new		£67.50
93 of 260	.917 gold proof, price new		£1,005.00

27.3 mm • 8.0 grammes • cupro-nickel • plain edge

COMMEMORATIVE TYPE 97
MARY ANNING (3 of 3)
Design by: Robert Nicholls
(Dimorphodon - one of three Mary Anning
dinosaur themed coins)

		As-New	Proof
2021	60,970 total BU	£8.00	
	Specimen in folder (12,673), price new	£10.00	
10,354 of 50k	Specimen in folder with added colour, price new	£20.00	
906 of 3,010	.925 sterling silver proof, price new		£62.50
3,574 of 7,410	.925 sterling silver proof with added colour, price new		£67.50
95 of 260	.917 gold proof, price new		£1,005.00

TEAM GB (dated 2021), See: COMMEMORATIVE TYPE 81

COMMEMORATIVE TYPE 98
WINNIE-THE-POOH - Pooh & Friends
Design by: © Disney
(The fourth of 9 Winnie-the-Pooh themed coins)
Obverse: As Type 97

		As-New	Proof
2021	74,777 total BU	£8.00	
	Specimen in folder (17,614), price new	£10.00	
13,335 of 45k	Specimen in folder with added colour, price new	£20.00	
7,602 of 18k	.925 sterling silver proof with added colour, price new		£69.50
151 of 535	.917 gold proof, price new		£1,195.00

COMMEMORATIVE TYPE 99
CHARLES BABBAGE
(Innovation in Science series no. 4)
Design by: Nigel Tudman and Jas Bhamra
(To mark 150 years since his death)
Obverse: As Type 97

		As-New	Proof
2021	46,292 total BU	£10.00	
	Specimen in folder (11,552), price new	£10.00	
1,702 of 3.5k	.925 sterling silver proof, price new		£59.50
731 of 1.5k	.925 sterling silver piedfort proof, price new		£110.00
82 of 250	.917 gold proof, price new		£1,195.00

COMMEMORATIVE TYPE 100
WINNIE-THE-POOH - Owl
Design by: © Disney
(The fifth of 9 Winnie-the-Pooh themed coins)
Obverse: As Type 97

		As-New	Proof
2021	73,884 total BU	£6.00	
	Specimen in folder (16,009), price new	£10.00	
11,147 of 45k	Specimen in folder with added colour, price new	£20.00	
6,040 of 18k	.925 sterling silver proof with added colour, price new		£69.50
136 of 535	.917 gold proof, price new		£1,195.00

COMMEMORATIVE TYPE 101
INSULIN
(Innovation in Science series no. 5)
Design by: Iris De La Torre
(To mark 100 years since the discovery of insulin)
Obverse: As Type 97

		As-New	Proof
2021	54,942 total BU	£7.00	
	Specimen in folder (15,123), price new	£10.00	
2,161 of 3.5k	.925 sterling silver proof, price new		£59.50
886 of 1.5k	.925 sterling silver piedfort proof, price new		£110.00
110 of 250	.917 gold proof, price new		£1,195.00

COMMEMORATIVE TYPE 103
SNOWMAN 4 (2021)
Design by: Robin Shaw
(Another Snowman coin to cash-in on Christmas.
The original Snowman commemorative was Type 69)
Obverse: As Type 97

		As-New	Proof
2021	80,274 total BU	£7.00	
	Specimen with greetings card (17,279), price new	£10.00	
10,086 of 10k!	Specimen in folder with added colour, price new	£20.00	
5,857 of 7k	.925 sterling silver proof with added colour, price new		£69.50
130 of 300	.917 gold proof, price new		£1,195.00

27.3 mm • 8.0 grammes • cupro-nickel • plain edge

COMMEMORATIVE TYPE 104
WINNIE-THE-POOH - Tigger
Design by: © Disney
(The sixth of 9 Winnie-the-Pooh themed coins)
Obverse: As Type 97

		As-New	Proof
2021	64,163 total BU	£8.00	
	Specimen in folder (16,292), price new	£11.00	
12,895 of 45k	Specimen in folder with added colour, price new	£20.00	
6,223 of 18k	.925 sterling silver proof with added colour, price new		£69.50
148 of 535	.917 gold proof, price new		£1,195.00

COMMEMORATIVE TYPE 105
2022 COMMONWEALTH GAMES
Design by: Natasha Preece
(To commemorate the
Commonwealth Games in Birmingham)

		As-New	Proof
2022	112,986 total BU	£8.00	
	Specimen in folder (12,469), price new	£11.00	
✴	Specimen in folder with added colour, price new	£20.00	
2,809 of 4k	.925 sterling silver proof with added colour, price new		£69.50
1,202	.925 sterling silver piedfort proof with added colour, price new		£120.00
88 of 250	.917 gold proof, price new		£1,195.00

*Four different coloured versions were sold, each with a different small symbol featured at the bottom of the reverse, representing Northern Ireland, Wales, England or Scotland. Total mintages were 4,928 for England and just short of 2,500 each, for the three other nations.

COMMEMORATIVE TYPE 106A / 106B
QUEEN'S 70th JUBILEE
Design by: Osborne Ross
(To mark the platinum jubilee)
Obverses: Type A - Queen on horseback,
design by John Bergdahl or
Type B - The standard Jody Clark portrait
(same obverse as Type 105, above)

		As-New
2022	5,000,070 for circulation (Obverse B)	£4.00
	BU example, e.g. from 2022 year-set (Obverse A)	£6.00
245,063	Specimen in folder (Obverse A), price new	£11.00
1,952	Specimens of both types in folder, price new	£29.00

COMMEMORATIVE TYPE 106A / 106B
(continued)

		Used	As-New	Proof
5,000	.925 sterling silver proof (Obverse A), price new			£59.50
700 max	.925 sterling silver proof, both types, price new			£135.00
2,497	.925 sterling silver piedfort proof (Obverse A), price new			£110.00
400	.917 gold proof (Obverse A), price new			£1,195.00
70	.917 gold proof, both types, price new			£2,400.00
50	.9995 platinum proof (Obverse A), price new			£1,465.00

COMMEMORATIVE TYPE 107
WINNIE-THE-POOH - Eeyore
Design by: © Disney
(The seventh of 9 Winnie-the-Pooh themed coins)
Obverse: As Type 105

		As-New	Proof
2022	61,094 total BU	£5.00	
	Specimen in folder (18,358), price new	£11.00	
12,098	Specimen in folder with added colour, price new	£20.00	
5,891	.925 sterling silver proof with added colour, price new		£69.50
131 of 150	.917 gold proof, price new		£1,195.00
5	.917 gold piedfort proof		no data

COMMEMORATIVE TYPE 108
PRIDE
Design by: Dominique Holmes
(50th anniversary of Pride UK)
Obverse: As Type 105

		Used	As-New	Proof
2022	5,000,000 for circulation	FV	£5.00	
	Specimen in folder (14,428), price new		£11.00	
33,825	Specimen in folder with added colour, price new		£20.00	
3,995	.925 sterling silver proof with added colour, price new			£69.50
1,446	.925 sterling silver piedfort proof with added colour, price new			£110.00
158 of 200	.917 gold proof, price new			£1,195.00
25	.917 gold piedfort proof			no data

Some also issued in combination with stamps.

27.3 mm • 8.0 grammes • cupro-nickel • plain edge

COMMEMORATIVE TYPE 109
ALAN TURING
(Innovation in Science series no. 6)
Design by: Matt Dent and Christian Davies
[To commemorate the life of Alan Turing]

		As-New	Proof
2022	52,092 total BU	£7.00	
	Specimen in folder (14,669), price new	£11.00	
2,689 of 3k	.925 sterling silver proof, price new		£59.50
1,315 of 1.5k	.925 sterling silver piedfort proof, price new		£110.00
148 of 200	.917 gold proof, price new		£1,195.00

COMMEMORATIVE TYPE 110
WINNIE-THE-POOH - Kanga & Roo
Design by: © Disney
[The eighth of 9 Winnie-the-Pooh themed coins]
Obverse: As Type 109

		As-New	Proof
2022	54,455 total BU	£5.00	
	Specimen in folder (16,080), price new	£11.00	
11,244 of 12.5k	Specimen in folder with added colour, price new	£20.00	
5,600 of 6k	.925 sterling silver proof with added colour, price new		£69.50
117 of 150	.917 gold proof, price new		£1,195.00

COMMEMORATIVE TYPE 111
WINNIE-THE-POOH - Pooh & Friends
Design by: © Disney
[The ninth of 9 Winnie-the-Pooh themed coins]
Obverse: As Type 109

		As-New	Proof
2022	55,390 total BU	£5.00	
	Specimen in folder (17,765), price new	£11.00	
12,234 of 12.5k	Specimen in folder with added colour, price new	£20.00	
5,888 of 6k	.925 sterling silver proof with added colour, price new		£69.50
136	.917 gold proof, price new		£1,195.00

COMMEMORATIVE TYPE 112
QEII MEMORIAL
Design by: Edgar Fuller and Cecil Thomas
(Issued shortly after the death of the Queen)

		Used	As-New	Proof
2022	9,600,000 for circulation	FV	£3.50	
	Specimen in folder (104,458), price new		£11.00	
21,422	.925 sterling silver proof, price new			£59.50
4,595	.925 sterling silver piedfort proof, price new			£110.00
1,105	.917 gold proof, price new			£1,195.00
86	.917 gold piedfort proof, price new			£2,395.00
106	.9995 platinum proof, price new			£1,465.00

COMMEMORATIVE TYPE 113
BBC
Design by: Henry Gray
(To commemorate the centenary of the BBC)
Obverse: As Type 109

		As-New	Proof
2022	86,522 total BU	£7.00	
	Specimen in folder (40,750), price new	£11.00	
3,498	.925 sterling silver proof, price new		£59.50
1,107	.925 sterling silver piedfort proof, price new		£110.00
247	.917 gold proof, price new*		£1,195.00

*Also sold as a gold pair with a 2022 sovereign.

COMMEMORATIVE TYPE 114
2022 HARRY POTTER SERIES - Coin 1 of 4
Design by: Jim Kay and Ffion Gwillim
(To commemorate the anniversary of the first book)
Obverse: As Type 109

		As-New	Proof
2022	99,873	£7.00	
	Specimen in folder (49,590), price new	£11.00	
34,782	Specimen in folder with added colour, price new	£20.00	
14,784 of 15k	.925 sterling silver proof with added colour, price new		£69.50
297	.917 gold proof, price new		£1,195.00

COMMEMORATIVE TYPE 115
SNOWMAN 4 (2022)
Design by: Robin Shaw
(Another Snowman Christmas themed coin.
The original Snowman commemorative was Type 69)
Obverse: As Type 109

			As-New	Proof
2022		62,229 total BU	£7.00	
		Specimen with greetings card (17,565), price new	£10.00	
8,500		Specimen in folder with added colour, price new	£20.00	
5,000		.925 sterling silver proof with added colour, price new		£69.50
120		.917 gold proof, price new		£1,195.00

COMMEMORATIVE TYPE 116
2022/23 HARRY POTTER SERIES - Coin 2 of 4
Design by: Jim Kay and Ffion Gwillim
(To commemorate the anniversary of the first book)
Obverse: As Type 109

			As-New	Proof
2022		85,426 total BU	£5.00	
		Specimen in folder (37,286), price new	£11.00	
27,885		Specimen in folder with added colour, price new	£20.00	
10,249		.925 sterling silver proof with added colour, price new		£69.50
240		.917 gold proof, price new		£1,195.00

1oz, 2oz and 5oz silver proof and 1/4oz and 2oz gold proof round versions with different face values were also sold.

COMMEMORATIVE TYPE 117
WINDRUSH GENERATIONS
Design by: Valda Jackson
(To mark 75 years of the Windrush Generations)
Obverse: As Type 118

			As-New	Proof
2023			£5.00	
		Specimen in folder, price new	£12.00	
		Specimen in folder with added colour, price new	£21.00	
1,948 max		.925 sterling silver proof with added colour, price new		£70.00
1,250 max		.925 sterling silver piedfort proof with added colour, price new		£128.00
75 max		.917 gold proof, price new		£1,220.00

COMMEMORATIVE TYPE 118
NATIONAL HEALTH SERVICE
Design by: Alice Lediard
(To commemorate 75 years of the NHS)

		As-New	Proof
2023		£5.00	
	Specimen in folder, price new	£12.00	
3,500 max	.925 sterling silver proof, price new		£65.00
250 max	.917 gold proof, price new		£1,355.00

COMMEMORATIVE TYPE 119
2022/23 HARRY POTTER SERIES - Coin 3 of 4
Design by: Jim Kay and Ffion Gwillim
(To commemorate the anniversary of the first book)
Obverse: As Type 118

		As-New	Proof
2023		£5.00	
	Specimen in folder, price new	£12.00	
	Specimen in folder with added colour, price new	£21.00	
15k max	.925 sterling silver proof with added colour, price new		£75.00
300 max	.917 gold proof, price new		£1,355.00

1oz, 2oz and 5oz silver proof and 1/4oz and 2oz gold proof round versions with different face values were also sold.

COMMEMORATIVE TYPE 120
2022/23 HARRY POTTER SERIES - Coin 4 of 4
Design by: Jim Kay and Ffion Gwillim
(To commemorate the anniversary of the first book)
Obverse: As Type 118

		As-New	Proof
2023		£5.00	
	Specimen in folder, price new	£12.00	
	Specimen in folder with added colour, price new	£21.00	
15k max	.925 sterling silver proof with added colour, price new		£75.00
?	.917 gold proof, price new		exists?

1oz and 5oz silver proof and 1/4oz and 2oz gold proof round versions with different face values were also sold.

27.3 mm • 8.0 grammes • cupro-nickel • plain edge

COMMEMORATIVE TYPE 121A / 121B

CORONATION OF CHARLES III
Design by: Natasha Jenkins (Westminster Abbey)
Obverses: Type A - Crowned effigy, or Type B - Bare head, both by Martin Jennings

		As-New	Proof
2023	5,000,000 for circulation (Obverse B)	£4.00	
	Specimen in folder (Obverse A), price new	£12.00	
12,500 max	.925 sterling silver proof (Obverse A), price new		£59.50
3,250 max	.925 sterling silver piedfort proof (Obverse A), price new		£118.00
500 max	.917 gold proof (Obverse A), price new		£1,220.00

COMMEMORATIVE TYPE 122

STAR WARS DUOS SERIES - Coin 1 of 4
C-3PO and R2-D2, **Design by:** Lucasfilm Ltd
(To loosely commemorate the 40th anniversary of Return of the Jedi)
Obverse: As Type 118

		As-New	Proof
2023		£5.00	
	Specimen in folder, price new	£12.00	
20k max	Specimen in folder with added colour, price new	£21.00	
12,500 max	.925 sterling silver proof with added colour, price new		£75.00
200 max	.917 gold proof, price new		£1,355.00

1oz, 2oz and 5oz silver proof and 1/4oz and 1oz gold proof round versions (different face values) were also sold.

COMMEMORATIVE TYPE 123

STAR WARS DUOS SERIES - Coin 2 of 4
Darth Vader and Emp. Palpatine, **Design by:** Lucasfilm Ltd
(To loosely commemorate the 40th anniversary of Return of the Jedi)
Obverse: As Type 118

		As-New	Proof
2023		£5.00	
	Specimen in folder, price new	£12.00	
20k max	Specimen in folder with added colour, price new	£21.00	
12,500 max	.925 sterling silver proof with added colour, price new		£75.00
200 max	.917 gold proof, price new		£1,355.00

1oz, 2oz and 5oz silver proof and 1/4oz and 1oz gold proof round versions (different face values) were also sold.

COMMEMORATIVE TYPE 124
THE LION, THE WITCH AND THE WARDROBE
Design by: Ffion Gwillim of Illustration by Pauline Baynes
(Tribute to the book by C. S. Lewis)
Obverse: As Type 118

		As-New	Proof
2023		£5.00	
	Specimen in folder, price new	£12.00	
10k max	Specimen in folder with added colour, price new	£21.00	
5k max	.925 sterling silver proof with added colour, price new		£75.00
100 max	.917 gold proof, price new		£1,355.00

COMMEMORATIVE TYPE 125
SNOWMAN 5 (2023)
Design by: Robin Shaw
(Another Snowman Christmas themed coin.
The original Snowman commemorative was Type 69)
Obverse: As Type 118

		As-New	Proof
2023		£5.00	
	Specimen with greetings card, price new	£12.00	
10k max	Specimen in folder with added colour, price new	£21.00	
5k max	.925 sterling silver proof with added colour, price new		£75.00
100 max	.917 gold proof, price new		£1,355.00

COMMEMORATIVE TYPE 126
STAR WARS DUOS SERIES - Coin 3 of 4
Luke Skywalker and Princess Leia, Design by: Lucasfilm Ltd
(To loosely commemorate the 40th anniversary of Return of the Jedi)
Obverse: As Type 118

		As-New	Proof
2023		£5.00	
	Specimen in folder, price new	£12.00	
20k max	Specimen in folder with added colour, price new	£21.00	
12,500 max	.925 sterling silver proof with added colour, price new		£75.00
200 max	.917 gold proof, price new		£1,355.00

1oz, 2oz and 5oz silver proof and 1/4oz and 1oz gold proof round versions (different face values) were also sold.

27.3 mm • 8.0 grammes • cupro-nickel • plain edge

COMMEMORATIVE TYPE 127
DINOSAURS, ICONIC SPECIMENS - Coin 1 of 3
Tyrannosaurus Design by: Robert Nicholls
(Another Dinosaur related series)
Obverse: As Type 129

		As-New	Proof
2024		£6.00	
	Specimen in folder, price new	£12.00	
15k max	Specimen in folder with added colour, price new	£21.00	
500 max	.925 sterling silver proof, price new		£65.00
5k max	.925 sterling silver proof with added colour, price new		£75.00
100 max	.917 gold proof, price new		£1,355.00

1oz silver proof and 1/4oz gold proof round versions (different face values) were also sold.

COMMEMORATIVE TYPE 128
ROYAL NATIONAL LIFEBOAT INSTITUTION
Design by: John Bergdahl
(200 year anniversary of the RNLI)
Obverse: As Type 129

		As-New	Proof
2024		£6.00	
	Specimen in folder, price new	£12.00	
7,500 max	Specimen in folder with added colour, price new	£21.00	
4k max	.925 sterling silver proof with added colour, price new		£65.00
1,824 max	.925 sterling silver proof piedfort with added colour, price new		£128.00
150 max	.917 gold proof, price new		£1,220.00

A 1/40oz gold proof round version was also sold for £99.50, max. 2,024.

COMMEMORATIVE TYPE 129
TEAM GB & PARALYMPICS GB
Design by: Charis Tsevis
(Paris 2024 Olympic and Paralympic Games)

		As-New	Proof
2024		£9.00	
	Specimen in folder, price new	£12.00	
12,500 max	Specimen in folder with added colour, price new	£21.00	
5k max	.925 sterling silver proof with added colour, price new		£75.00
2,024 max	.925 sterling silver proof piedfort with added colour, price new		£128.00
150 max	.917 gold proof, price new		£1,220.00

COMMEMORATIVE TYPE 130
STAR WARS DUOS SERIES - Coin 4 of 4
Han Solo and Chewbacca, Design by: Lucasfilm Ltd
(To loosely commemorate the 40th anniversary of Return of the Jedi)
Obverse: As Type 129

		As-New	Proof
2024		£5.00	
	Specimen in folder, price new	£12.00	
20k max	Specimen in folder with added colour, price new	£21.00	
12,500 max	.925 sterling silver proof with added colour, price new		£75.00
200 max	.917 gold proof, price new		£1,355.00

1oz, 2oz and 5oz silver proof and 1/4oz and 1oz gold proof round versions (different face values) were also sold.

COMMEMORATIVE TYPE 131
DINOSAURS, ICONIC SPECIMENS - Coin 2 of 3
Stegosaurus Design by: Robert Nicholls
(Another Dinosaur related series)
Obverse: As Type 129

		As-New	Proof
2024		£5.00	
	Specimen in folder, price new	£12.00	
15k max	Specimen in folder with added colour, price new	£21.00	
500 max	.925 sterling silver proof, price new		£65.00
5k max	.925 sterling silver proof with added colour, price new		£75.00
100 max	.917 gold proof, price new		£1,355.00

1oz silver proof and 1/4oz gold proof round versions (different face values) were also sold.

COMMEMORATIVE TYPE 132
DINOSAURS, ICONIC SPECIMENS - Coin 3 of 3
Diplodocus Design by: Robert Nicholls
(Another Dinosaur related series)
Obverse: As Type 129

		As-New	Proof
2024		£5.50	
	Specimen in folder, price new	£12.00	
15k max	Specimen in folder with added colour, price new	£21.00	
500 max	.925 sterling silver proof, price new		£61.00
5k max	.925 sterling silver proof with added colour, price new		£75.00
100 max	.917 gold proof, price new		£1,355.00

1oz silver proof and 1/4oz gold proof round versions (different face values) were also sold.

COMMEMORATIVE TYPE 133
STAR WARS VEHICLES SERIES - Coin 1 of 4
TIE Fighter, Design by: Lucasfilm Ltd
(Another Star Wars franchise TIE-in!)
Obverse: As Type 129

		As-New	Proof
2024		£5.50	
	Specimen in folder, price new	£12.00	
20k max	Specimen in folder with added colour, price new	£21.00	
7,500 max	.925 sterling silver proof with added colour, price new		£75.00
100 max	.917 gold proof, price new		£1,355.00

1oz, 2oz and 5oz silver proof and 1/4oz and 1oz gold proof round versions (different face values) were also sold.

COMMEMORATIVE TYPE 134
HARRY POTTER - WINGED KEYS
Design by: Bella Briggs
(Another Harry Potter franchise coin)
Obverse: As Type 129

		As-New	Proof
2024		£5.50	
	Specimen in folder, price new	£12.00	
20k max	Specimen in folder with added colour, price new	£21.00	
8k max	.925 sterling silver proof with added colour, price new		£75.00
200 max	.917 gold proof, price new		£1,355.00

1oz silver proof (£2 FV) and 1/40oz gold proof (50p FV) round versions were also sold.

COMMEMORATIVE TYPE 135
STAR WARS VEHICLES SERIES - Coin 2 of 4
Millennium Falcon, Design by: Lucasfilm Ltd
(Another Star Wars franchise tie-in!)
Obverse: As Type 129

		As-New	Proof
2024		£5.50	
	Specimen in folder, price new	£12.00	
20k max	Specimen in folder with added colour, price new	£21.00	
7,500 max	.925 sterling silver proof with added colour, price new		£75.00
100 max	.917 gold proof, price new		£1,355.00

1oz, 2oz and 5oz silver proof and 1/4oz and 1oz gold proof round versions (different face values) were also sold.

COMMEMORATIVE TYPE 136
D-DAY 80th ANNIVERSARY
Design by: David Lawrence
(To Commemorate the 80th Anniversary of D-Day)
Obverse: As Type 129

		As-New	Proof
2024		£5.50	
	Specimen in folder, price new	£12.00	
5k max	.925 sterling silver proof, price new		£65.00
1,944 max	.925 sterling silver piedfort proof, price new		£118.00
350 max	.917 gold proof, price new		£1,355.00

1/40oz, 1/4oz and 2oz gold proof round versions (different face values) were also sold.

COMMEMORATIVE TYPE 137
STAR WARS VEHICLES SERIES - Coin 3 of 4
X-Wing, Design by: Lucasfilm Ltd
(Another Star Wars franchise tie-in!)
Obverse: As Type 129

		As-New	Proof
2024		£5.50	
	Specimen in folder, price new	£12.00	
20k max	Specimen in folder with added colour, price new	£21.00	
7,500 max	.925 sterling silver proof with added colour, price new		£75.00
100 max	.917 gold proof, price new		£1,355.00

1oz, 2oz and 5oz silver proof and 1/4oz and 1oz gold proof round versions (different face values) were also sold.

COMMEMORATIVE TYPE 138
STAR WARS VEHICLES SERIES - Coin 4 of 4
Death Star II, Design by: Lucasfilm Ltd
(Another Star Wars franchise tie-in!)
Obverse: As Type 129

		As-New	Proof
2024		£5.50	
	Specimen in folder, price new	£12.00	
20k max	Specimen in folder with added colour, price new	£21.00	
7,500 max	.925 sterling silver proof with added colour, price new		£75.00
100 max	.917 gold proof, price new		£1,355.00

1oz, 2oz and 5oz silver proof and 1/4oz and 1oz gold proof round versions (different face values) were also sold.

What's currently legal tender?

None of the old round pound coins can be spent, but they can be credited into most UK bank accounts. Coins with mismatching reverse design, date and/or edge type are invariably fakes.

Which are hard to find?

Now they have been removed from every day use, all of the old pounds are harder to find, but none are rare. The most expensive old £1 coins are currently 1998, 1999, the 2015 with shield reverse (and 5th portrait of the Queen), the 2016 with shield reverse and the 2016 heraldic beasts coin as those were only made for year sets or packages so were unlikely to be found in circulation.

The obverses used for pound coins correspond to the obverse types shown on pages six and seven.

UK Royal Arms design by Eric Sewell Edge: DECUS ET TUTAMEN

			Used	As-New	Proof
1983	443,053,510		FV	£5.00	£6.00
	Specimen in folder			£9.00	
	50,000 .925 sterling silver proof				£25.00
	10,000 .925 sterling silver piedfort proof				£60.00
1993	114,744,500		FV	£5.00	£6.00
	50,000 .925 sterling silver proof				£18.00
	10,000 .925 sterling silver piedfort proof				£20.00
1998	(BU sets only)		£7.00	£11.00	£20.00
	13,863 .925 sterling silver proof				£25.00
	10,000 .925 sterling silver piedfort proof				£30.00
2003	61,596,500		FV	£3.50	£8.00
	15,830 .925 sterling silver proof				£20.00
	9,871 .925 sterling silver piedfort proof				£25.00
2008	3,910,000 (BU packs: 18,336)		FV	£8.00	£10.00
	9,134 .925 sterling silver proof				£20.00
	7,894 .925 sterling silver piedfort proof				£30.00
	2,005 Set of 14 £1 coins, all designs 1983 - 2008. Silver with gold coloured 'silhouette' details. All dated 2008				£300.00
	As above, as a gold proof set				no data

The following 4 coins ("Coronet" series) were designed by Leslie Durbin.

Scottish Thistle in Coronet. Edge: NEMO ME IMPUNE LACESSIT

1984	146,256,501		FV	£5.00	£6.00
	27,960 Specimen in folder			£9.00	
	44,855 .925 sterling silver proof				£20.00
	15,000 .925 sterling silver piedfort proof				£35.00
1989	70,580,501		FV	£5.00	£5.00
	25,000 .925 sterling silver proof				£12.00
	10,000 .925 sterling silver piedfort proof				£20.00

Welsh Leek in Coronet. Edge: PLEIDIOL WYF I'M GWLAD

1985	228,430,749		FV	£5.00	£6.00
	24,850 Specimen in folder			£9.00	
	50,000 .925 sterling silver proof				£20.00
	15,000 .925 sterling silver piedfort proof				£25.00
1990	97,269,302		FV	£4.00	£5.00
	25,000 .925 sterling silver proof				£18.00

22.5 mm • 9.5 grammes • nickel-brass • lettered edge

N.I. Flax in Coronet. Edge: DECUS ET TUTAMEN

		Used	As-New	Proof
1986	10,409,501	FV	£5.00	£6.00
	19,908 Specimen in folder		£9.00	
	37,958 .925 sterling silver proof			£20.00
	15,000 .925 sterling silver piedfort proof			£25.00
1991	38,443,575	FV	£5.00	£8.00
	25,000 .925 sterling silver proof			£18.00

English Oak in Coronet. Edge: DECUS ET TUTAMEN

1987	39,298,502	FV	£4.00	£6.00
	72,607 Specimen in folder		£9.00	
	50,500 .925 sterling silver proof			£20.00
	15,000 .925 sterling silver piedfort proof			£22.00
1992	36,320,487	FV	£4.00	£5.00
	25,000 .925 sterling silver proof			£18.00

Royal Shield by Derek Gorringe. Edge: DECUS ET TUTAMEN
(one year only design)

1988	7,118,825	£2.00	£5.00	£8.00
	29,550 Specimen in folder		£12.00	
	50,000 .925 sterling silver proof			£20.00
	10,000 .925 sterling silver piedfort proof			£22.00

The following 4 coins ("Heraldic" series) were designed by Norman Sillman.

Scottish Lion Rampant. Edge: NEMO ME IMPUNE LACESSIT

1994	29,752,525	FV	£5.00	£8.00
	Specimen in folder		£8.00	
	25,000 .925 sterling silver proof			£15.00
	11,722 .925 sterling silver piedfort proof			£20.00
1999	(BU packs only)	£7.00	£11.00	£20.00
	25,000 .925 sterling silver proof			£20.00
	2,000 .925 sterling "Special Frosted Finish" proof			£20.00
	10,000 .925 sterling silver piedfort proof			£25.00

Welsh Dragon. Edge: PLEIDIOL WYF I'M GWLAD

		Used	As-New	Proof
1995	34,503,501	FV	£5.00	£7.00
	Specimen in folder		£7.00	
	Specimen in folder (Welsh text)		no data	
	27,445 .925 sterling silver proof			£20.00
	8,458 .925 sterling silver piedfort proof			£25.00
2000	109,496,500	FV	£4.00	£8.00
	40,000 .925 sterling silver proof			£20.00
	2,000 .925 sterling "Special Frosted Finish" proof			£25.00
	10,000 .925 sterling silver piedfort proof			£25.00

N.I. Celtic Cross. Edge: DECUS ET TUTAMEN

		Used	As-New	Proof
1996	89,886,000	FV	£4.50	£7.00
	Specimen in folder		£10.00	
	25,000 .925 sterling silver cased proof			£20.00
	10,000 .925 sterling silver piedfort cased proof			£25.00
2001	63,968,065	FV	£4.50	£8.00
	13,237 .925 sterling silver proof			£25.00
	2,000 .925 sterling "Special Frosted Finish" proof			£35.00
	8,464 .925 sterling silver piedfort proof			£25.00

English Three Lions. Edge: DECUS ET TUTAMEN

		Used	As-New	Proof
1997	57,117,450	FV	£4.00	£7.00
	56,996 Specimen in folder		£8.00	
	20,137 .925 sterling silver proof			£20.00
	10,000 .925 sterling silver piedfort proof			£25.00
2002	77,818,000	FV	£5.00	£8.00
	17,693 .925 sterling silver proof			£20.00
	2,000 .925 sterling "Special Frosted Finish" proof			£25.00
	6,599 .925 sterling silver piedfort proof			£25.00

The 4 coins that follow ("Bridge" series) were designed by Edwina Ellis. The edges all feature a decorative pattern.

2004   Scotland - Forth Bridge

		Used	As-New	Proof
39,162,000		FV	£7.00	£11.00
24,014	Specimen in folder		£15.00	
11,470	.925 sterling silver proof			£20.00
7,013	.925 sterling silver piedfort cased proof			£25.00
2,618	.917 gold proof			£500.00

2005 Wales - Menai Bridge

		Used	As-New	Proof
99,429,500		FV	£5.00	£11.00
24,802	Specimen in folder		£15.00	
8,371	.925 sterling silver proof			£20.00
6,007	.925 sterling silver piedfort cased proof			£25.00
1,195	.917 gold proof			£500.00

Also sold in packs with the 2005 £2 (Gunpowder plot) and 2005 50p (Johnson's Dictionary). Value: £20

2006 Northern Ireland - Egyptian Arch

		Used	As-New	Proof
38,938,000		FV	£5.00	£11.00
23,856	Specimen in folder		£15.00	
14,765	.925 sterling silver proof			£20.00
5,129	.925 sterling silver piedfort cased proof			£25.00
728	.917 gold proof			£550.00

2007 England - Millennium Bridge

		Used	As-New	Proof
26,180,160		FV	£6.00	£11.00
5,326	Specimen in folder		£15.00	
10,110	.925 sterling silver proof			£20.00
5,739	.925 sterling silver piedfort cased proof			£25.00
1,122	.917 gold proof			£550.00

Large shield part of the UK Royal coat of Arms by: Matthew Dent. With Obverse 4 or 5. Edge: DECUS ET TUTAMEN

		Used	As-New	Proof
2008	43,827,300	FV	£7.00	£10.00
5,000	.925 sterling silver proof			£35.00
2,456	.925 sterling piedfort proof			£50.00
860	.917 gold proof			£700.00
2009	27,625,600	FV	£7.00	£10.00
	Standard BU pack		£10.00	
	.925 sterling silver BU issue		£20.00	
	.925 sterling silver proof			£30.00
	.917 gold proof			£600.00
2010	57,120,000	FV	£4.00	£10.00
	Silver proofs sold in sets only			
2011	25,415,000	FV	£4.00	£10.00
	Silver proofs sold in sets only			

Large shield part of the UK Royal coat of Arms (continued)

		Used	As-New	Proof
2012	35,700,030	FV	£7.00	£10.00
1,234	.925 sterling silver proof			no data
	.925 silver BU			no data
	Also seen as silver proof with gold plated shield detail			
2013	13,090,500	FV	£7.00	£10.00
	.925 sterling silver proof (available in sets only)			no data
	.925 silver 'Royal Birth' BU (4,414 of 10k max)			£30.00?
	.917 gold proof (17 sold, plus 59 in sets)			no data
2014	79,305,200	FV	£6.00	£10.00
	.925 sterling silver proof (available in sets only)			£40.00
750	.925 sterling silver BU			no data
2015	29,580,000 (Obverse 4)	FV	£8.00	£10.00
	(Obverse 5) (in sets only, 23,643 total)		£14.00	£20.00
	Silver proofs sold in sets only			no data
2016	(Obv 5) Available in sets only (38,502 total)		£28.00	£30.00

The 4 Capital Cities series were designed by Stuart Devlin (all Obverse 4).

2010 Belfast. Edge: PRO TANTO QUID RETRIBUAMUS

	Used	As-New	Proof
6,205,000 (BU packs: 6,767)	£1.50	£7.00	£14.00
.925 sterling silver proof			£25.00
.925 sterling silver piedfort proof			£30.00

2010 London. Edge: DOMINE DIRIGE NOS

	Used	As-New	Proof
2,635,000 (BU packs: 8,584)	£3.00	£9.00*	£15.00
.925 sterling silver proof			£25.00
.925 sterling silver piedfort proof			£40.00

* Some of the BU packs contained the 2010 Shield reverse coin in error.
4,023 BU packs containing both 2010 coins were sold.

2011 Cardiff. Edge: Y DDRAIG GOCH DDYRY CYCHWYN

	Used	As-New	Proof
1,615,000	£4.00	£8.00	£15.00
.925 sterling silver proof (5,553 sold)			£30.00
.925 sterling silver piedfort proof (1,615 sold)			£35.00
.917 gold proof (524 sold)			no data

Incorrect die alignment (rotated over 90 degrees) Cardiff coins noted.

2011 Edinburgh. Edge: NISI DOMINUS FRUSTRA

		Used	As-New	Proof
935,000		£4.00	£14.00	£2500
	.925 sterling silver proof (4,973 sold)			£40.00
	.925 sterling silver piedfort proof (2,696 sold)			£50.00
	.917 gold proof (499 sold)			no data

3,198 BU packs containing both 2011 coins were sold.

The 4 Floral Symbols series were designed by Timothy Noad (all Obverse 4).

2013 England. Edge: DECUS ET TUTAMEN

	5,270,000	£1.50	£10.00	£15.00
1,858	.925 sterling silver proof*			£40.00
1,071	.925 sterling silver piedfort proof			£50.00
185	.917 gold proof (plus 99 in sets with Wales)			no data

2013 Wales. Edge: PLEIDIOL WYF I'M GWLAD

	5,270,000	£1.50	£10.00	£15.00
1,618	.925 sterling silver proof*			£40.00
860	.925 sterling silver piedfort proof			£50.00
175	.917 gold proof (plus 99 in sets with England)			-

This coin also exists with incorrect (rotated) die alignment.
* Plus an additional 1,476 2013 silver proof coins sold in pairs.
6,112 BU packs of both 2013 coins were sold.
30th anniversary of £1, set of 3 coins (1983 design, 1988 design and a normal 2013 Matthew Dent shield reverse coin) all dated 2013. 1,311 .925 sterling silver proof sets sold. 17 .917 gold proof sets sold.   No data

2014 Scotland. Edge: NEMO ME IMPUNE LACESSIT

	5,185,000	£1.50	£15.00	£20.00
1,540	.925 sterling silver proof			£50.00
	.925 sterling silver piedfort proof			£70.00?
154	.917 gold proof			no data

2014 Northern Ireland. Edge: DECUS ET TUTAMEN

	5,780,000	£1.50	£15.00	£20.00
1,502	.925 sterling silver proof			£50.00
788	.925 sterling silver piedfort proof			£70.00?
166	.917 gold proof			no data

3,832 BU packs of both 2014 coins were sold.

2015   The Royal Arms - by Timothy Noad
Edge: DECUS ET TUTAMEN

		Used	As-New	Proof
All with Obverse 5				
	129,616,985	FV	£8.00	
9,294	BU pack		£15.00	
3,500 max	.925 sterling silver proof			£60.00
2,000 max	.925 sterling piedfort proof			£150.00?
500 max	.917 gold proof (price new £850)			no data

2016   Four Heraldic beast symbols of the UK -
by Gregory Cameron, Bishop of St Asaph.
'The last round pound'. Edge: DECUS ET TUTAMEN

238,238	Non-circulated, had to be purchased*	£10.00	£20.00
7,491	.925 sterling silver proof		£40.00
2,993	.925 sterling piedfort proof		£120.00?
499	.917 gold proof		no data

*These coins were also sold in pairs (9,850 total) - combined with a cross-crosslet mint marked new pound coin. This coin and the new pound were also sold as pairs in gold proof guise. An additional 68,537 'BU' coins were sold in tubes to other retailers, a further 22,786 were included in the 2016 annual (non-proof) sets and 128 were contained in framed pairs including a larger version of the coin design cast in plaster!

The New Twelve-Sided £1 Coin, introduction and specifications

On the 19th March 2014 the Chancellor of the Exchequer announced that a completely new £1 coin would be produced to replace the round pound coin. The coins feature a 'hologram' at the bottom of the obverse, which depending on the angle it is viewed from, will either show a '£' symbol or a '1'.

The new 12-sided pound first appeared for sale on the 1st January 2017 within the 2017 BU and proof sets. During March 2017 the coins started to appear in circulation, the first were dated 2016 and were closely followed by coins dated 2017.

Specifications of the new £1 coin:
Diameter (2015 onwards): 23.03mm flat to opposing flat, 23.43mm point to opposing point.
Weight (2015 onwards): 8.75 grammes.
Alloy (2015 onwards): Centre part - Nickel-brass plated in nickel. Outer ring - Nickel brass.
Edge: The edge has alternately milled and plain sections.

2014 - 2016, Royal Mint new £1 coin 'TRIAL PIECES'

Trial Piece 2014 £1 coin
(monometallic)

Trial Piece 2015 £1 coin

			Used
2014	Inverted MMXIV edge lettering	(bi-metallic)	? (two seen)
2014 20k?	Monometallic, very few seen		£300 - £400?
2015	Mintage number said to be 234,586*	(bi-metallic)	£30
2016	Mintage number said to be 1,000*	(bi-metallic)	£300
no date	'double tailed' - reverse of 2015/16 trial coin struck on both sides		? (two reported)

*About 15,000 2015/16 are known to have been returned to the mint, as originally stipulated.

Note: there are known fakes of the trial coins! They almost certainly originate from China and examples I've seen omit the micro 'ONE POUND' lettering around the obverse rim. They are all over eBay, often described as 'fillers', which seems to be eBay-speak for 'forgery'!

A variety of note, which is known to affect all current circulation coins (on the opposite page), concerns the rim milling (ridges) on the alternate flat sides of the edge. When the coin is held with the monarch up the right way, at the bottom point (below the hologram) most coins have a milled edge on the edge section to the right of the hologram. Some have the milled section to the left and the latter seems a little scarcer. Many other types of errors are known, some of which are quite common. Fakes also exist. See the checkyourchange.co.uk website for further details.

The 12-sided £1 coin, circulation type

Elizabeth II, 2016 - 2022 £1 coin

Charles III, 2023 onwards £1 coin

<u>Used</u>   As-New   Proof

TYPE 1 (Elizabeth II with Nations of the Crown reverse, designed by David Pearce)

2016	648,936,536		FV	£1.50
	Mule, with 2017 reverse (tiny 2017 micro dates around reverse rim)			
		£400 - £600 (no recent sales)		
	Error, mono-metallic in nickel-brass	Only 1 known		
	With small cross-crosslet mintmark*, sold in packs with a 'last round pound',			
	base metal: £60.00 (9,850 made), in gold: £1995 (new price, max. 100 made)			
	Error, non-plated golden centre piece	no data		
2017	749,616,200 (+80,850 BU versions)		FV	£3.00	£8.00
	Error, mono-metallic nickel-brass	£350 - £400		
	Error, non-plated golden centre piece	£50 - £150		
	.925 sterling silver proof, 25k max. - £40.00 piedfort proof, ? max. - £75.00			
	.917 gold proof, 2,017 max., price new				£950.00
2018	130,560,000		FV	£3.00	£5.00
2018	Error, non-plated golden centre piece	no data		
2019	138,635,000		FV	£5.00	£6.00
2020	55,840,169		FV	£4.00	£6.00
2021	21,760,000		FV	£10.00	£10.00
2022	7,735,000		FV	£10.00	£10.00

TYPE 2 (Charles III with Bees reverse, designed by Royal Mint in-house)

2023	10,030,000		FV	£9.00	
2023	With crown privy mark, from sets			£9.00	£9.00
2024	Currently in 2024 sets only		FV	£9.00	£9.00

* The small cross-crosslet mintmark is located above the 'E' of 'ONE' on the silver part, below the crown and looks like this: ╬

| 28.40 mm • 15.98 grammes • nickel-brass • various edge

What's currently legal tender?

All £2 coins dated from 1986 to date are legal tender. The earlier single metal type coins dated 1986 to 1996 are not often seen in circulation and therefore may not be accepted by some merchants who are unfamiliar with them. All of the single metal coins tend to be worth a little more than face value, even in used condition. Note that there are fake £2 coins in circulation, mostly with commemorative designs. They seem to originate from China.

Which are hard to find?

All of the 1986 to 1996 (single alloy) £2 coins are now hard to find in circulation. The scarcest £2 coin is probably COMMEMORATIVE TYPE 3, the 'Claim of Right' coin, as this was minted in much smaller quantities than the other 1989 £2 coin, and was only issued in Scotland. Some of the more recent £2 coins do sell for more than face value, even in used condition. No £2 coins have been struck for circulation since 2016.

COMMEMORATIVE TYPE 1

A thistle encircled by a laurel wreath, superimposed on St. Andrew's Cross
(1986 Commonwealth Games, Edinburgh)
Reverse design by: Norman Sillman
Edge: XIII COMMONWEALTH GAMES SCOTLAND 1986

			Used	As-New	Proof
1986	8,212,184	(+104,591 Proofs)	£3.00	£4.00	£10.00
		Specimen in folder		£10.00	
	58,881	.500 silver UNC		£17.00	
	59,779	.925 sterling silver proof			£27.00
		.917 gold proof			£1,100.00

COMMEMORATIVE TYPE 2

Intertwined W & M (monogram of William & Mary)
House of Commons Mace, English Crown TERCENTENARY of the BILL of RIGHTS 1689-1989
Reverse design by: John Lobban
Edge: MILLED

			Used	As-New	Proof
1989	4,432,000	(+84,704 Proofs)	£3.00	£5.00	£10.00
		Partially non frosted proof*			£18.00
		Specimen in folder		£12.00	
	25,000	.925 sterling silver proof pair with type 3			£60.00
	10,000	.925 sterling silver piedfort proof pair, with type 3			£65.00

*Proofs that were part of a Bass Charrington promotion appear to have a non frosted bust of the Queen. More comparison is needed at this stage.

96

COMMEMORATIVE TYPE 3
Intertwined W & M
(monogram of William & Mary)
House of Commons Mace, Scottish Crown
TERCENTENARY of the CLAIM of RIGHT
1689-1989
Reverse design by: John Lobban
Edge: MILLED

			Used	As-New	Proof
1989	345,891	(+84,704 Proofs)	£20.00	£25.00	£35.00
		Specimen in folder		£40.00	
	Specimen folder, including both versions ('Bill' & 'Claim')			£50.00	
	24,852	.925 sterling silver proof pair, with type 2			£60.00
	10,000	.925 sterling silver piedfort proof pair with type 2			£65.00

COMMEMORATIVE TYPE 4
Intertwined W & M
(monogram of William & Mary)
Britannia Seated
BANK of ENGLAND 1694-1994
Reverse design by: Leslie Durbin
Edge: SIC VOS NON VOBIS

✽

			Used	As-New	Proof
1994	1,443,116	(+67,721 Proofs)	£4.50	£6.00	£10.00
		Specimen in folder		£14.00	
	27,957	.925 sterling silver proof			£25.00
	9,569	.925 sterling silver piedfort proof			£30.00
	1,000	.917 gold proof			£1,200.00
	? Est. 300	Gold proof mule with wrong obverse✽			£2,000.00+

✽The obverse of the double sovereign £2 coin was used in error on some of the gold proof issue. As shown above, the head is larger, legend more abbreviated and it omits the words 'TWO POUNDS'.

COMMEMORATIVE TYPE 5
Dove of Peace
(Commemorating 50 years' peace,
since the end of World War II)
Reverse design by: John Mills
Edge: 1945 IN PEACE GOODWILL 1995

			Used	As-New	Proof
1995	4,391,248	(+60,639 Proofs)	£3.00	£6.00	£12.00
		Specimen in folder		£20.00	
	50,000	.925 sterling silver proof			£27.00
	10,000	.925 sterling silver piedfort proof			£30.00
	2,500	.917 gold proof			£1,300.00

COMMEMORATIVE TYPE 6
UN logo, array of flags
NATIONS UNITED FOR PEACE 1945 - 1995
(50th Anniversary - United Nations)
Reverse design by: Michael Rizzello
Edge: MILLED

			Used	As-New	Proof
1995	1,665,257		£8.00	£11.00	
		Specimen in folder		£22.00	
	175,000	.925 sterling silver proof			£27.00
	10,000	.925 sterling silver piedfort proof			£35.00
		.917 gold proof			£1,200.00

COMMEMORATIVE TYPE 7
Football design, with date, 1996, in centre
(10th European Championship)
Reverse design by: John Mills
Edge: TENTH EUROPEAN CHAMPIONSHIP

			Used	As-New	Proof
1996	5,141,350		£6.00	£9.00	£15.00
		Specimen in folder		£20.00	
	50,000	.925 sterling silver proof			£35.00
	10,000	.925 sterling silver piedfort proof			£35.00
	2,098	.917 gold proof (slight varieties exist*)			£1,300.00

*concerning the type of blank used. Some are flatter, not concave.

BI-METALLIC £2 COINS (1997 onwards)

OBVERSES

OBVERSE 1
(dated 1997 only, but actually issued in 1998)
ELIZABETH II DEI GRA REGINA F D
Elizabeth II, Dei Gratia Regina, Fidei Defensor
(Elizabeth II, By the Grace of God Queen and Defender of the Faith)
Portrait by: Raphael Maklouf

OBVERSE 2
(used 1998 to 2015)
(Also used on commemoratives 8 to 17, 19, 21 and 32)
ELIZABETH II DEI GRATIA REGINA FID DEF
Elizabeth II, Dei Gratia Regina, Fidei Defensor
(Elizabeth II, By the Grace of God Queen and Defender of the Faith)
Portrait by: Ian Rank-Broadley

OBVERSE 2b   **OBVERSE 2c**   **OBVERSE 2d**

Variations of obverse 2 - Some of the later esigns featuring the Ian Rank-Broadley portrait don't include a date, the face value or both, so these have been incorporated into the obverse legend.

2b: 'TWO POUNDS' at bottom
2c: no denomination on obverse, **DATE** at bottom
2d: 'TWO POUNDS' and **DATE** at bottom

OBVERSE 3
(used 2015 to 2022)
ELIZABETH II DEI GRA REG FID DEF + date
Elizabeth II, Dei Gratia Regina, Fidei Defensor
(Elizabeth II, By the Grace of God Queen and Defender of the Faith)
Portrait by: Jody Clark

99

OBVERSES (continued)

OBVERSE 3b   OBVERSE 3c   OBVERSE 3d   OBVERSE 3e

Variations of obverse 3 - Due to the commemorative reverse designs not stating the face value or already featuring the date, there are four variations of the Jody Clark portrait obverse (Obverse 3)

3b: With denomination '2 POUNDS', no date.
3c: No denomination, no date.
3d: With denomination 'TWO POUNDS' and date at top.
3e: With denomination '2 POUNDS' and date at top.

OBVERSE 4
(used 2023 onwards for the definitive floral £2 coins)
CHARLES III DEI GRA REX FID DEF + date
Charles III, Dei Gratia Rex, Fidei Defensor
(Charles III, By the Grace of God King and Defender of the Faith)
Portrait by: Martin Jennings

OBVERSE 4b
(used on the commemorative £2 coins)

Similar to above, but includes the denomination written as
'2 POUNDS'

STANDARD (non commemorative) REVERSES:

REVERSE 1 (standard non-commemorative reverse)
(used 1997 to 2015)
Rings, representing stages of development:
from centre, outward: IRON AGE, INDUSTRIAL REVOLUTION
(cogs), ELECTRONIC AGE (silicon chips), INTERNET AGE
Edge: STANDING ON THE SHOULDERS OF GIANTS
Design by: Bruce Rushin

REVERSES (continued)

REVERSE 2 (standard non-commemorative reverse)
(used 2015 to 2022)
Britannia facing left, holding trident.
Edge: QUATUOR MARIA VINDICO (I claim the four seas)
Design by: Anthony Dufort

REVERSE 3 (standard non-commemorative reverse)
(Charles III, used 2023 onwards)
UK national flowers and CIII monograms.
Edge: IN SERVITIO OMNIUM (in the service of all)
Design by: Royal Mint in-house

TRIAL TYPES
Sailing ship, representing the Mayflower
The 1994 bi-metallic trial £2 coin. Although dated 1994, they were actually released in 1998. The coins were all issued in packs which also contained examples of round nickel-brass (outer) and cupro-nickel (inner) blanks and a nickel-brass ring. The obverse used is a modified OBVERSE 1 - very similar, but the trial obverse has minor differences, for example, a dot instead of a small cross between the 'D' and 'ELIZABETH'.

Edge: DECUS ET TUTAMEN ANNO REGNI XLVI
Value: The bi-metallic pack tends to sell for between £200 and £220.
(loose trial coins are £120 - £140. BEWARE, fakes exist)

Monometallic all-brass £2 trial, dated 1994 and marked 'ROYAL MINT TRIAL' on both sides, also featuring the ship design on the reverse. This particular coin was never made available to the public. They are very rare. **Value £1,000.00 - £2,000.00**

101

28.40 mm • 12.0 grammes • bi-metal • various edge

DEFINITIVE TYPE 1 (obverse 1, reverse 1)

Year	Mintage		Used	As-New	Proof
1997	13,734,625		FV	£5.00	£7.50
		Specimen in folder		£9.00	
	29,910	.925 silver proof			£20.00
	10,000	.925 silver piedfort proof			£30.00
	2,482	.917 gold proof			£1,300.00

DEFINITIVE TYPE 2 (obverse 2, reverse 1)

Year	Mintage		Used	As-New	Proof
1998	91,110,375	100,000 proofs	FV	£5.00	£7.50
1999*	33,719,000		FV	£80.00	£80.00+
2000	25,770,000		FV	£6.00	£7.50
2001	34,984,750		FV	£8.00	£9.00
2002	13,024,750		FV	£6.00	£7.50
2003	17,531,250		FV	£6.00	£7.50
2004	11,981,500		FV	£5.00	£7.50
2005	3,837,250		FV	£6.00	£7.50
2006	16,715,000		FV	£6.00	£7.50
2007	10,270,000		FV	£6.00	£7.50
2008	30,107,000		FV	£7.00	£8.00
2009	8,775,000		FV	£6.00	£7.50
2010*	6,890,000		FV	£4.00	£7.00
2011	24,375,030		FV	£4.00	£7.50
2012	3,900,000		FV	£14.00	£14.00
2013	15,860,250		FV	£14.00	£14.00
2014	18,200,000		FV	£6.00	£7.50
2015	35,360,058**		FV	£8.00	£9.00

* 1999 was not issued in the proof or BU sets that year and very few people seem to have saved them new from change. It is therefore scarce to almost unheard of in top condition. 2010 coins exist with an interesting doubled-die error obverse, most evident on lettering below the queen.

DEFINITIVE TYPE 3 (obverse 3, reverse 2) - The definitive Britannia coin.

Year	Mintage		Used	As-New	Proof
2015	650,000**		£3.00	£10.00	£15.00
	15,597	Specimen in folder		£20.00	
		.925 silver proof/piedfort			£50.00/£65.00
		.917 gold proof			£1,300.00
2016	2,925,000			£11.00	£15.00
		.917 gold proof			£1,200.00
2017	47,626	Available in sets only		£30.00	
2018	29,909	Available in sets only		£33.00	
2019	36,050	Available in sets only		£22.00	
2020	Unknown	Available in sets only		£10.00	
2021	Unknown	Available in sets only		£15.00	
2022	Unknown	Currently available in sets only		£14.00	

**Many 2015 £2 coins (both types) have been observed with die rotation errors. The 2015 technology coin is also known to exist as a mono-metallic brass alloy coins, struck in error on an unpierced outer ring.

DEFINITIVE TYPE 3 (obverse 4, reverse 3) - New Charles III floral design

			As-New	Proof
2023	with privy mark*	Available in sets only	£12.00	£20.00
2024	Not yet known	Currently available in sets only	£9.00	£20.00

* The privy mark is a small crown to the right of the King's head, see page 37. No 2023 £2 coins were struck for circulation.

BI-METALLIC COMMEMORATIVE COINS

Note that some Brilliant Uncirculated bi-metallic £2 folders that are still sealed in original plastic wrappers can be worth more than the values shown.

COMMEMORATIVE TYPE 8
Symbolic representation of a stadium with rugby ball and goalposts. '1999' above, 'TWO POUNDS' below
(1999 Rugby World Cup)
Design by: Ron Dutton
Edge: RUGBY WORLD CUP 1999

			Used	As-New	Proof
1999	4,933,000		FV	£7.50	£10.00
		Specimen in folder		£26.00	
	9,665	.925 sterling silver proof			£40.00
	10,000	.925 sterling silver hologram piedfort proof			£70.00
	311	.917 gold proof			£1,300.00

Noted with incorrect (rotated) die alignment of about 90 degrees.

COMMEMORATIVE TYPE 9
Symbolic representation of Marconi's successful transatlantic wireless transmission of 1901, 'TWO POUNDS' below
Design by: Robert Evans
Edge: WIRELESS BRIDGES THE ATLANTIC...MARCONI 1901...

			Used	As-New	Proof
2001	4,558,000		FV	£8.00	£10.00
		Specimen in folder		£25.00	
	11,488	.925 sterling silver proof			£28.00
	6,759	.925 sterling silver piedfort proof			£33.00
	1,658	.917 gold proof			£1,200.00

a  b  c  d

COMMEMORATIVE TYPE 10
XVII COMMONWEALTH GAMES 2002
around athlete holding banner, (1 of 4) national flags
(17th Commonwealth Games, Manchester)
Design by: Matthew Bonaccorsi
Edge: SPIRIT OF FRIENDSHIP MANCHESTER 2002

			Used	As-New	Proof
2002	650,500	10a English flag	£10.00	£30.00	£35.00
	485,500	10b N. Ireland flag	£35.00	£65.00	£65.00
	771,750	10c Scottish flag	£9.00	£25.00	£30.00
	588,500	10d Welsh flag	£14.00	£30.00	£35.00

The NI coin looks very similar to the England coin. The NI flag has a crowned hand in the centre.

Sets of the 4 Type 10 coins:	Specimens in BU card (19,229)	£170.00
	base metal proof set (3,552 felt box. 747 in plastic box)	£180.00
2,553	.925 sterling silver proof set	£200.00
3,497?	.925 sterling silver piedfort set (coloured flags)	£400.00
315	.917 gold proof set	no data

COMMEMORATIVE TYPE 11
DNA Double Helix pattern, DNA DOUBLE HELIX,
1953 TWO POUNDS 2003
(50th Anniversary - Discovery of DNA)
Design by: John Mills
Edge: DEOXYRIBONUCLEIC ACID

			Used	As-New	Proof
2003	4,299,000		FV	£7.50	£15.00
	14,105	Specimen in folder		£22.00	
	11,204	.925 sterling silver proof			£30.00
	8,728	.925 sterling silver piedfort proof			£35.00
	1,500	.917 gold proof			£1,200.00

COMMEMORATIVE TYPE 12
Steam locomotive TWO POUNDS R.TREVITHICK
1804 INVENTION INDUSTRY PROGRESS 2004
(200th anniversary - Steam Locomotive)
Design by: Robert Lowe
Edge: pattern of arcs & curves, representing viaducts

			Used	As-New	Proof
2004	5,004,500		FV	£7.50	£15.00
	14,447	Specimen in folder		£20.00	
	1,923 max.	.925 sterling silver BU version in pack			£40.00?
	10,233 of 25k	.925 sterling silver proof			£30.00
	5,303 of 10k	.925 sterling silver piedfort proof			£35.00
	1,500	.917 gold proof			£1,200.00

COMMEMORATIVE TYPE 13
Swords, Maces, Croziers in a star-burst pattern,
1605-2005, TWO POUNDS
(400th anniversary - Gunpowder Plot)
Design by: Peter Forster
Edge: REMEMBER REMEMBER THE FIFTH OF NOVEMBER*

			Used	As-New	Proof
2005	5,140,500		FV	£8.00	£15.00
	12,044	Specimen in folder		£30.00	
	4,394	.925 sterling silver proof			£30.00
	4,584	.925 sterling silver piedfort proof			£40.00
	914	.917 gold proof			£1,300.00

* These very often end up having missing tails on the 'R's of the edge lettering, so that they can in extreme cases read PEMEMBEP PEMEMBEP THE FIFTH OF NOVEMBEP. This problem with certain edge letters has also been noted on some other £2 and £1 coins. It makes them a little more interesting, but it is my opinion that such errors should have no real influence on value.

> **INFO**
> Some £2 coins still sealed in original 'specimen' BU packaging have been known to sell for considerably more than shown.

105

| 28.40 mm • 12.0 grammes • bi-metal • various edge

COMMEMORATIVE TYPE 14
St. Paul's Cathedral, floodlit with spotlights.
1945-2005, TWO POUNDS
(60th anniversary - End of World War II)
Design by: Robert Elderton
Edge: IN VICTORY: MAGNANIMITY, IN PEACE: GOODWILL

			Used	As-New	Proof
2005	10,191,000		FV	£7.50	
	13,904	(folder including special medallion)		£25.00	
	21,734	.925 sterling silver proof			£30.00
	Not Known	*Error edge: REMEMBER REMEMBER THE FIFTH OF			
		NOVEMBER .925 silver proof			£400.00?
	4,798	.925 sterling silver piedfort proof			£40.00
	2,924**	.917 gold proof			no data

Noted with slightly incorrect (rotated) die alignment.

* The edge error 60th Anniversary of the End of WWII £2 coin incorrectly has the edge inscription of the other themed £2 coin struck that year to commemorate the gunpowder plot.

**Of the gold proof total, 1,578 were boxed single coins and a further 1,346 were sold in allied nation coin sets.

COMMEMORATIVE TYPE 15
Portrait of Isambard Kingdom Brunel in front of machinery
TWO POUNDS | 2006
(200th anniversary - Birth of Isambard Kingdom Brunel)
Design by: Rod Kelly
Edge: 1806-59 . ISAMBARD KINGDOM BRUNEL . ENGINEER

			Used	As-New	Proof
2006	7,928,250		FV	£6.50	£15.00
	10,941	Specimens in folder (with Type 16)		£24.00	
	7,251 of 20k	.925 sterling silver proof			£34.00
	3,199 of 5k	.925 sterling silver piedfort proof			£40.00
	1,071 of 1,500	.917 gold proof			£1,200.00

Known to exist with its outer ring made from a 2006 heroic acts 50p! Believed unique.

The words 'TWO POUNDS' above Mr Brunel on the reverse often looks more like 'TWO DOUNDS', due to the tail of the 'P' being obscured by the join between the inner and outer metal types.

The Brunel coins (types 15 and 16) were also sold in pairs in a folder and also cased as silver proofs.

COMMEMORATIVE TYPE 16

Representation of the engineering achievements of I.K.Brunel,
2006 | BRUNEL | TWO POUNDS
(200th anniversary - Birth of Isambard Kingdom Brunel)
Design by: Robert Evans
Edge: **SO MANY IRONS IN THE FIRE**

			Used	As-New	Proof
2006	7,452,250		FV	£6.50	£15.00
	10,941	Specimens in folder (with Type 15)		£24.00	
	5,375 of 20k	.925 sterling silver proof			£25.00
	Not Known	.925 sterling silver proof with no edge lettering			£300.00?
	3,018 of 5k	.925 sterling silver piedfort proof			£45.00
	746 of 1,500	.917 gold proof*			£1,300.00

* Noted with certificate no. 1054, which shouldn't be possible! Printing mix up with Type 15?

COMMEMORATIVE TYPE 17

Jigsaw pieces of the English rose and Scottish thistle,
TWO | 2007 | POUNDS | 1707
(300th anniversary - Act of Union between England and Scotland)
Design by: Yvonne Holton
Edge: **UNITED INTO ONE KINGDOM**

			Used	As-New	Proof
2007	7,545,000		FV	£6.00	£15.00
	8,863	Specimen in folder		£40.00	
	8,310	.925 sterling silver proof			£25.00
	4,000	.925 sterling silver piedfort proof			£30.00
	750	.917 gold proof			£1,300.00

COMMEMORATIVE TYPE 18 (A & B)

Five link chain with broken link as the nought in 1807,
AN ACT FOR THE ABOLITION OF THE SLAVE TRADE | 2007
(200th anniversary - Abolition of the British slave trade)
Design by: David Gentleman
Edge: **AM I NOT A MAN AND A BROTHER**
Obverse: 2b

			Used	As-New	Proof
2007	B	8,445,000	(no 'DG' initials)	FV	Hard to find	
	A	8,688	Specimen in folder ('DG' to right of chain) £40.00			
	A	7,095	.925 sterling silver proof ('DG' to right of chain)			£35.00*
	A	3,990	.925 sterling silver piedfort proof			£45.00
	A	1,000 max	.917 gold proof			£1,200.00

Type A has 'DG' initials to the right of the '1807'. Type B has no initials and a textured background.
A silver proof version of this coin is known to exist with the 'THE 4TH OLYMPIAD LONDON'
edge legend, obviously meant for Type 19. See also the note under Type 14.

107

| 28.40 mm • 12.0 grammes • bi-metal • various edge

COMMEMORATIVE TYPE 19
Running Track
LONDON OLYMPIC CENTENARY | 1908 | TWO POUNDS | 2008
(Centenary - 1908 London Olympics)
Design by: Thomas T Docherty
Edge: THE 4TH OLYMPIAD LONDON
Obverse: 2

		Used	As-New	Proof
2008	910,000	£4.00	£14.00	£20.00
	14,426 of 100k Specimen in folder		£30.00	
	6,841 of 20k .925 sterling silver proof			£40.00
	1,619 of 2,000 .925 sterling silver piedfort proof			£65.00
	1,908 .917 gold proof			£1,300.00

COMMEMORATIVE TYPE 20
Olympic flag and two hands
BEIJING 2008 | LONDON 2012
(Olympic handover ceremony)
Design by: Royal Mint in House
Edge: I CALL UPON THE YOUTH OF THE WORLD
Obverse: 2b

		Used	As-New	Proof
2008	918,000	£5.00	£16.00	
	57,346 of 250k Specimen in folder		£40.00	
	30,000 .925 sterling silver proof			£40.00
	3,000 .925 sterling silver piedfort proof			£50.00
	3,250 .917 gold proof			£1,200.00

COMMEMORATIVE TYPE 21
Darwin facing ape
1809 DARWIN 2009 | TWO POUNDS
(200th anniversary - birth of Charles Darwin)
Design by: Suzie Zamit
Edge: ON THE ORIGIN OF SPECIES 1859
Obverse: 2

		Used	As-New	Proof
2009	3,903,000	FV	£20.00	£25.00
	18,658 of 25k Specimen in folder		£40.00	
	9,357 .925 sterling silver proof			£45.00
	3,282 .925 sterling silver piedfort proof			£50.00
	1,000 .917 gold proof			£1,200.00

COMMEMORATIVE TYPE 22
Burns quote
1759 ROBERT BURNS 1796 | TWO POUNDS
(250 years anniversary - birth of Robert Burns)
Design by: Royal Mint in House
Edge: SHOULD AULD ACQUAINTANCE BE FORGOT
Obverse: 2c

			Used	As-New	Proof
2009	3,253,000		FV	£11.00	£15.00
	23,455	Specimen in folder		£40.00	
	9,188	.925 sterling silver proof			£40.00
	3,500	.925 sterling silver piedfort proof			£45.00
	1,000	.917 gold proof			no data

COMMEMORATIVE TYPE 23
Nurses hands feeling for a pulse
1820 - FLORENCE NIGHTINGALE - 1910 | TWO POUNDS
(150 years of modern nursing and to the centenary of the
death of Florence Nightingale)
Design by: Gordon Summers
Edge: 150 YEARS OF NURSING
Obverse: 2c

			Used	As-New	Proof
2010	6,175,000		FV	£8.00	£15.00
	14,905 of 25k	Specimen in folder		£40.00	
	5,117 of 20k	.925 sterling silver proof			£45.00
	2,770 of 3,5k	.925 sterling silver piedfort proof			£60.00
	472 of 1,000	.917 gold proof			no data

An error struck on a nickel plated steel blank is known to exist - it is thought to be a blank
intended for a Gambian 50 Butots (the Royal Mint also strike coins for many other countries).

COMMEMORATIVE TYPE 24
King James' Bible
KING JAMES BIBLE | 1611 - 2011
(400 years anniversary - King James' Bible)
Design by: Paul Stafford & Benjamin Wright
Edge: THE AUTHORISED VERSION
Obverse: 2b

			Used	As-New	Proof
2011	975,000		£4.00	£20.00	£30.00
	11,317 of 25k	Specimen in folder		£55.00	
	4,494 of 20k	.925 sterling silver proof			£60.00
	2,394 of 3,5k	.925 sterling silver piedfort proof			£120.00
	355 of 1000	.917 gold proof			£1,300.00

109

COMMEMORATIVE TYPE 25
Mary Rose
THE MARY ROSE | TWO POUNDS
(500 Years - Mary Rose)
Design by: John Bergdahl
Edge: 1511 . YOUR NOBLEST SHIPPE .
Obverse: 2c

			Used	As-New	Proof
2011	1,040,000		£4.00	£16.00	£25.00
	8,277 of 25k	Specimen in folder		£50.00	
	6,618 of 20k	.925 sterling silver proof			£60.00
	2,680 of ?2k	.925 sterling silver piedfort proof			£70.00
	692 of 1,511	.917 gold proof			£1,200.00

COMMEMORATIVE TYPE 26
Olympic Handover
LONDON 2012 | RIO 2016
(Olympic handover ceremony)
Design by: Jonathan Olliffe
Edge: I CALL UPON THE YOUTH OF THE WORLD
Obverse: 2d

			Used	As-New	Proof
2012	845,000		£4.00	£30.00	
	18,275	Specimen in folder		£50.00	
	3,781 of 12k	.925 sterling silver proof			£50.00
	2000 sold	.925 sterling silver piedfort proof			£80.00
	771 of 1200 max	.917 gold proof			£1,200.00

COMMEMORATIVE TYPE 27
Charles Dickens
1812 CHARLES DICKENS 1870
(200th anniversary - birth of Charles Dickens)
Design by: Matthew Dent
Edge: SOMETHING WILL TURN UP
Obverse: 2d

			Used	As-New	Proof
2012	8,190,000		FV	£16.00	£18.00
	15,035*	Specimen in folder		£40.00	
	2,631 of 8k	.925 sterling silver proof			£45.00
	1,279 of 2k	.925 sterling silver piedfort proof			£85.00
	202 of 1,000	.917 gold proof, price new			£1,400.00

*Plus 7,726 in packages combining stamps with the coin.

COMMEMORATIVE TYPE 28
Underground Roundal
1863 | UNDERGROUND | 2013
(150th anniversary - The London Underground)
Design by: Edwina Ellis
Edge: MIND THE GAP
Obverse: 2b

		Used	As-New	Proof
2013	1,560,000	£3.00	£18.00	£20.00
	11,647 pairs of coins* Type 28 and 29 Specimens in folder £25.00			
	1,185 of 12.5k	.925 sterling silver proof		£60.00
	162 of 2.5k	.925 sterling silver piedfort proof		no data
	21 of 750	.917 gold proof, price new (111 also sold in pairs)		no data

* Plus another 9,250 pairs of Underground coins combined with stamps.
Errors: Noted completely in brass, struck on an un-pierced outer ring. Also seen with incorrect patterned edge design of Type 29.

COMMEMORATIVE TYPE 29
Underground Train
1863 | LONDON UNDERGROUND | 2013
(150th anniversary - The London Underground)
Design by: Edward Barber and Jay Osgerby
Edge: A pattern of circles connected by lines.
Obverse: 2b

		Used	As-New	Proof
2013	1,690,000	£3.00	£18.00	£20.00
	2,023 of 12k	.925 sterling silver proof*		£60.00
	186 of 2.5k	.925 sterling silver piedfort proof		no data
	29 of 750	.917 gold proof, price new (111 also sold in pairs)		no data

* A further 2,204 silver proof pairs of both Underground coins were sold : £140
Piedfort proof pair of both Underground coins : £175.00

COMMEMORATIVE TYPE 30
Spade Guinea
ANNIVERSARY OF THE GOLDEN GUINEA | 2013
(350th anniversary - the Guinea)
Design by: Anthony Smith
Edge: WHAT IS A GUINEA? 'TIS A SPLENDID THING
Obverse: 2b

		Used	As-New	Proof
2013	2,990,000	FV	£20.00	£25.00
	10,340	Specimen in folder	£40.00	
	1640 of 12k	.925 sterling silver proof		£60.00
	969 of 4,013	.925 sterling silver piedfort proof		no data
	284 of 1,200	.917 gold proof		no data

COMMEMORATIVE TYPE 31
Design from Kitchener recruitment poster
THE FIRST WORLD WAR 1914 - 1918 | 2014
(Centenary - Start of WWI)
Design by: John Bergdahl
Edge: THE LAMPS ARE GOING OUT ALL OVER EUROPE
Obverse: 2b

			Used	As-New	Proof
2014	5,720,000		FV	£10.00	£15.00
	40,357	Specimen in folder*		£20.00	
	4,983 of 8,014	.925 sterling silver proof			£40.00
	2,496 of 4,514	.925 sterling silver piedfort proof			£50.00
	734 of 825	.917 gold proof			£1,300.00

*10,490 were also combined with stamps. **Errors:** One with outer ring made from a 2014 standard 50p. Two seen completely in brass and a mule has been seen with incorrect Obv 2, instead of 2b (i.e. missing 'TWO POUNDS').

COMMEMORATIVE TYPE 32
Top of a Lighthouse
1514 TRINITY HOUSE 2014 | TWO POUNDS
(500 years of Trinity house)
Design by: Joe Whitlock Blundell and David Eccles
Edge: SERVING THE MARINER
Obverse 2

			Used	As-New	Proof
2014	3,705,000		FV	£18.00	£25.00
	10,521	Specimen in folder, price new		£35.00	
	1,285 of 4,714	.925 sterling silver proof, price new			£50.00
	652 of 3,514	.925 sterling silver piedfort proof, price new			£170.00
	204 of 375	.917 gold proof			£1,400.00

COMMEMORATIVE TYPE 33a
Royal Navy Battleship
THE FIRST WORLD WAR 1914 - 1918 | 2015
(Centenary - WWI, Royal Navy themed coin)
Design by: David Rowlands
Edge: THE SURE SHIELD OF BRITAIN
With Obverse type 2b, shown to right

			As-New	Proof
2015	39,009	(not issued for circulation)	£12.00	£20.00
		Specimen in folder	£20.00	
	3,030 of 8.5k	.925 sterling silver proof		£80.00
	4,000 max.	.925 sterling silver piedfort proof		£100.00
	406 of 900	.917 gold proof		£1,200.00

COMMEMORATIVE TYPE 33b
Royal Navy Battleship
THE FIRST WORLD WAR 1914 - 1918 | 2015
(Centenary - WWI, Royal Navy themed coin)
Design by: David Rowlands
Edge: THE SURE SHIELD OF BRITAIN
With Obverse type 3b, shown to right

			Used	As-New*
2015				
	650,000		£4.00	£15.00
	?	.925 sterling silver proof, price new		no data
	?	.925 sterling silver piedfort proof		no data
	99	.917 gold proof		no data

* Hard to find in very high grade as this coins is a circulation type only. Noted with incorrect (rotated) die alignment. Also of note are the 'flag' and 'cat on mast' types, which are colloquial terms for extra features at the top of the mast, both of which have been caused by die damage.

COMMEMORATIVE TYPE 34a
King John with bishop and a baron
MAGNA CARTA | 1215 - 2015
(King John signing the Magna Carta)
Design by: John Bergdahl
Edge: FOUNDATION OF LIBERTY
With Obverse type 2d, shown to right

			Used	As-New	Proof
2015	32,818	(not issued for circulation) £5.00		£15.00	£25.00
		Specimen in folder		£25.00	
	1500	.925 sterling silver proof, in sets only*			£75.00?
	?	.925 sterling silver piedfort proof*			no data
	?	.917 gold proof*			no data

*Available in the full annual silver/gold proof set, as well as the 5-coin commemorative silver/gold proof sets.

COMMEMORATIVE TYPE 34b
King John with bishop and a baron
MAGNA CARTA | 1215 - 2015
(King John signing the Magna Carta)
Design by: John Bergdahl
Edge: FOUNDATION OF LIBERTY
Obverse type 3d, shown to right

			Used	As-New*	Proof
2015	1,495,000		£3.00	£10.00	
	2,995 of 3k	.925 sterling silver proof			£60.00
	2,000 max.	.925 sterling silver piedfort proof			£60.00
	399 of 400	.917 gold proof			£1,300.00

* Hard to find in perfect condition due to the general poor standard of current circulation coins.

113

The 2015 Commemorative £2 coins on the previous pages lack continuity and can be confusing. For each of the two coins (First World War Navy and Magna Carta) two different obverses were used during the year, one with the 4th portrait of the Queen and the other with the new 5th portrait. There are therefore four basic designs. The whole thing is further complicated by the proof issues, which for the Navy coin all use the 4th portrait and for the Magna Carta coin, use the 5th portrait, except for the base metal proof coin (from sets) which features the 4th portrait and early versions of the Magna Carta silver proof coins which were sold in sets of 2015 commemorative coins and feature the 4th portrait.

COMMEMORATIVE TYPE 35
Stylised representation of 'Pals Battalion'
THE FIRST WORLD WAR 1914 - 1918 | 2016
(Centenary - WWI, Army themed coin)
Design by: Tim Sharp of the creative agency Uniform
Edge: FOR KING AND COUNTRY
Obverse 3b

			Used	As-New	Proof
2016	9,550,000		FV	£8.00	£15.00
	19,066	Specimen in folder		£20.00	
	1,703 of 8.5k	.925 sterling silver proof			£60.00
	931 of 2,500	.925 sterling silver piedfort proof			£70.00
	279 of 950	.917 gold proof			£1,400.00

COMMEMORATIVE TYPE 36
Scene from the Great Fire of London
1666 THE GREAT FIRE OF LONDON 2016 | TWO POUNDS
(350th Anniversary of the Great Fire of London)
Design by: Aaron West
Edge: THE WHOLE CITY IN DREADFUL FLAMES
Obverse 3c

			Used	As-New	Proof
2016	1,625,000		£3.00	£13.00	£20.00
	23,215*	Specimen in folder		£24.00	
	1,649 of 10,5k	.925 sterling silver proof			£40.00
	1,356 of 3,500	.925 sterling silver piedfort proof			£60.00
	259 of 1,000	.917 gold proof			£1,400.00

* 4,857 sold in tubes to other retailers.

Types 35 & 36 have been seen completely in brass without the inner silver coloured part (a mint error). Both were contained within BU sets.

COMMEMORATIVE TYPE 37
Marotte and Jester's hat
WILLIAM SHAKESPEARE | 2016
(300th Anniversary of Shakespeare's death. Comedy theme)
Design by: John Bergdahl
Edge: ALL THE WORLDS A STAGE (in italic on proofs?)
Obverse 3b

			Used	As-New	Proof
2016	4,355,000		FV	£8.00	£15.00
	22,060 each	*The 3 Shakespeare coins in folder		£40.00	
	951 of 8k	.925 sterling silver proof			£55.00
	533 of 2,500	.925 sterling silver piedfort proof			£80.00
	152 of 450	.917 gold proof			no data

COMMEMORATIVE TYPE 38
Crown and Sword
WILLIAM SHAKESPEARE | 2016
(300th Anniversary of Shakespeare's death. History theme)
Design by: John Bergdahl
Edge: THE HOLLOW CROWN (in italic on proofs?)
Obverse 3b

			Used	As-New	Proof
2016	5,655,000		FV	£8.00	£15.00
	965 of 8k	.925 sterling silver proof			£55.00
	624 of 2,500	.925 sterling silver piedfort proof			£80.00
	156 of 450	.917 gold proof			no data

COMMEMORATIVE TYPE 39
Skull and Rose
WILLIAM SHAKESPEARE | 2016
(300th Anniversary of Shakespeare's death. Tragedy theme)
Design by: John Bergdahl
Edge: WHAT A PIECE OF WORK IS A MAN
(in italic script on proofs)
Obverse 3b

			Used	As-New	Proof
2016	4,615,000		FV	£8.00	£15.00
	Error	FOR KING AND COUNTRY WWI edge. Used: £35			
	679 of 2,500	.925 sterling silver proof			£55.00
	209 of 450	.925 sterling silver piedfort proof			£100.00
	209 of 450	.917 gold proof			no data

*The three coins on this page in 'Brilliant Uncirculated' form were only sold together. In addition to that, 3,500 Comedy, 6,341 History and 6,550 Tragedy coins were sold in tubes to other retailers. Other higher denomination and precious metal Shakespeare themed coins were also sold.

115

COMMEMORATIVE TYPE 40
Jane Austen Silhouette and signature
JANE AUSTEN 1817 - 2017 | TWO POUNDS
(200th Anniversary of Jane Austen's death)
Design by: Dominique Evans
Edge: THERE IS NO DOING WITHOUT MONEY
Obverse 3

			As-New	Proof
2017	54,729	(All in RM packs)	£25.00	
3,531 of 8k		.925 sterling silver proof		£60.00
2,155 of 4k		.925 sterling silver piedfort proof		£90.00
307 of 884		.917 gold proof		£1,400.00

COMMEMORATIVE TYPE 41
Biplane from above
1914 - 1918 | THE WAR IN THE AIR
(Centenary - WWI, Aviation themed coin)
Design by: tangerine (design agency)
Edge: THE SKY RAINED HEROES
Obverse 3e

			As-New	Proof
2017	Total sold: 62,448	(54,159 in RM packs, remainder in PNCs)	£20.00	
2,924 of 7k		.925 sterling silver proof		£50.00
1,535 of 3,5k		.925 sterling silver piedfort proof		£60.00
302 of 634		.917 gold proof		no data

COMMEMORATIVE TYPE 42
'FRANKENSTEIN' in a style reminiscent of an ECG
Above: BICENTENARY OF MARY SHELLEY'S
Below: 1818 THE MODERN PROMETHEUS 2018
(200th Anniversary of Mary Shelley's Frankenstein novel)
Design by: Thomas T. Docherty
Edge: A SPARK OF BEING
Obverse 3b

			As-New	Proof
2018	Total sold: 34,759	(17,280 in RM packs)	£23.00	£25.00
2,198 of 8k		.925 sterling silver proof		£40.00
1,041 of 1,818		.925 sterling silver piedfort proof		£50.00
115 of 400		.917 gold proof		no data

COMMEMORATIVE TYPE 43
Badge of the Royal Air Force
THE 100th ANNIVERSARY OF THE ROYAL AIR FORCE |
1918 - 2018
(Centenary - The establishment of the Royal Air Force, 1 of 5)
Design by: Rhys Morgan
Edge: PER ARDUA AD ASTRA
Obverse 3b

			As-New	Proof
2018 Total sold: 77,350	(29,077 in RM packs)		£19.00	£20.00
5,706 of 10k	.925 sterling silver proof			£50.00
1,256 of 3k	.925 sterling silver piedfort proof			£100.00
255 of 1,918	.917 gold proof			no data

COMMEMORATIVE TYPE 44
Stylised 'THE TRUTH UNTOLD THE PITY OF WAR'
THE FIRST WORLD WAR - ARMISTICE - 1918 |
TWO POUNDS
(Centenary - WWI, Armistice themed coin)
Design by: Stephen Raw
Edge: WILFRED OWEN KILLED IN ACTION 4 NOV 1918
Obverse 3

			As-New	Proof
2018 Total sold: 48,736	(19,615 in RM packs)		£28.00	£30.00
2,627 of 8k	.925 sterling silver proof			£75.00
1,172 of 2.5k	.925 sterling silver piedfort proof			£110.00
185 of 1,000	.917 gold proof			no data

Seen with incorrect die alignment (approx. 80 degrees out) contained within a BU set.
Other precious metal higher value Armistice themed coins, with different designs, were also sold.

COMMEMORATIVE TYPE 45
Spitfire
SPITFIRE RAF | 1918 - 2018
(Centenary - The establishment of the Royal Air Force, 2 of 5)
Design by: Richard Talbot & Neil Talbot
Edge: PER ARDUA AD ASTRA
Obverse 3b

			As-New	Proof
2018 Total sold: 73,052	(31,725 in RM packs)		£20.00	£25.00
5,960 of 10k	.925 sterling silver proof			£50.00
1,490	.925 sterling silver piedfort proof			£120.00
287 of 1,918	.917 gold proof			no data

COMMEMORATIVE TYPE 46
Vulcan
RAF 1918 - 2018 | VULCAN
(Centenary - The establishment of the Royal Air Force, 3 of 5)
Design by: Richard Talbot & Neil Talbot
Edge: PER ARDUA AD ASTRA
Obverse 3b

			As-New	Proof
2018 Total sold: 60,538	(26,893 in RM packs)		£23.00	no data
4,795 of 10k	.925 sterling silver proof			£70.00
971 of 3k	.925 sterling silver piedfort proof			£100.00
167 of 1,918	.917 gold proof			no data

COMMEMORATIVE TYPE 47
Captain James Cook (1)
1768 - 2018 | CAPTAIN JAMES COOK | 250
(To commemorate the HM Bark Endeavour voyage, 1 of 3)
Design by: Gary Breeze
Edge: OCEANI INVESTIGATOR ACERRIMVS
Obverse 3b

			As-New	Proof
2018 Total sold: 48,909	(24,660 in RM packs)		£30.00	no data
4,778 of 5k	.925 sterling silver proof, price new			£67.50
339 of 350	.917 gold proof			£1,400.00

BU version also sold as a PNC with stamps.

COMMEMORATIVE TYPE 48
Sea King
SEA KING | RAF 1918 - 2018
(Centenary - The establishment of the Royal Air Force, 4 of 5)
Design by: Richard Talbot & Neil Talbot
Edge: PER ARDUA AD ASTRA
Obverse 3b

			As-New	Proof
2018 Total sold: 52,052	(23,161 in RM packs)		£23.00	no data
4,163 of 10k	.925 sterling silver proof			£50.00
911 of 3k	.925 sterling silver piedfort proof			£110.00
118 of 1,918	.917 gold proof			no data

| 28.40 mm • 12.0 grammes • bi-metal • various edge | TWO POUNDS 2019 |

COMMEMORATIVE TYPE 49
Lightning II
RAF 1918 - 2018 | LIGHTNING II
(Centenary - The establishment of the Royal Air Force, 5 of 5)
Design by: Richard Talbot & Neil Talbot
Edge: PER ARDUA AD ASTRA
Obverse 3b

			As-New	Proof
2018 Total sold: 49,423	(20,532 in RM packs)		£40.00	no data
4,072 of 10k	.925 sterling silver proof			£60.00
786 of 3k	.925 sterling silver piedfort proof			£140.00
120 of 1,918	.917 gold proof			no data

COMMEMORATIVE TYPE 50
75th Anniversary of D-Day
D-DAY 75TH ANNIVERSARY | 2019
(To mark the 75th Anniversary of the Normandy landings)
Design by: Stephen Taylor
Edge: THE LONGEST DAY
Obverse 3b

			As-New	Proof
2019 Total sold: 74,967	(25,935 in RM packs)		£11.00	£15.00
4,050 of 5k *	.925 sterling silver proof			£40.00
1,594 of 2k	.925 sterling silver piedfort proof			£100.00
400 of 750 *	.917 gold proof			£1,400.00

* 1,850 individual silver proofs also sold to trade customers. 50 gold proofs also sold to trade customers.
Also available as silver (191 sold) or gold (20 sold) proofs accompanied by old newspapers.

COMMEMORATIVE TYPE 51
Wedgwood
WEDGWOOD | 1759 - 2019
(260 years since the establishment of Wedgwood)
Design by: Wedgwood Design Team
Edge: EVERYTHING GIVES WAY TO EXPERIMENT
Obverse 3b

			As-New	Proof
2019 Total sold: 33,005	(15,529 in RM packs)		£14.00	£15.00
1,951 of 4.5k	.925 sterling silver proof			£60.00
968 of 1,250	.925 sterling silver piedfort proof			no data
142 of 350	.917 gold proof			no data

28.40 mm • 12.0 grammes • bi-metal • various edge

COMMEMORATIVE TYPE 52
Samuel Pepys
SAMUEL PEPYS DIARIST | 1669 - 2019
(To mark 350 years since the last diary entry by Samuel Pepys)
Design by: Gary Breeze
Edge: THE GOOD GOD PREPARE ME
Obverse 3b

		As-New	Proof
2019 Total sold: 31,754	(14,278 in RM packs)	£15.00	£20.00
1,878 of 4.5k max.	.925 sterling silver proof		£50.00
841 of 1,019 max.	.925 sterling silver piedfort proof		£80.00
138 of 350 max.	.917 gold proof		no data

COMMEMORATIVE TYPE 53
Captain James Cook (2)
1768 - 2018 | CAPTAIN JAMES COOK | 250
(To commemorate the HM Bark Endeavour voyage, 2 of 3)
Design by: Gary Breeze
Edge: OCEANI INVESTIGATOR ACERRIMVS
Obverse 3b

		As-New	Proof
2019 Total sold: 39,278	(21,778 in RM packs)	£18.00	
4,326 of 5k max.	.925 sterling silver proof		£50.00
340 of 350 max.	.917 gold proof		£1,400.00

COMMEMORATIVE TYPE 54
Agatha Christie
100 YEARS OF MYSTERY | 1920 | (signature) | 2020
(100 years since the publication of Agatha Christie's first novel)
Design by: David Lawrence
Edge: LITTLE GREY CELLS
Obverse 3b

		As-New	Proof
2020 Total sold: 55,288	(16,838 in RM packs)	£8.00	
2,210 of 3,255	.925 sterling silver proof, price new		£70.00
794	.925 sterling silver piedfort proof, price new		no data
194 of 355	.917 gold proof		no data

COMMEMORATIVE TYPE 55
VE-Day 75th Anniversary
1945 - 2020 | VICTORY IN EUROPE DAY
(To mark the 75th Anniversary of VE-Day)
Design by: Dominique Evans
Edge: **JUST TRIUMPH AND PROUD SORROW**
Obverse 3b

		As-New	Proof
2020 Total sold: 92,377	(31,322 in RM packs)	£6.00	
4,741 of 7,250	.925 sterling silver proof		£40.00
1,635	.925 sterling silver piedfort proof		£80.00
475 of 661	.917 gold proof		£1,300.00

Also made available in various postal numismatic covers and a variant as 1/2oz silver proof.

COMMEMORATIVE TYPE 56
Mayflower Commemorative
1620 | 2020 | MAYFLOWER
(400 Years since the voyage of the Mayflower)
Design by: Chris Costello
Edge: **UNDERTAKEN FOR THE GLORY OF GOD**
Obverse 3b

		As-New	Proof
2020 Total sold: 59,803	(18,82 in RM packs)	£7.00	
3,991 of 5,505	.925 sterling silver proof		£50.00
1,990	.925 sterling silver piedfort proof, price new		£115.00
397 of 585	.917 gold proof		£1,300.00

Different Mayflower related bi-national coin/medal pairs were also sold in conjunction with the US mint. Some of the silver and gold proof coins were also 'slabbed' as 'PF70' by US third party coin grader NGC and offered for sale via the Royal Mint. Gold NGC version £1,450 new (max. 100). Silver NGC version £72.50 new (max. 500).

COMMEMORATIVE TYPE 57
Captain James Cook (3)
1768 - 2018 | CAPTAIN JAMES COOK | 250
(To commemorate the HM Bark Endeavour voyage, 3 of 3)
Design by: Gary Breeze
Edge: **OCEANI INVESTIGATOR ACERRIMVS?**
Obverse 3b

		As-New	Proof
2020 Total sold: 36,710	(19,715 in RM packs)	£14.00	
4,793 of 5,000	.925 sterling silver proof		£50.00
2,000 max?	.925 sterling silver piedfort proof, price new		exists?
339	.917 gold proof		£1,400.00

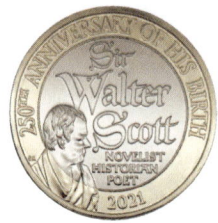

COMMEMORATIVE TYPE 58
Sir Walter Scott
250th ANNIVERSARY OF HIS BIRTH | SIR WALTER SCOTT | NOVELIST | HISTORIAN | POET | 2021
(250th Anniversary)
Design by: Stephen Raw
Edge: THE WILL TO DO THE SOUL TO DARE
Obverse 3b

		As-New	Proof
2021 Total sold: 46,871	(8,931 in RM packs)	£8.00	
1,232 of 2,581	.925 sterling silver proof		£50.00
647 of 771	.925 sterling silver piedfort proof, price new		£117.50
73 of 280	.917 gold proof		no data

COMMEMORATIVE TYPE 57
H.G. Wells
2021 | H.G. WELLS
(To mark 75 years since the death of H.G. Wells)
Design by: Chris Costello
Edge: GOOD BOOKS ARE THE WAREHOUSES OF IDEAS
Obverse 3b

		As-New	Proof
2021 Total sold: 56,214	(9,827 in RM packs)	£7.00	
1,406 of 3,135	.925 sterling silver proof		£50.00
671	.925 sterling silver piedfort proof		£100.00
116 of 330	.917 gold proof		no data

BU, silver proof and gold proof coins were also sold as PNC's, combined with Sci-Fi themed stamps.

COMMEMORATIVE TYPE 58
Dame Vera Lynn
DAME VERA LYNN | 1917 - 2020
(General Dame Vera Lynn commemorative)
Design by: Royal Mint in-house
Edge: WE'LL MEET AGAIN
Obverse 3e, as shown

		As-New	Proof
2022 Total sold: 38,863	(10,566 in RM packs)	£8.00	
1,739 of 3.5k	.925 sterling silver proof		£50.00
483 of 1,175	.925 sterling silver piedfort proof, price new		£125.00
236 of 350	.917 gold proof, price new		£1,225.00

5oz silver and 5oz gold proofs were also sold - mintage 60 and 30 respectively.

COMMEMORATIVE TYPE 59
Alexander Graham Bell
ALEXANDER GRAHAM BELL
(To mark the centenary of his death)
Design by: Henry Gray
Edge: INNOVATION IN SCIENCE • BELL
Obverse 3e

	As-New	Proof
2022 Total sold: 49,463 (15,917 in RM packs)	£8.00	
2,194 of 2.5k .925 sterling silver proof, price new		£75.00
997 .925 sterling silver piedfort proof, price new		£125.00
125 .917 gold proof, price new		£1,225.00

COMMEMORATIVE TYPE 60
FA CUP
CELEBRATING 150 YEARS OF THE FA CUP
(To mark 150 years of the FA Cup)
Design by: Matt Dent & Christian Davies
Edge: FOOTBALL'S GREATEST CUP COMPETITION
Obverse 3e

	As-New	Proof
2022 Total sold: 79,126 (36,380 in RM packs)	£8.00	
3,721 .925 sterling silver proof, price new		£75.00
1,149 .925 sterling silver piedfort proof		£100.00
193 .917 gold proof		£1,500.00

BU, silver proof and gold proof coins were also sold as PNC's, combined with FA Cup related stamps. A monometallic silver coloured error coin has been reported.

COMMEMORATIVE TYPE 61
Anniversary of the modern £2 coin
TWO POUNDS / 1997
(To mark 25 years of the modern £2 coin)
Design by: Bruce Rushin
Edge: STANDING ON THE SHOULDERS OF GIANTS

	As-New	Proof
2022 Total sold: 26,842 (12,844 in RM packs)*	£12.00	
1,804 of 2,525 .925 sterling silver proof, price new		£75.00
918 of 1,425 .925 sterling silver piedfort proof, price new		£125.00
213 of 275 .917 gold proof, price new		£1,225.00

A further 1,698 were sold in the £2 'Effigies Set'.

28.40 mm • 12.0 grammes • bi-metal • various edge

COMMEMORATIVE TYPE 62
J R R Tolkien
1892 J R R TOLKIEN 1973 | WRITER - POET - SCHOLAR
(Fifty years since his death)
Design by: David Lawrence
Edge: NOT ALL THOSE WHO WANDER ARE LOST
Obverse 4b

		As-New	Proof
2023	(not issued for circulation)	£10.00	
4,500 max.	.925 sterling silver proof, price new		£78.50
2,000 max.	.925 sterling silver piedfort proof, price new		£128.50
225 max.	.917 gold proof, price new		£1,250.00

COMMEMORATIVE TYPE 63
Flying Scotsman
FLYING SCOTSMAN | LNER 4472 | 1923 - 2023
(One hundred years of the Flying Scotsman)
Design by: John Bergdahl
Edge: LIVE FOR THE JOURNEY
Obverse 4b

		As-New	Proof
2023	(not issued for circulation)	£9.00	
15k max.	Coloured BU version, price new		£22.00
2,500 max.	.925 sterling silver coloured proof, price new		£78.50
1,250 max.	.925 sterling silver coloured piedfort proof, price new		£128.50
300 max.	.917 gold proof, price new		£1,250.00

The silver proof version and gold proof version were also sold including a 1923 half-crown or a 1923 sovereign respectively. Various PNC version were also issued with themed stamps.

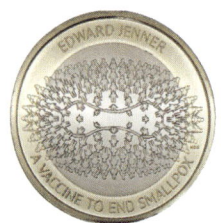

COMMEMORATIVE TYPE 64
Edward Jenner
EDWARD JENNER | A VACCINE TO END SMALLPOX
(Two hundred years since his death)
Design by: Henry Gray
Edge: INNOVATION IN SCIENCE JENNER
Obverse 4b

		As-New	Proof
2023	(not issued for circulation)	£9.00	
2,500 max.	.925 sterling silver proof, price new		£78.50
1,250 max.	.925 sterling silver piedfort proof, price new		£128.50
150 max.	.917 gold proof, price new		£1,250.00

COMMEMORATIVE TYPE 65
Ada Lovelace
ADA LOVELACE | COMPUTER VISIONARY 1815 - 1852 |
discoverer of the hidden realities of nature
(General Ada Lovelace commemorative)
Design by: Osborne Rees
Edge: INNOVATION IN SCIENCE LOVELACE
Obverse 4b

		As-New	Proof
2023	(not issued for circulation)	£10.00	
1,750 max.	.925 sterling silver proof, price new		£78.50
750 max.	.925 sterling silver piedfort proof, price new		£128.50
75 max.	.917 gold proof, price new		£1,250.00

COMMEMORATIVE TYPE 66
National Gallery
200 YEARS OF THE NATIONAL GALLERY
(200 years existence of The National Gallery)
Design by: Edwina Ellis
Edge: MAJORUM GLORIA PSTERIS LVMEN EST
Obverse 4b

		As-New	Proof
2024	(not issued for circulation)	£9.00	£20.00
2,500 max.	.925 sterling silver proof, price new		£82.00
700 max.	.925 sterling silver piedfort proof, price new		£135.00
2,024 max.	Gold proof 1/40 oz (50p), price new (milled edge)		£99.50
150 max.	.917 gold proof, price new		£1,390.00

COMMEMORATIVE TYPE 67
Winston Churchill
150TH ANNIVERSARY OF THE BIRTH OF WINSTON CHURCHILL | 1874 - 1965
(One hundred and fifty years since his birth)
Design by: Natasha Seaward
Edge: PAVE THE WAY FOR PEACE AND FREEDOM
Obverse 4b

		As-New	Proof
2024	(not issued for circulation, from sets)	£9.00	£20.00
? max.	.925 sterling silver proof, price new	not yet available Nov '24	
? max.	.925 sterling silver piedfort proof	not yet available Nov '24	
? max.	.917 gold proof	not yet available Nov '24	

What's currently legal tender?
All £5 coins are technically legal tender but are not widely accepted in shops as people are simply not familiar with them. Ever since the silver £20/£50/£100 coin debacle and the Royal Mint's January 2016 memo to banks asking them not to accept higher value coins, the acceptance and status of cupro-nickel £5 coins was also affected - so these £5 coin only have £5 face value to those who accept them as such.

Look out for non UK £5 coins being offered for face value as these are often from smaller provinces/islands and are therefore not legal tender in the United Kingdom (and usually aren't even legal tender in the province stated on them either). Particularly relevant are the coins from Tristan da Cunha, a tiny island group with a population of less than 300. So-called £5 coins from Tristan da Cunha often look very British but have 'TDC' somewhere in the legend.

Which are hard to find?
All of these large coins are hard to find in circulation because those that circulated tended to get hoarded by the public when they were new and all recent issues were made available in card packages only. They are also heavy and not really practical to carry around for day-to-day transactions.

Recently released mintage figures reveal that many of the newest coins (that were never made available at £5 face value in post offices, like they used to be) were struck in fairly low numbers. This is simply because when they were new and sold in packs, there wasn't much demand for them. The recent obsession with mintage numbers and the publication of the figures instantly created more demand for them, resulting in a few that have risen in value over the last few years. Remember these are coins that were fairly unpopular when new; it is only the publication of mintage numbers and basically a little social media/eBay frenzy that has caused them to go up in value now. In the future they may end up being just as unpopular as they were when they were sold new.

Reorganisation in this book
The Royal Mint have increased the output of different £5 crown coins they produce substantially. It used to be (way back) a special coin for coronations, jubilees and important Royal-relevant events - A coin struck every few years. They diversified to include other occasions related to senior royals, such as weddings, birthdays, anniversaries etc, but in recent years they've gone a bit mad and are churning out £5 coins at an alarming rate! During the entire 100 year period 1900-1999 there were 27 crowns issued. In 2021 alone, there were 15!

The whole thing has been complicated further by the issuance of silver-proof-only coins in a number of different themed series and the production of cu-ni coins based on the designs of what were originally silver/gold bullion issues. I'm not sure if many people really care much either; In comparison to lower denominations I hear general low demand for £5 coins on the grapevine. Modern £5 coin issues seem to lack any kind of structure, have no real direction and while there are some hardcore collectors of them, I feel many people have been put off by the sheer number of them and their complicated offshoots.

In an attempt to put it all in some kind of order I have decided to split the FIVE POUNDS section into two parts....

FIVE POUNDS Pt. 1 contains all pre 2009 coins plus any newer coins that commemorate Royal events or are available in humble base metal form at a cost of less than £16.00 when bought new.

FIVE POUNDS Pt.2 contains the post 2008 silver-proof only coins that don't have a royal theme (or a very loose one!) plus special sets of £5 coins and any derived oddities like the bullion based Queen's beast series of cu-ni £5 coins that I also feel don't belong within the main £5 crowns section.

COMMEMORATIVE TYPE 1
Standard portrait of QE II
Design by: Raphael Maklouf
Double "E" monogram, crowned
Design by: Leslie Durbin
Edge: Milled

			As-New	Proof
1990	2,761,431		£6.00	£10.00
	Specimen in card/folder		£10.00	
	56,102	.925 sterling silver proof		£25.00
	2,500	.917 gold proof		no data

COMMEMORATIVE TYPE 2
Mary Gillick portrait of QEII
Design by: Robert Elderton
St. Edward's crown
Design by: Robert Elderton
Edge: Milled

			As-New	Proof
1993	1,834,655		£7.00	£10.00
	Specimen in folder		£9.00	
	58,877*	.925 sterling silver proof		£25.00
	2,500	.917 gold proof		no data

* Oddly, a higher certificate with number 58,879 has been seen.

COMMEMORATIVE TYPE 3

Standard portrait of QE II
Design by: Raphael Maklouf
Windsor Castle and Pennants
Design by: Avril Vaughan
Edge:
VIVAT REGINA ELIZABETHA

			As-New	Proof
1996	2,396,100		£7.00	£10.00
		Specimen in folder	£9.00	
	75,000	.925 sterling silver proof		£25.00
	2,750	.917 gold proof		£2,600.00

COMMEMORATIVE TYPE 4

Conjoined busts of Elizabeth II
and Prince Philip
Design by: Philip Nathan
Arms of the Royal Couple,
crown, anchor. Design by: Leslie
Durbin. Edge: Milled

			As-New	Proof
1997	1,733,000		£7.00	£10.00
		Specimen in folder	£9.00	
	33,689	.925 sterling silver proof		£25.00
	2,750	.917 gold proof		£2,600.00

COMMEMORATIVE TYPE 5

Standard portrait of QE II
Design by: Ian Rank-Broadley
Prince Charles, "The Prince's Trust
Design by: Michael Noakes
Edge: Milled

			Used	As-New	Proof
1998	1,407,300		£6.00	£7.00	£10.00
	43,465	Specimen in folder		£9.00	
	35,000	.925 sterling silver proof			£25.00
	2,000	.917 gold proof			£2,600.00

COMMEMORATIVE TYPE 6
Standard portrait of QEII
Design by: Ian Rank-Broadley
Portrait of Princess Diana
Design by: David Cornell
Edge: Milled

			As-New	Proof
1999	4,900,000		£7.00	£9.00
	358,991	Specimen in folder	£12.00	
	49,545	.925 sterling silver proof		£35.00
	2,750	.917 gold proof		£2,900.00

COMMEMORATIVE TYPE 7
Standard portrait of QE II
(Dated either 1999 or 2000)
Design by: Ian Rank-Broadley
Clock at midnight, with map
of the British Isles
Design by: Jeffrey Matthews
Edge:
WHAT'S PAST IS PROLOGUE

			Used	As-New	Proof
Dated 1999 on Obverse	3,700,000		£9.00	£10.00	£12.00
		Specimen in folder		£14.00	
	49,057	.925 sterling silver cased proof			£25.00
	2,500	.917 gold cased proof			£2,500.00
Dated 2000 on Obverse (not shown)	3,197,739		£9.00	£10.00	£16.00
	27,546	Specimen in folder		£16.00	
	14,255	.925 sterling silver proof*			£40.00
	1,487	.917 gold proof			£2,600.00

*Features gold highlights British Isles and clock hands.

COMMEMORATIVE TYPE 7a (SEE NEXT PAGE)

As above, with special dome mint-mark, available only at the Millennium Dome.

2000	Specimen in folder	£25.00

TYPE 7a: Picture showing the location of the dome mint-mark, to the upper right of 'ANNO DOMINI'.

COMMEMORATIVE TYPE 8
Standard portrait of QE II
Design by: Ian Rank-Broadley
Portrait of the Queen Mother
Design by: Ian Rank-Broadley
Edge: Milled

			Used	As-New	Proof
2000	3,217,000		£6.00	£7.00	£10.00
	31,316	Specimen in folder		£10.00	
	100,000	.925 sterling silver proof			£30.00
	14,850	.925 sterling silver Piedfort proof			£35.00
	2,750	.917 gold proof			£2,600.00

COMMEMORATIVE TYPE 9
Standard portrait of QEII
Design by: Ian Rank-Broadley
Wyon portrait of Victoria
Design by: Mary Milner Dickens
Edge: Milled

			Used	As-New	Proof
2001	851,491		£6.00	£8.00	£10.00
	44,090	Specimen in folder		£11.00	
	19,812	.925 sterling silver proof			£30.00
	733	.925 sterling silver proof, reverse frosted			no data
	2,831	.917 gold proof			£2,600.00
	596	.917 gold proof, reverse frosted			no data

COMMEMORATIVE TYPE 10
Queen Elizabeth II on horseback
Design by: Ian Rank-Broadley
Queen wearing robes and diadem
Design by: Ian Rank-Broadley
Edge: Milled

			Used	As-New	Proof
2002	3,469,243		£6.00	£7.00	£10.00
	340,230	Specimen in folder		£10.00	
	54,012	.925 sterling silver proof			£30.00
	3,461	.917 gold proof			£2,700.00

COMMEMORATIVE TYPE 11
Standard portrait of QEII
Design by: Ian Rank-Broadley
Portrait of Queen Mother
Design by: Avril Vaughan.
Edge: STRENGTH DIGNITY LAUGHTER

			Used	As-New	Proof
2002	Inc. above, with Type 10		£6.00	£7.00	£10.00
		Specimen in folder		£10.00	
	35,000	.925 sterling silver proof			£30.00
	2,750	.917 gold proof			£2,600.00

COMMEMORATIVE TYPE 12
Sketched portrait of QE II
Design by: Tom Philips
"GOD SAVE THE QUEEN"
Design by: Tom Philips
Edge: Milled

			Used	As-New	Proof
2003	1,307,147		£6.00	£7.00	£10.00
	100,481	Specimen in folder		£10.00	
	75,000	.925 sterling silver proof			£30.00
	3,500	.917 gold proof			£2,600.00

38.61 mm • 28.28 grammes • cupro-nickel • various edge

COMMEMORATIVE TYPE 13
Standard portrait of QEII
Design by: Ian Rank-Broadley
Conjoined Britannia and Marianne
Design by: David Gentlemen
Edge: Milled

2004			Used	As-New	Proof
2004	1,205,594	(+ 16,507 in folders)	£6.00	£7.00	£10.00*
	11, 295 of 15k	.925 sterling silver proof			£30.00
	2,500	.925 sterling silver piedfort proof			£60.00
	926 of 1,500	.917 gold proof			£2,600.00
	501	.9995 platinum cased proof (3.0271 troy oz)			no data

* Was also sold as a cased base metal proof with certificate, value £20 - £25.

COMMEMORATIVE TYPE 14
Standard portrait of QE II
Design by: Ian Rank-Broadley
Portrait of Horatio Nelson
Design by: James Butler
Edge (precious metal only): ENG-LAND EXPECTS EVERYMAN WILL DO HIS DUTY

2005			Used	As-New	Proof
2005	1,075,516 inc. Type 15 (milled edge)		£6.00	£13.00	£14.00
	79,868	Specimen in folder (milled edge)		£20.00	
	12,852	.925 sterling silver proof*			£30.00
	1,760	.917 gold proof			£2,600.00
	200 max	Platinum piedfort proof			no data

COMMEMORATIVE TYPE 15
Standard portrait of QEII
Design by: Ian Rank-Broadley
HMS Victory & Temeraire
Design by: Clive Duncan
Edge (precious metal only): ENGLAND EXPECTS EVERYMAN WILL DO HIS DUTY

2005			Used	As-New	Proof
2005	Inc. above, with Type 14 (milled edge)		£6.00	£12.00	£14.00
	79,868	Specimen in folder (milled edge)		£20.00	
		Specimen set (contains both 2005 folders, in sleeve)		£25.00	
	21,448	.925 sterling silver proof*			£30.00
	1,805	.917 gold proof			£2,600.00

COMMEMORATIVE TYPE 16

Standard portrait of QEII
Design by: Ian Rank-Broadley
**Ceremonial Trumpets
with Banners**
Design by:
Danuta Solowiej-Wedderburn
Edge (precious metal only):
DUTY SERVICE FAITH

			Used	As-New	Proof
2006	52,267	(milled edge)	£6.00	£8.00	£10.00
	330,790	Specimen in folder (milled edge)		£12.00	
	20,790 of 50k	.925 sterling silver proof			£30.00
	5,000	.925 sterling silver piedfort proof			£60.00
	2,750	.917 gold proof			£2,600.00

COMMEMORATIVE TYPE 17

Standard portrait of QEII
Design by: Ian Rank-Broadley
**The North Rose Window at
Westminster Abbey**
Design by: Emma Noble
Edge (precious metal only):
MY STRENGTH AND STAY

			Used	As-New	Proof
2007	30,561	(milled edge)	£6.00	£7.00	£10.00
	260,856	Specimen in folder (milled edge)		£12.00	
	15,186 of 35k	.925 sterling silver proof			£40.00
	2,000 of 5,000	.925 sterling silver piedfort proof			£60.00
	2,380 of 2,500	.917 gold proof			£2,600.00
	250	Platinum piedfort proof			£4,000.00

*On the previous page: pairs of both 2005 coins were sold in silver piedfort guise. 2,818 were sold.

COMMEMORATIVE TYPE 18
Standard portrait of QEII
Design by: Ian Rank-Broadley
Portrait of Elizabeth I
Westminster Abbey
Design by: Rod Kelly
Edge (precious metals only): I
HAVE REIGNED WITH YOUR
LOVES

			Used	As-New	Proof
2008	20,047 'circulation' + 30,649 '£5 for £5'?*		£7.00	£12.00	£18.00
	26,700	Specimen in folder*		£20.00	
	9,216 of 20k	.925 sterling silver proof			£40.00
	1,602 of 2k	.925 sterling silver piedfort proof			£60.00
	1,500	.917 gold proof			£2,600.00
	125 of 150	Platinum piedfort proof			£4,000.00

*Plain milled edge.

COMMEMORATIVE TYPE 19
Standard portrait of QEII
Design by: Ian Rank-Broadley
Portrait of the Price of Wales
Design by: Ian Rank-Broadley
Edge (precious metals only):
SIXTIETH BIRTHDAY

			Used	As-New	Proof
2008	14,088	(milled edge)	£7.00	£10.00	£16.00
	54,746	Specimen in folder (milled edge)		£17.00	
	6,264	.925 sterling silver proof			£35.00
	1,088 of 5k	.925 sterling silver piedfort proof			£60.00
	867 of 1,500	.917 gold proof			£2,600.00
	54 of 150	Platinum piedfort proof			£4,000.00

COMMEMORATIVE TYPE 20
Standard portrait of QEII
Design by: Ian Rank-Broadley
Henry VIII
Design by: John Bergdahl
Edge (precious metals only):
ROSA SINE SPINA

		Used	As-New	Proof
2009	(all originally sold in folders/proof sets)*	£7.00	£10.00	£20.00
67,119	Specimen in folder*		£18.00	
10,419 of 20k	.925 sterling silver proof			£35.00
3,580 of 4,009	.925 sterling silver piedfort proof			£60.00
1,130 of 1,509	.917 gold proof			£2,800.00
100	Platinum piedfort proof			£4,000.00

*Plain milled edge.

COMMEMORATIVE TYPE 21
Standard portrait of QEII
Design by: Ian Rank-Broadley
Countdown '3'
Design by: Claire Aldridge
Edge: Milled

		Used	As-New	Proof
2009	(all originally sold in folders/proof sets)	£7.00	£8.00	
184,921	Specimen in folder		£15.00	
26,645 of 30k	.925 sterling silver proof			£40.00
4,874 of 6k	.925 sterling silver piedfort proof			£60.00
1,860 of 4k	.917 gold proof			£2,600.00

COMMEMORATIVE TYPE 22
Standard portrait of QEII
Design by: Ian Rank-Broadley
1660 Restoration of Monarchy
Design by: David Cornell
Obverse: Type as no. 20
Edge (precious metals only):
A QUIET AND PEACEFUL
POSSESSION

		Used	As-New	Proof
2010	(all originally sold in folders/proof sets)*	£8.00	£10.00	£14.00
30,247	Specimen in folder*		£14.00	
6,518 of 20k	.925 sterling silver proof			£30.00
4,435 of 5k	.925 sterling silver piedfort proof			£60.00
1,182 of 1,200	.917 gold proof			£2,600.00
100 max	Platinum piedfort proof			no data

*Plain milled edge.

COMMEMORATIVE TYPE 23
Standard portrait of QEII
Design by: Ian Rank-Broadley
Countdown '2'
Design by: Claire Aldridge
Edge: Milled

		Used	As-New	Proof
2010	(all originally sold in folders)	£7.00	£8.00	
153,080	Specimen in folder		£14.00	
20,159 of 30k	.925 sterling silver proof			£50.00
4,435	.925 sterling silver piedfort proof			£60.00
1,562 of 3k	.917 gold proof			£2,600.00

Higher face value coins were also issued. In silver: a £10 with a diameter of 65mm and weight of 5oz (155.5g) featuring the winged horse pegasus. A £500 with a diameter of 100mm and weight of one kilogram, featuring the stylised words 'XXX OLYMPIAD'.

Gold olympic themed coins consisted of 6x £25 coins (2 each for 'faster', 'higher' and 'stronger'), 3x £100 coins (one each for 'faster', 'higher' and 'stronger') and a crude looking one kilogram gold coin with a face value of £1000.

COMMEMORATIVE TYPE 24
Standard portrait of QEII
Design by: Ian Rank-Broadley
Royal Wedding of William &
Catherine
Design by: Mark Richards
Edge: Milled

			Used	As-New	Proof
2011	(all originally sold in folders)		£9.00	£10.00	
	250,000	Specimen in folder		£20.00	
	26,069 of 50k	.925 sterling silver proof/or 7,451 max gold plated coin*			£55.00
	2,991 of 3k	.925 sterling silver piedfort proof			£80.00
	2,066 of 3k	.917 gold proof			£2,600.00
	133 of 200	Platinum piedfort proof			£4,000.00

*The previous gold plated maximum mintage of 3,000 seems to have been raised.

COMMEMORATIVE TYPE 25
Standard portrait of QEII
Design by: Ian Rank-Broadley
Countdown '1'
Design by: Claire Aldridge
Edge: Milled

			Used	As-New	Proof
2011	(all originally sold in folders)		£8.00	£9.00	
	163,235	Specimen in folder		£15.00	
	25,877 of 30k	.925 sterling silver proof			£35.00
	4,000	.925 sterling silver piedfort proof			£55.00
	1,300 of 3k	.917 gold proof			£2,600.00

137

COMMEMORATIVE TYPE 26
Standard portrait of QEII
Design by: Ian Rank-Broadley
Prince Philip 90th Birthday
Design by: Mark Richards
Edge: Plain

		Used	As-New	Proof
2011	(all originally sold in folders/proof sets)	£18.00	£20.00	£25.00
18,730	Specimen in folder		£25.00	
4,599 of 20k	.925 sterling silver proof			£60.00
2,659 of 4k	.925 sterling silver piedfort proof			£80.00
636 of 1,200	.917 gold proof			no data
49 of 90	Platinum piedfort proof			£4,000.00

COMMEMORATIVE TYPE 27
Standard portrait of QEII
Design by: Ian Rank-Broadley
Countdown '0'
Design by: Claire Aldridge
Edge: Milled

		Used	As-New	Proof
2012	(all originally sold in folders)	£20.00	£30.00	
52,261*	Specimen in folder/card		£35.00	
12,670 of 30k	.925 sterling silver proof			£50.00
2,324 of 4k	.925 sterling silver piedfort proof			£70.00
1,007 of 3k	.917 gold proof			no data

* Plus 13,014 in packaging combining stamps with the coin.

COMMEMORATIVE TYPE 28
Standard portrait of QEII
Design by: Ian Rank-Broadley
London 2012 Olympics Commemorative
Design by: Siaman Miah
Obverse: Type as no. 24
Edge: Milled

			Used	As-New	Proof
2012	(all originally sold in folders)		£8.00	£10.00	
	315,983*	Specimen in folder		£14.00	
	20,810 of 100k	.925 sterling silver proof			£30.00
	5,946 of 7k	.925 sterling silver piedfort proof			£50.00
	8,180 of 12.5k	.925 sterling silver, gold plating*			£60.00
	1,045 of 5k	.917 gold proof			no data

* Plus 13,959 in packaging combining stamps with the coin.

20x 2012 £1000 face value gold Olympic games coins were sold. Other proof gold coins included six classical Olympics themed £25 coins and three £100 coins. Full sets are still available new for £10,500. 5,056 5oz silver coins were sold and 910x £500FV 1kg coins were sold.

COMMEMORATIVE TYPE 29
Standard portrait of QEII
Design by: Ian Rank-Broadley
London 2012 Paralympics Commemorative
Design by: Pippa Sanderson
Obverse: Type as no. 24
Edge: Milled

			Used	As-New	Proof
2012	(all originally sold in folders)		£8.00	£12.00	
	50,143*	Specimen in folder		£20.00	
	10,000/3,000*	.925 sterling silver proof / or gold plated version			£40.00
	2,012 max	.925 sterling silver piedfort proof			£65.00
	5,000 max	.917 gold proof			no data

* Plus 13,014 in packaging combining stamps with the coin.

38.61 mm • 28.28 grammes • cupro-nickel • various edge

COMMEMORATIVE TYPE 30
Special portrait of QEII
Design by: Ian Rank-Broadley
Queen's Diamond Jubilee
Design by: Ian Rank-Broadley
Edge (precious metals only):
A VOW MADE GOOD

		As-New	Proof
2012	(milled edge)	£6.00	
	(961 base metal proofs sold separately - milled edge)		£12.00
484,775*	Specimen in folder (milled edge)	£12.00	
16,820 of 75k	.925 sterling silver proof		£40.00
3,187 of 3,250	.925 sterling silver piedfort proof		£50.00
12,112 of 12.5k	.925 sterling silver, gold plated*		£80.00
1,085 of 3,850	.917 gold proof		£2,600.00
20 of 250	Platinum piedfort proof		no data

To mark the Jubilee there was also a £10 coin (as silver or gold proof) with a diameter of 65mm - these have the same obverse as above and feature the queen enthroned and facing on the reverse. Prices new were about £450 for the silver version (1933 sold) and £9,500 for the gold coin (they sold 140). One kilogram silver (£500FV, 206 sold) and one kilogram gold (£1000FV, 21 sold) coins were also made to mark the Queens jubilee. Both use the same obverse as above and show the full Royal Arms on the reverse.

* Plus 18,948 in packages combining stamps with the coin.

COMMEMORATIVE TYPE 31
Standard portrait of QEII
Design by: Ian Rank-Broadley
Anniversary of Coronation
Design by: Emma Noble
Obverse: Type as no. 24
Edge: Milled

		Used	As-New	Proof
2013	(all originally sold in folders/proof sets)	£7.00	£10.00	£20.00
57,262*	Specimen in folder		£20.00	
6,667 of 15k	.925 sterling silver proof			£40.00
3,185 of 3,250	.925 sterling silver piedfort proof			£50.00
2,547 of 12.5k	.925 sterling silver, gold plated			£50.00
458 of 2,000	.917 gold proof, price new			£2,600.00
106 of 100 max!	Platinum piedfort proof, price new			no data

*Plus 11,642 in packages combining stamps with the coin.
301 x £500 1kg silver proofs were sold. 1604 x 5oz silver proofs were also sold.

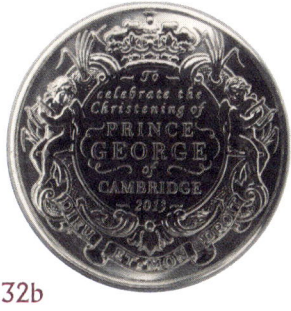

32a   32b

COMMEMORATIVE TYPES 32a & 32b
Standard portrait of QEII
Design by: Ian Rank-Broadley
32a: Birth of Prince George
32b: Christening of George
Design by: Benedetto Pistrucci
(Birth). John Bergdahl (Christen')
Obverses: Both as Type no. 23
Edge: Milled (both types)

			Used	As-New	Proof
2013	7,460*	(32a) .925 sterling silver proof only			£60.00
		(32b)	£10.00	£11.00	
	56,014	(32b) Specimen in folder		£17.00	
	7,264 of 75k	(32b) .925 sterling silver proof			£60.00
	2,251 of 2.5k	(32b) .925 sterling silver piedfort proof			£70.00
	486 of 1,000	(32b) .917 gold proof			£2,600.00
	38 of 100	(32b) Platinum piedfort proof			no data

*Shortly after the birth of Prince George, a silver proof only £5 Crown was released with the Pistrucci St. George Reverse. This was the first coin that the Royal Mint refused to sell to other businesses, offering it exclusively to their customers for £80. Apparently 25 platinum proof versions of the birth coin were also made.

Note that for both the 2013 coronation (no. 31) and Prince George (no.32b) one kilo versions with a face value of £500 were struck in silver. These were both available new for £2,600. Gold kilo versions of no. 32b were also sold.

COMMEMORATIVE TYPE 33
Standard portrait of QEII
Design by: Ian Rank-Broadley
300th Anniversary of the Death of Queen Anne
Design by: Mark Richards
Obverse: Type as no. 24
Edge: Milled

			Used	As-New	Proof
2014		(all originally sold in folders/proof sets)	£40.00	£50.00	£55.00
	12,181	Specimen in folder		£75.00	
	2,212 of 3,100	.925 sterling silver proof			£80.00
	627 of 1,665	.925 sterling silver, gold plated			£80.00
(was 2014 max)	4,028 max*	.925 sterling silver piedfort proof			£100.00
	253 of 375	.917 gold proof, price new			no data
	250 max?	Platinum piedfort proof			no data

* 636 were sold.

COMMEMORATIVE TYPE 34
Standard portrait of QEII
Design by: Ian Rank-Broadley
Re-used 1953/1960 reverse to
mark the 1st birthday
of Prince George
Design by:
Edgar Fuller & Cecil Thomas
Edge: Milled

Proof

2014

7,451 of 7,500	.925 sterling silver proof only	£55.00

COMMEMORATIVE TYPE 35
Standard portrait of QEII
Design by: Ian Rank-Broadley
Winston Churchill - 50th Anniversary of his death
Design by: Mark Richards
Obverse: Type as no. 24
Edge (precious metals only): NEVER FLINCH, NEVER
WEARY, NEVER DESPAIR

		Used	As-New	Proof
2015	(milled edge)	£10.00	£14.00	£15.00
18,163*	Specimen in folder (milled edge)		£20.00	
3,863 of 7.5k	.925 sterling silver proof			£40.00
1,150 of 2k	.925 sterling silver piedfort proof			£60.00
275 of 620	.917 gold proof			no data
65	Platinum piedfort proof			no data

* Plus a further 4,987 sold in packs including the 1965 Churchill Crown (sourced 2nd hand) and 9,896 in packs including commemorative Royal Mail stamps. Various other larger silver/gold Churchill themed coins were also sold.

COMMEMORATIVE TYPE 36a and 36b
Standard portrait of QEII
Design by: Ian Rank-Broadley (36a) or Jody Clark (36b)
Battle of Waterloo - 200th Anniversary
Design by: David Lawrence
Obverse: Type as no. 24 (for 36a) or as no. 41 (for 36b)
Edge (precious metals only): THE NEAREST RUN THING YOU EVER SAW

			Used	As-New	Proof
2015	24,554*	(36a) Loose coin, ex pack	£8.00	£14.00	£16.00
		(36a) Specimen in folder		£20.00	
	2,523 of 9.5k	(36b) .925 sterling silver proof			£50.00
	1,500 max	(36a) .925 sterling silver proof, from a set			£100.00?
	896 of 1,500	(36b) .925 sterling silver piedfort proof			£75.00
	273 of 350	(36b) .917 gold proof			no data

The individually boxed silver proof coins of this type (36b) feature the 5th portrait. Some were also made as silver proof with the 4th portrait, available only in sets of 5x 2015 silver proof coins. A £2 coin with a diameter of 38.61mm, featuring the reverse design of the Waterloo coin was also sold as part of a set of three Waterloo commemorative coins marketed by the Dutch Mint.

* Plus another 8,576 sold in packs including commemorative Royal Mail stamps.

COMMEMORATIVE TYPE 37
Standard portrait of QEII
Design by: Jody Clark
Birth of Princess Charlotte
Design by: John Bergdahl
Edge: Milled

			Used	As-New	Proof
2015			£9.00	£10.00	£20.00
	30,926	Specimen in folder		£25.00	
	4,342 of 4.5k*	.925 sterling silver proof			£40.00
	250*	.917 gold proof			no data

* +500 'First Strike' coins in silver and 100 in gold.

See also COMMEMORATIVE TYPE 39 for the Princess Charlotte Christening coin.

143

38.61 mm • 28.28 grammes • cupro-nickel • various edge

COMMEMORATIVE TYPE 38
Alternative portrait of QEII
Design by: James Butler
Longest Reigning Monarch
Design by: James Butler
Edge (on precious metal proofs):
LONG TO REIGN OVER US

		Used	As-New	Proof
2015	48,848 (all originally sold in folders)	£8.00	£11.00	
	Specimen in folder		£15.00	
10,249 of 9k??	.925 sterling silver proof			£40.00
3,171 of 3.7k	.925 sterling silver piedfort proof			£80.00
899 of 1,650	.917 gold proof			£2,600.00
88 of 63??	Platinum proof, price new			no data

See also the Longest Reigning Monarch £20 coin, the design of which was also used on larger size silver and gold proof coins, which were very expensive new and are rarely offered for sale.

COMMEMORATIVE TYPE 39
Standard Fifth portrait of QEII
Design by: Jody Clark
Christening of Princess Charlotte
Design by: John Bergdahl
Edge: Milled

		Proof
2015		
4,342*	.925 sterling silver proof only	£60.00
250*	.917 gold proof	no data

* +500 'First Strike' coins in silver and 100 in gold.

COMMEMORATIVE TYPE 40
Standard Fifth portrait of QEII
Design by: Jody Clark
Second Birthday of Prince George
Design by: Christopher Le Brun
Obverse: Same as TYPE 39
Edge: Milled

		Proof
2015		
4,009 of 7.5k	.925 sterling silver proof only	£100.00

COMMEMORATIVE TYPE 41
Standard Fifth portrait of QEII
Design by: Jody Clark
Queen's 90th Birthday
Design by: Christopher Hobbs
Edge (on precious metal proofs):
FULL OF HONOUR AND YEARS

		Used	As-New	Proof
2016	74,195 (only sold in RM packs/sets)	£7.00	£8.00	£10.00
	8,947 of 13k	.925 sterling silver proof		£35.00
	3,099 of 7k	.925 sterling silver piedfort proof		£50.00
	906 of 1,200	.917 gold proof		£2,600.00
	77 of 90	Platinum piedfort proof		no data

This coin design was also used for 5oz silver, gold and 1kg silver coins. They are rarely offered. A further 10,181 BU coins were sold in tubes to other retailers.

COMMEMORATIVE TYPE 42
Standard Fifth portrait of QEII
Design by: Jody Clark
King Canute
Design by: Lee R. Jones
Edge (on precious metal proofs):
TIME AND TIDE WAIT FOR NO
MAN

		Used	As-New	Proof
2017	26,950 (only sold in RM packs/proof sets)	£6.00	£7.00	£15.00
	2,953 of 3k	.925 sterling silver proof, price new		£82.50
	1,071 of 1,500	.925 sterling silver piedfort proof, price new		£155.00
	150	.917 gold proof		no data

COMMEMORATIVE TYPE 43
Standard Fifth portrait of QEII
Design by: Jody Clark
House of Windsor
Design by: Timothy Noad
Edge (on precious metal proofs):
THE CHRISTENING OF A
DYNASTY

		Used	As-New	Proof
2017	30,344 (only sold in RM packs/proof sets)	£6.00	£7.00	£15.00
	3,701 of 10k	.925 sterling silver proof, price new		£82.50
	1,480 of 4k	.925 sterling silver piedfort proof, price new		£155.00
	440 of 750	.917 gold proof		£2,700.00

145

COMMEMORATIVE TYPE 44
Standard Fifth portrait of QEII
Design by: Jody Clark
Sapphire Jubilee
Design by: Glyn Davis
Edge (on precious metal proofs):
SHINE THROUGH THE AGES

		Used	As-New	Proof
2017	75,440 (only sold in RM packs / proof sets)	£7.00	£10.00	£16.00
	7,794	.925 sterling silver proof		£30.00
	2,579	.925 sterling silver piedfort proof		£50.00
	650	.917 gold proof		£2,600.00

Other 'Sapphire Jubilee' coins were also made available.

COMMEMORATIVE TYPE 45
Standard Fifth portrait of QEII
Design by: Etienne Millner
Royal Wedding Anniversary
Design by: John Bergdahl
Edge (on precious metal proofs):
FELICES JUNXIT CONUBIALIS
AMOR

		Used	As-New	Proof
2017	43,608 (only sold in RM packs / proof sets)	£7.00	£9.00	£16.00
	6,955 of 15k	.925 sterling silver proof		£35.00
	2,319 of 4k	.925 sterling silver piedfort proof		£70.00
	724 of 1,250	.917 gold proof		£2,600.00

5oz silver and 5oz gold proof coins as well as 1kg silver and 1kg gold proof coins were also made for the Royal Wedding anniversary, both featuring different designs.

 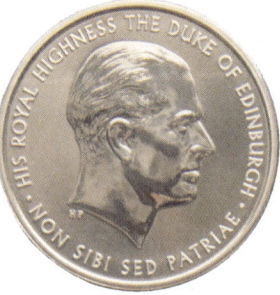

COMMEMORATIVE TYPE 46
Standard Fifth portrait of QEII
Design by: Jody Clark
Service of Prince Philip
Design by: T 'Humphrey' Paget
Edge: Milled for base metal -
Plain on precious metal proofs.

		Used	As-New	Proof
2017	29,384 (only sold in RM packs / proof sets)	£8.00	£9.00	£15.00
	2,547 of 3k	.925 sterling silver proof		£40.00
	1,199	.925 sterling silver piedfort proof		£80.00
	299	.917 gold proof		no data

COMMEMORATIVE TYPE 47
Standard Fifth portrait of QEII
Design by: Jody Clark
Remembrance Day 2017
Design by: Stephen Taylor
Edge: Milled

		Used	As-New	Proof
2017	(10,771 originally sold in RM packs)	£13.00	£20.00	
3,483 of 5k	.925 sterling silver proof, price new			£50.00
1,319 of 1,500	.925 sterling silver piedfort proof, price new			£155.00

COMMEMORATIVE TYPE 48
Standard Fifth portrait of QEII
Design by: Jody Clark
Christmas 2017
Design by: Edwina Ellis
Edge: Milled

		As-New
2017	39,413 (only sold within a blank Christmas card)	£9.00

COMMEMORATIVE TYPE 49
Standard Fifth portrait of QEII
Design by: Jody Clark
Prince George's fifth birthday
Design by: Jody Clark
Edge: Milled on all versions

		Used	As-New	Proof
2018	(all originally sold in folders/proof sets)	£7.00	£9.00	£16.00
1,569 of 7,000	.925 sterling silver proof			£70.00
338 of 1,000	.925 sterling silver piedfort proof (only sold in silver sets)			?
175 max??	.917 gold proof – doesn't appear to exist			no data

147

COMMEMORATIVE TYPE 50
Standard Fifth portrait of QEII
Design by: Jody Clark
4 Generations of Royal Family
Design by: Timothy Noad
Edge: Milled for base metal
(Precious metal edges are plain)

		Used	As-New	Proof
2018	Total sold: 22,393 (13,911 in RM packs)	£10.00	£12.00	£20.00
3,275 of 5k	.925 sterling silver proof			£55.00
1,189 of 2k	.925 sterling silver piedfort proof, price new			£155.00
340 of 500	.917 gold proof			£2,700.00
399 of 1,000	Silver 5oz £10 coin (larger), price new			£415.00
736 of 1,100	Gold proof 1/4oz £25 coin (smaller), price new			£475.00
67 of 100	Gold proof 5oz £10 coin (larger), price new			£8,450.00

Just in case the base metal version plus the usual silver and gold proofs of this rather uninspired design (no disrespect to the designer) simply wasn't enough for you, fortunately there are another three different versions to satisfy your collecting needs.

I do wonder if they've got something wrong in the blurb on their website - the 1/4oz gold proof has a face value of £25 and the 5oz gold proof has a face value of £10? Surely if 0.25oz is £25 then 5oz should be £500? Perhaps they used an incorrect obverse picture showing the wrong face value.

COMMEMORATIVE TYPE 51
Standard Fifth portrait of QEII
Design by: Jody Clark
65th Anniversary of Coronation
Design by: Stephen Taylor
Edge (on precious metal proofs):
SHINE THROUGH THE AGES

		Used	As-New	Proof
2018	Total sold: 18,296 (11,947 in RM packs)	£7.00	£9.00	
3,910 of 6.5k	.925 sterling silver proof, price new			£82.50
1,610 of 1,953	.925 sterling silver piedfort proof			£160.00
460 of 550	.917 gold proof			£2,700.00

Further coins were also made to mark 65 years since the coronation. They include a £10 gold proof, £10 silver proof, £500 silver kilo and £25 1/4oz gold coin.

COMMEMORATIVE TYPE 52
Standard Fifth portrait of QEII
Design by: Jody Clark
Wedding of Harry & Meghan
Design by: Jody Clark
Edge: Milled for base metal
(Precious metal edges are plain)

	Used	As-New	Proof
2018 Total sold: 60,699 (39,132 in RM packs)	£6.00	£7.00	
4,852 of 15k .925 sterling silver proof			£40.00
1,153 of 2,018 .925 sterling silver piedfort proof			£70.00
255 .917 gold proof			no data

Also available as a "Strike Your Own" - prices silly-high for that packaging!

COMMEMORATIVE TYPE 53
Standard Fifth portrait of QEII
Design by: Jody Clark
Remembrance Poppy 2018
Design by: Laura Clancy
Edge: Milled on all versions

	Used	As-New	Proof
2018 Total sold: 15,941 (10,443 in RM packs)	£10.00	£13.00	
2,992 of 3.5k .925 sterling silver proof			£45.00
846 of 1,500 .925 sterling silver piedfort proof			£145.00

COMMEMORATIVE TYPE 54
Standard Fifth portrait of QEII
Design by: Jody Clark
Prince Charles 70th Birthday
Design by: Robert Elderton
Edge: Milled for base metal
(Precious metal edges are plain)

	Used	As-New	Proof
2018 Total sold: 26,246 (9,984 in RM packs)	£8.00	£10.00	
2,207 of 4.5k .925 sterling silver proof			£60.00
770 of 1,000 .925 sterling silver piedfort proof			£75.00
203 of 300 .917 gold proof			no data
28 of 70 .9995 platinum piedfort proof, price new			£4,000.00

Also available in a smaller, platinum 1/4oz £25 guise.

149

38.61 mm • 28.28 grammes • cupro-nickel • various edge

COMMEMORATIVE TYPE 55
Standard Fifth portrait of QEII
Design by: Jody Clark
Christmas 2018 coin
Design by: Harry Brockway
Edge: Milled

		Used	As-New
2018	Total sold: 39,337 (26,857 in Xmas card RM packs)	£8.00	£10.00

COMMEMORATIVE TYPE 56
Standard Fifth portrait of QEII
Design by: Jody Clark
200th Anniversary of the birth of Queen Victoria
Design by: John Bergdahl
Edge (on precious metal proofs): WORKSHOP OF THE WORLD

			As-New	Proof
2019	36,328	(all originally sold in folders/proof sets)	£8.00	£16.00
	3,854*	.925 sterling silver proof		£80.00
	1,236*	.925 sterling silver piedfort proof, price new		£155.00
	583*	.917 gold proof		£2,700.00

*Other weights in silver and gold were available. Sales figures include trade and other presentations.

COMMEMORATIVE TYPE 57
Standard Fifth portrait of QEII
Design by: Jody Clark
Remembrance Poppy 2019
Design by: Harry Brockway
Edge: Milled on all versions

			As-New	Proof
2019	27,920	(all originally sold in folders)	£15.00	
	2,097	.925 sterling silver proof		£70.00
	775	.925 sterling silver piedfort proof, price new		£155.00
	130 total	.917 gold proof		no data

The 2019 coin that never came
A 2019 Christmas themed coin was planned, but never materialised.

COMMEMORATIVE TYPE 58
Standard Fifth portrait of QEII
Design by: Jody Clark
200th Anniversary since end of George III's reign
Design by: Dominique Evans
Edge: (on precious metal proofs)
I GLORY IN THE NAME OF BRITON

			As-New	Proof
2020	Total made: 75,762*	(6,925 in RM packs)	£6.00	£12.00
	1,861 of 2,500	.925 sterling silver proof		£50.00
	542	.925 sterling silver piedfort proof		£130.00
	249	.917 gold proof		no data

* Including those contained within annual sets. 45x gold 1oz coins were also sold.

COMMEMORATIVE TYPE 59
Standard Fifth portrait of QEII
Design by: Jody Clark
Remembrance 2020
The Unknown Warrior
Design by: Natasha Preece
Edge: Milled on all versions

			As-New	Proof
2020	Total sold: 17,398	(10,898 in RM packs - with colour)	£12.00	
	1,911	.925 sterling silver proof (with colour)		£55.00
	592 of 700	.925 sterling silver piedfort proof (with colour), new		£182.50

COMMEMORATIVE TYPE 60
Standard Fifth portrait of QEII
Design by: Jody Clark
Queen's 95th Birthday
E II R
Design by: Timothy Noad
Edge: Milled on all versions

			As-New	Proof
2021	Total sold: 67,767	(23,984 in RM packs)	£13.00	£15.00
9,525	BU version in 'premium pack' with 'wave-milled' edge		£18.00	
7,567	.925 sterling silver proof			£60.00
1,923	.925 sterling silver piedfort proof			£80.00
99	Silver 2oz (£5) proof, price new			£180.00
949	Silver 5oz (£10) proof, price new*			£455.00
149	Silver 1kg (£500) proof, price new*			£2,270.00
947	Gold 1/4oz (£25) proof, price new			£595.00
654	.917 gold proof, price new			£2,590.00
200	Gold 2oz (£200) proof, price new			£4,370.00
149	Gold 5oz (£10!?), price new*			£10,525.00

* Features a different design, by Gary Breeze. 15x gold 1kg and 1x gold 9.5kg were also sold.
There is inconsistency again with the marked face values - The 2oz gold coin has been deemed a £200 coin and yet the 5oz gold version has a face value of only £10. Also sold were PNC's containing coins, prints by the coin designers, sets involving old coins (that would normally cost pennies without the fancy packaging) and also items involving gold sovereigns. The first £5 coin to mark the Queen's birthday was the 1996 coin for her 70th. That was the only £5 issued that year. This 2021 coin is one of fifteen £5 coins dated 2021 and numismatically the Queen shared her special event with (among others) the Mr. Men, Peter Rabbit and an ox!

COMMEMORATIVE TYPE 61
Standard Fifth portrait of QEII
Design by: Jody Clark
Alfred the Great
Inspired by the Alfred Jewel
Design by: John Bergdahl
Edge: (on precious metal proofs)
AELFRED MEC HEHT
GEWYRCAN

			As-New	Proof
2021	Total sold: 10,882	(6,400 in RM packs)	£13.00	£16.00
1,488 of 2,250	.925 sterling silver proof			£90.00
709 of 900	.925 sterling silver piedfort proof, price new			£167.50
159	.917 gold proof			£3,500.00
	125x 2oz and 45x 5oz gold proofs were also sold.			

COMMEMORATIVE TYPE 62
Standard Fifth portrait of QEII
Design by: Jody Clark
Prince Philip
Design by: Ian Rank-Broadley
Edge: Milled

		As-New	Proof
2021 Total sold: 43,855	(21,314 in RM packs)	£10.00	
894 of 1,000	Silver 2oz (£5) proof, price new*		£190.00
343 of 750	Silver 5oz (£10) proof, price new*		£480.00
68 of 300	Gold 2oz (£200) proof, price new		£5,215.00
29 of 150	Gold 5oz (£500) proof, price new		£12,500.00
9 of 200	Gold 10oz (£200) proof, price new		£22,250.00

Various other weight gold / silver proofs were also struck. Two different PNC's were also sold.

COMMEMORATIVE TYPE 63
Standard Fifth portrait of QEII
Design by: Jody Clark
2021 Remembrance
Design by: Gary Breeze
Edge: Milled

		As-New	Proof
2021 Total sold: 17,904	(9,631 in RM packs - with colour)	£13.00	
1,542 of 2,021	.925 sterling silver proof (with colour)		£70.00
597	.925 sterling silver piedfort proof (with colour)		£100.00

COMMEMORATIVE TYPE 64A / 64B
Platinum Jubilee
Obverses: Type A - The standard Jody Clark portrait (same as TYPE 61) or Type B - Queen on horseback, design by John Bergdahl
Reverse by: John Bergdahl
Edge: SERVE YOU ALL THE DAYS OF MY LIFE (on special versions)

153

COMMEMORATIVE TYPE 64A / 64B (continued)

				As-New	Proof
2022	57,915	64A	From annual set, conventional obverse	£10.00	£15.00
	308,400	64B	A Standard BU version	£14.50	
	10k	64B	A BU version with edge motto	£16.50	
	4,998	64B	.925 sterling silver proof		£90.00
	1,950	64B	.925 sterling silver piedfort proof		£90.00
	1,000	64B	Silver 2oz (£5) proof*		£160.00
	400	64B	.917 gold proof, price new		£2,975.00
	51	64B	.9995 platinum piedfort proof, price new		£5,770.00

Note also that none of TYPE 64A/64B coins have a marked face-value.

COMMEMORATIVE TYPE 65
Standard Fifth portrait of QEII
Design by: Jody Clark
Duke of Cambridge 40th
Design by:
Edge: HRH THE DUKE OF CAM-
BRIDGE on some proofs

			As-New	Proof
2022	Total sold: 24,140	(15,653 in RM packs)	£12.00	
	2,722 of 3,500	.925 sterling silver proof, price new		£95.00
	1,048 of 1,500	.925 sterling silver piedfort proof		£100.00
	494	Gold 1/4oz (£25) proof, price new*		£725.00
	298	.917 gold proof, price new		£2,975.00
	89 of 52 max??	Gold 2oz (£200) proof, price new		£5,215.00

5oz gold proofs were also sold.

COMMEMORATIVE TYPE 66
Honours & Investitures
Standard Fifth portrait of QEII
Design by: Jody Clark
Queen's Reign 1 of 3
Design by: P J Lynch
Edge: DEVOTED TO YOUR
SERVICE on some proofs

			As-New	Proof
2022	Total sold: 49,345	(37,820 in RM packs)	£10.00	
	3,998	.925 sterling silver proof		£70.00
	1,491	.925 sterling silver piedfort proof		£160.00
	499	Gold 1/4oz (£25) proof*		£600.00
	250	.917 gold proof, price new		£2,975.00

* has plain milled edge, unlike the other proof versions. Other silver/gold kg and oz coins were sold.

COMMEMORATIVE TYPE 67
Charity & Patronage
Standard Fifth portrait of QEII
Design by: Jody Clark
Queen's Reign 2 of 3
Design by: P J Lynch
Edge: DEVOTED TO YOUR
SERVICE on some proofs

		As-New	Proof
2022 Total sold: 40,272	(30,793 in RM packs)	£10.00	
3,992	.925 sterling silver proof		£70.00
1,497	.925 sterling silver piedfort proof		£160.00
497	Gold 1/4oz (£25) proof*		£600.00
246	.917 gold proof, price new		£2,975.00

COMMEMORATIVE TYPE 68
The Commonwealth
Standard Fifth portrait of QEII
Design by: Jody Clark
Queen's Reign 3 of 3
Design by: P J Lynch
Edge: DEVOTED TO YOUR
SERVICE on some proofs

		As-New	Proof
2022 Total sold: 49,161	(39,201 in RM packs)	£10.00	
3,827 of 4k	.925 sterling silver proof		£70.00
1,500	.925 sterling silver piedfort proof		£160.00
498	Gold 1/4oz (£25) proof*		£600.00
249	.917 gold proof, price new		£2,975.00

* has plain milled edge, unlike the other proof versions.

COMMEMORATIVE TYPE 69
New portrait of CIII
Design by: Martin Jennings
QE2 Memorial
Designs by: John Bergdahl
Edge: • ELIZABETH II • DEVOTED TO YOUR SERVICE - on .925 silver and .917 gold proofs

			As-New	Proof
2022	Total sold: 176,230	(120,002 in RM packs)	£12.00	
	-			
22,491		.925 sterling silver proof		£95.00
4,956		.925 sterling silver piedfort proof, price new		£180.00
24,935		Silver 1oz (£5) proof, price new*		£99.50
2,603 of 3k		Silver 5oz (£10) proof, price new*		£570.00
854 of 1,000		Silver 10oz (£10?!) proof, price new*		£1,050.00
243 of 500		Silver 1kg (£500) proof, price new		£2,580.00
1,140		.917 gold proof, price new		£2,975.00
1,262		Gold 1oz (£100) proof, price new		£2,725.00
561 of 650		Gold 2oz (£200), price new*		£5,455.00
202 of 250		Gold 5oz (£500) proof, price new		£13,395.00

* No edge motto and features a different design, also by John Bergdahl. Other weights were sold in what the RM call the 'Ounce Range', which also included gold 1kg, 2kg, 5kg, 15kg and platinum 1oz.

COMMEMORATIVE TYPE 70
Portrait of CIII
Design by: Martin Jennings
75th Birthday of the King
Design by: Dan Thorne
Edge: RESTORING HARMONY WITH NATURE - on .925 silver and .917 gold proofs

	As-New	Proof
2023	£15.50	

		Proof
3k max	.925 sterling silver proof, price new	£106.00
1,000 max	.925 sterling silver piedfort proof, price new	£200.00
5k max	Silver 1/2oz (£1) proof, price new	£78.00
200 max	.917 gold proof, price new	£3,340.00
2,023 max	Gold 1/40oz (50p) proof, price new	£99.50
500 max	Gold 1/4oz (£25), price new	£750.00
75 max	Gold 2oz (£200) proof, price new	£5,890.00

Some coins were also sold accompanied with older coins and also in PNC envelopes with a stamp.

COMMEMORATIVE TYPE 71
Crowned Portrait of CIII
Design by: Martin Jennings
King's Coronation
Design by: Timothy Noad
Edge: Milled

	As-New	Proof
2023	£15.50	

		Proof
17.5k max	Silver 1oz (£2) proof, price new	£110.00
1,000 max	Silver 2oz (£5) proof, price new	£213.00
1,500 max	Silver 5oz (£10) proof, price new	£520.00
200 max	Silver 1kg (£500) proof, price new	£2,716.00
2,023 max	Gold 1/40oz (50p) proof, price new	£85.00
500 max	Gold 1oz (£100) proof, price new	£2,995.00
300 max	Gold 2oz (£200), price new	£5,890.00
15 max	Gold 1kg (£1000), price new	£86,945.00

The proof coins feature a different reverse design by John Bergdahl. Bullion 1oz silver and 1/10oz gold coins were also sold, also with a different design (CIIIR monogram by John Bergdahl). Gold sovereign based coins with the crowned portrait of the King were also sold in special coronation packaging.

£5 coins that don't commemorate royal events or were only made available in precious metals, are now found here, in part 2 of the Five Pounds section

CELEBRATION OF BRITAIN: Mind, Body and Spirit (2009 and 2010)

The Royal Mint issued a whopping eighteen different crowns in conjunction with the London 2012 Olympics, eleven of which are shown on the following pages. Starting in June 2009, one was issued every twenty-eight days until late 2010. The eighteen coins were made available as a complete set (one of which, with original packaging, box etc sold for nearly £900.00) as well as being available in groups of six (themed: 'Mind', 'Body' and 'Spirit').

They were all struck as sterling silver proofs. Three of them: the Clock-face (1), London (15) and Churchill (16) coins were also struck in cupro-nickel. The obverse design is the same as that used for COMMEMORATIVE TYPE 24, but dated either 2009 or 2010, as indicated. The reverse designs are all of a high standard and by Shane Greeves. Each design is accompanied by some wise words with a very loose connection to the subject matter of the design featured.

CAUTION: Chinese made forgeries of this series exist. The fakes have inconsistently frosted details and poorly executed colouring of the '2012' logos.

The coins were issued as follows:

1. Clock-face of the Palace of Westminster (green logo)
2. Stonehenge (green logo)
3. The Angel of the North (green logo)
4. The Flying Scotsman (green logo)
5. A sculpture of Isaac Newton (green logo)
6. The Globe theatre (green logo)
7. Rhossili Bay (red logo)
8. Giant's Causeway (red logo)
9. River Thames (red logo)
10. A Barn owl (red logo)
11. Oak leaves and an acorn (red logo)
12. Weather-vane (red logo)
13. Floral emblems of the UK (blue logo)
14. White rabbit from Alice in Wonderland (blue logo)
15. View down the Mall, London (blue logo)
16. Winston Churchill statue (blue logo)
17. Musical instruments (blue logo)
18. Image of Olaudah Equiano (blue logo)

| All | .925 Sterling silver proof version (95k max.) | £30-£40 |
| All | Cupro-Nickel proof version (100k max.) | £20-£25 |

No. 17 is shown above right.

THE QUEEN'S PORTRAIT SET (2013)

Reverse

Gillick Obverse

Machin Obverse

Coins featuring the four Portraits of the Queen used on coinage -
Three previous obverses and the current obverse of the time,
by: Mary Gillick, Arnold Machin, Raphael Maklouf and Ian Rank-Broadley
Reverse Design (common to all), the Royal Arms by: James Butler

This set of four coins produced in 2013, available only in sets struck in either .925 silver or .917 gold. All four coins share the same reverse. The obverses used are as follows:
Coin 1: A re-worked Mary Gillick obverse with 'FIVE POUNDS' under the bust.
Coin 2: A re-worked Arnold Machin obverse with new legend to incorporate 'FIVE POUNDS'.
Coin 3: Appears to be the same reverse as used on the 1990 Crown (Commemorative Type 1).
Coin 4: One of the standard obverses of the time which first appeared on the 2002 Crown (Commemorative Type 11).

Proof

| 2013 | 1,465 of 4,800 max | .925 silver proof set of 4, price new | £400.00 |
| | 150 of 450 | .917 gold proof set of 4, price new | £7,200.00 |

THE PORTRAIT OF BRITAIN SET (2014)

In 2014 a set of four .925 sterling silver proof coins dubbed 'The Portrait of Britain Collection' was sold new for £360.00. The reverses by Glyn Davies and Laura Clancy featured Tri-Chromatic pad printed images of The Elizabeth Tower (Big Ben), Buckingham Palace, Tower Bridge and Trafalgar Square. Maximum mintage was 3,500 (1,299 were sold). Sorry, no pictures!

THE FIRST WORLD WAR, SIX COIN SET (2014)

And if that wasn't enough, the first set of six .925 sterling silver proof only coins were produced to mark WWI, using the same obverse type as COMMEMORATIVE TYPE 24 . This set was £450.00 new and a maximum of 1,914 complete sets were produced (839 were sold). Sorry, no pictures!

FIRST WORLD WAR, SIX COIN SET (2015)

Albert Ball VC   Animals at war   Submarines

Edith Cavell   Merchant Navy   Gallipoli

The second set of six coins produced to mark WWI, struck in .925 silver. All six coins share the same obverse (the same used on Commemorative Type 41). The reverses used are as follows:

Coin 1: Albert Ball VC, by David Cornell. Edge: BY FAR THE BEST ENGLISH FLYING MAN.
Coin 2: Animals at war, by David Lawrence. Edge: PATIENT EYES COURAGEOUS HEARTS.
Coin 3: Submarines, by Edwina Ellis. Edge: IN LITTLE BOXES MADE OF TIN.
Coin 4: Edith Cavell, by David Cornell. Edge: SHE FACED THEM GENTLE AND BOLD.
Coin 5: Merchant Navy, by David Rowlands. Edge: SEPULCHRED IN THE HARBOUR OF THE DEEP.
Coin 6: Gallipoli, by John Bergdahl. Edge: HEROES THAT SHED THEIR BLOOD.

Proof

2015	1,915 max	.925 silver proof set of 6, price new		£465.00

Maximum mintage for each coin was 2,500 with the exception of the Gallipoli coin, that one was max. 5,000 as it was also sold as part of an international 3-coin set.

They don't seem to have been very popular though, as they were available for some time, until the Royal Mint offered them at a discount via their eBay account - I was able to purchase a set for about £260.00, hence the more extensive coverage and my own photographs on this page.

THE PORTRAIT OF BRITAIN SET (2016)

In 2016 a second (the first set was sold in 2014) set of four .925 sterling silver proof coins dubbed 'Portrait of Britain 2016 UK £5 Silver Collection' was sold new for £295.00. The reverses by Glyn Davies and Laura Clancy feature Tri-Chromatic pad printed images of The White Cliffs of Dover, Giants Causeway, Lake District and Snowdonia. 1,098 out of a maximum mintage of 2,016 were sold. Interesting to note the reductions in both price and mintage over the 2014 set. Sorry, no pictures!

FIRST WORLD WAR, SIX COIN SET (2016)

And another set of six coins produced in 2016, the third set to mark WWI, struck in .925 silver. All six coins share the same obverse (the same used on Commemorative Type 41.) Themes of the six coins are 'The Boy Hero of Jutland (Jack Cornwell)', 'The Battle of Jutland', 'Dreadnought', 'The Somme', 'The Army', and 'Poetry and Language'. The Somme coin was available separately and is shown below.

				Proof
2016	499 of 1,916	.925 silver proof set of 6, price new		£450.00
2016	25 of 450	.917 gold proof set of 6, price new		£10,500.00

COMMEMORATIVE TYPE SOMME
Standard Fifth portrait of QEII
Design by: Jody Clark
Battle of the Somme, 100th Anniversary.
Design by: John Bergdahl
Edge:
DEAD MEN CAN ADVANCE NO FURTHER
Obverse: As Type 41.

Proof

2016			
	3,678 of 6k	.925 sterling silver proof only, price new	£82.50

*Apparently the boxed proof coins are limited to 1,916. The total maximum mintage is 6,000. I'm not sure how the others were sold.

THE PORTRAIT OF BRITAIN SET (2017)

In 2017 a third set of four .925 sterling silver proof coins (max. mintage 1,500) dubbed 'Portrait of Britain 2017 UK £5 Silver Collection' was sold new originally for £295.00 (they were still available mid-2020 for £350). The reverses by Glyn Davies and Laura Clancy feature Tri-Chromatic pad printed images of Downing Street, Edinburgh Castle, Hampton Court Palace and Westminster Abbey. Maximum mintage is apparently 1,500. Sorry, no pictures!

FIRST WORLD WAR, SIX COIN SET (2017)

And the fourth set of six coins produced in 2017 to mark WWI, struck in .925 silver. All six coins share the same obverse (the same used on Commemorative Type 41.) Themes of the six coins are 'Noel Chavasse', 'Medical Services', 'Sopwith Camel', 'Art and Poetry', 'Gas', and 'Battle of Arras'.

2017	1,917 max	.925 silver proof set of 6, price new	£465.00
2017	450 max	.917 gold proof set of 6, price new	£11,000.00

THE PORTRAIT OF BRITAIN SET (2018)

The 2018 Portrait of Britain set of four .925 silver proof coins (max. mintage 1,500) show: Tenby harbour with the inscription 'TENBY' Blackpool Tower with the inscription 'BLACKPOOL', a view of Brighton Pier with the inscription 'BRIGHTON' and a view of Southwold beach with the inscription "SOUTHWOLD".

This set is still available in mid-2020 for £350. Clearly not a big sales success and it looks like they've given up on them now, as there doesn't appear to have been 2019 or 2020 'Portrait of Britain' sets.

THE QUEEN'S BEASTS, 2017 to 2021 range

Originally a silver bullion issue, these unexpectedly appeared in base-metal guise. There are 11 coins - a series of 10 actual beasts, plus a 'completer' coin:

1. Lion of England (2017) - 31,838 sold. Value in BU pack £10.
2. Unicorn of Scotland (2017) - 31,978 sold. Value in BU pack £10.
3. Red Dragon of Wales (2018) - 25,753 sold. Value in BU pack £20.
4. Black Bull of Clarence (2018) - 17,763 sold. Value in BU pack, around £85.
5. Falcon of the Plantagenets (2019) - 19,694. Value in BU pack, £14.
6. Yale of Beaufort (2019) - 17,437 sold. Value in BU pack £13.
7. White Lion of Mortimer (2020). 18,227 sold. Value in BU pack £13.
8. White Horse of Hanover (2020). 16,905 sold. Value in BU pack £10.
9. Greyhound of Richmond (2021). 17,184 sold. Value in BU pack £12.
10. Griffin of Edward III (2021). 17,184 sold. Value in BU pack £10.
(11.) Queen's Beasts completer coin (2021). 30,588 sold. Value in BU pack £13.

THE QUEEN'S BEASTS, 2017 to 2021 range (continued) •

All of the reverses are shown below and on the following page. The beasts depicted on the coins by Jody Clark, originally stood guard in statue form at the Queen's coronation in 1953. They are connected to a Royal event (the coronation) but don't actually commemorate it, so I've decided to put them here, in part 2 of the £5 coin section. Note that there are design differences for the silver/gold versions, including different marked face values, different arrangement of the legend and textured backgrounds. Each coin is available in many guises. It's all rather complicated!

Base metal:
Marked as £5 face value, sold new in card packs for £13.00. The 'Black Bull of Clarence' all of a sudden became more sought-after when the sales figures were released and it was discovered that it sold less than the others (for which sales figures are known) despite the fact that the sales numbers for all are relatively low.

Bullion Issues, new prices (struck to BU standard):
2 oz silver (£5 marked face value), available for about £51.00. 10 oz silver (£10 marked face value), available for about £240.00

Proof Issues, new prices (2021):
1 oz silver proof, sold new for £92.50. 5 oz silver proof, sold new for £465.00. 1/4 oz gold proof, sold new for £650.00. 10 oz silver proof, sold new for £865.00. 1 oz gold proof, sold new for £2,315.00. 1kg silver proof, sold new for £2,330.00. 5 oz gold proof, sold new for £11,125.00. 1kg gold proof, sold new for A LOT

THE QUEEN'S BEASTS 2017 - 2021, Coins 1 to 6

THE QUEEN'S BEASTS 2017 - 2021, Coins 7 to 10, the 'completer' and the common obverse

THE TUDOR BEASTS, 2022 onwards

Another series of Beast related coins, 10 are planned. At the time of writing the first seven have been made available. As usual, they come in standard BU form and are also available as proofs in umpteen different weights, in silver or gold. Of note is that the 2023 dated Beaufort Yale coin featured the late Queen, despite her passing during 2022.

1. Seymour Panther (2022 QEII), BU price new £14.50.
2. Lion of England (2022 QEII), BU price new £14.50.
3. The Beaufort Yale (dated 2023, available late 2022 QEII), BU price new £14.50.
4. Bull of Clarence (2023 KCIII), BU price new £14.50
5. Seymour Unicorn (2024), BU price new £14.50.
6. Tudor Dragon (2024), BU price new £15.50.
7. Queen's Panther (dated 2025, available late 2024), BU price new £15.50.

The Seymour panther and Beaufort Yale are shown to the right.

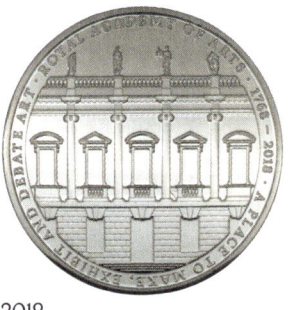

COMMEMORATIVE TYPE ACADEMY
Standard Fifth portrait of QEII
Design by: Jody Clark
250th Anniversary of the Royal Academy of Arts
Design by: Sir David Chipperfield RA
Edge: Milled
Obverse: Same as that shown on previous page.

		As-New	Proof
2018			
11,988 of 12k	Base metal version, not available directly*	£12.00	
2,750 max.	.925 sterling silver proof only		£40.00

*In an unusual marketing tactic (that I am pleased to see has not been repeated) this coin in BU form was not available to buy directly from the Royal Mint and instead, had to be purchased via a single third party. It was only about £11.00 to buy new but did increase in value initially, caused no doubt by the usual factors that seem to play a role when certain coins sell out. The value is now back down to a more realistic level.

COMMEMORATIVE TYPE LION 2018
An unplanned, fairly spontaneous (from what I can tell) 2018 dated 'Lion of England' coin was sold in special packs to cash in on England doing better than was expected in the Football World Cup. The design used was the same as that for the 'Lion of England' Queen's Beast coin, as shown in the Queen's Beasts 2017-2021 range. Current value is about £20.00.

COMMEMORATIVE TYPE TOWER 2019 1 (of 4)
Standard Fifth portrait of QEII
Design by: Jody Clark
Tower of London Raven
Design by: Glyn Davies
Edge: (on proofs) ON INTO TWILIGHT WITHIN WALLS OF STONE.

			As-New	Proof
2019	20,199	(not issued for circulation)	£10.00	
	2,864 of 4k max.	.925 sterling silver proof		£50.00
	951 of 950 max.	.925 sterling silver piedfort proof		£120.00
	200 of 325 max.	.917 gold proof		no data
	225 of 800 max	[£25 face value] .917 gold 1/4oz proof (smaller), price new		£480.00

This raven coin is one of four that was sold to commemorate the Tower of London (in 2019 - another four came in 2020). The other 2019 coins, shown on the next page, are themed 'The Crown Jewels' (March 2019), 'The Yeoman Warders' (June 2019) and 'The Ceremony of the Keys' (August 2019). 5oz silver proof and 5oz gold proof versions (both with £10 face value) were also sold.

COMMEMORATIVE TYPE TOWER 2019 2 (of 4)

Standard Fifth portrait of QEII
Design by: Jody Clark
Crown and wall diagram
Design by: Glyn Davies
Edge: (on proofs) ON INTO TWILIGHT WITHIN WALLS OF STONE.

		As-New	Proof
2019	18,986	(not issued for circulation)	£13.00
2,389 of 3.8k max.	.925 sterling silver proof		£50.00
712 of 950 max.	.925 sterling silver piedfort proof		£120.00
181 of 325 max.	.917 gold proof, price new		£2,495.00
168 of 800 max.	(£25 face value) .917 gold 1/4oz proof (smaller), price new		£555.00

COMMEMORATIVE TYPE TOWER 2019 3 (of 4)

Standard Fifth portrait of QEII
Design by: Jody Clark
Beefeater
Design by: Glyn Davies
Edge: (on proofs) ON INTO TWILIGHT WITHIN WALLS OF STONE.

		As-New	Proof
2019	17,145	(not issued for circulation)	£12.00
2,222 of 3.8k max.	.925 sterling silver proof		£60.00
601 of 950 max.	.925 sterling silver piedfort proof		£120.00
150 of 325 max.	.917 gold proof, price new		£2,495.00
146 of 800 max.	(£25 face value) .917 gold 1/4oz proof (smaller), price new		£555.00

COMMEMORATIVE TYPE TOWER 2019 4 (of 4)

Standard Fifth portrait of QEII
Design by: Jody Clark
Lamp and Keys
Design by: Glyn Davies
Edge: (on proofs) ON INTO TWILIGHT WITHIN WALLS OF STONE.

		As-New	Proof
2019	16,475	(not issued for circulation)	£11.00
2,134 of 3.8k max.	.925 sterling silver proof		£60.00
548 of 950 max.	.925 sterling silver piedfort proof		£120.00
145 of 325 max.	.917 gold proof, price new		£2,495.00
110 of 800 max.	(£25 face value) .917 gold 1/4oz proof (smaller), price new		£555.00

COMMEMORATIVE TYPE LION 2019

Another spontaneous re-issue of the 'Lion of England' design (top left on page 164), this time to cash-in on England winning the Cricket World Cup. Current value seems to be around £25.00. 6,845 were sold.

COMMEMORATIVE TYPE LUNAR YEAR OF THE RAT

Standard Fifth portrait of QEII
Design by: Jody Clark
Rat and Chinese symbol
Design by: P J Lynch
Edge: Milled on all versions.

		As-New	Proof
2020	Total sold: 19,178	(14,428 in RM packs)	£55.00	
2,585	Silver 1oz (£2) proof		£44.00
188 of 88??	Silver 5oz (£10) proof, price new		£420.00
25	Silver 1kg (£500) proof, price new		£2,270.00
822	Gold 1oz (£100) proof, price new		£2,315.00
28	Gold 5oz (£500) proof, price new		£10,525.00

The original Lunar series of coins were precious metal proofs only (see page 208). This was the first to be sold in BU-pack format. Various other versions in silver and gold with various face values were also sold. Instead of the usual .925 silver and .917 gold alloys, it would seem a lot of precious metal proofs from 2020 onwards are being struck in 999.9 alloys, probably aimed more towards bullion stackers. 8x 1kg gold coins were also sold.

COMMEMORATIVE TYPE WORDSWORTH

Standard Fifth portrait of QEII
Design by: Jody Clark
Scene with name and years of birth and death.
Design by: David Lawrence
Edge: (on proofs)
I WANDERED LONELY AS A CLOUD

		As-New	Proof
2020	Total sold: 18,202	(7,945 in RM packs)	£10.00	
1,463 of 3k	.925 sterling silver proof, price new		£82.50
not issued	.925 sterling silver piedfort proof		
136 of 300	.917 gold proof, price new		£2,495.00

A piedfort proof version wasn't made. The BU and silver proof versions were also sold in combination with stamps.

COMMEMORATIVE TYPE
TOWER 2020 1 (of 4)
Standard Fifth portrait of QEII
Design by: Jody Clark
The White Tower
Design by: Timothy Noad
Edge: (on precious metal proofs):
THE WHITE TOWER

		As-New	Proof
2020 Total sold: 14,689	(9,690 in RM packs)	£10.00	
1,567 of 2,500	.925 sterling silver proof		£70.00
438	.925 sterling silver piedfort proof, price new		£155.00
125	.917 gold proof, price new		£2,495.00

COMMEMORATIVE TYPE
MUSIC LEGENDS 1 (of ?)
Standard Fifth portrait of QEII
Design by: Jody Clark
The Band Queen (instruments)
Design by: Chris Facey
Edge: (on the 1oz silver proof):
Mercury, Taylor, Deacon and May

		As-New	Proof
2020 Total sold: 96,456	(75,457 in RM packs)*	£13.00	
15,088	Silver 1/2oz (£1) proof, price new		£60.00
7,498	Silver 1oz (£2) proof, with gold detail, price new		£90.00
481	Silver 2oz (£5) proof, price new		£180.00
150	Silver 5oz (£10) proof		no data
1,249	Gold 1/4oz (£25) proof, price new		£510.00
300	Gold 1oz (£100) proof, price new		£2,195.00
53	Gold 2oz (£200) proof		no data

*In addition to the standard BU folder, three other BU folders were sold for £15 each, featuring the artwork of the albums 'Hot Space', 'Live', and 'A Kind of Magic'. 34,756 total is for all packages combined. 6x gold 1kg and 50x 5oz gold coins were also sold.

Note that the precious metal versions all have different marked face values and that the two smallest silver coins have lower face values than their cupro-nickel BU counterparts.

COMMEMORATIVE TYPE
JAMES BOND 1 (of 3)
Standard Fifth portrait of QEII
Design by: Jody Clark
Aston Martin DB5
Design by: Matt Dent and
Christian Davies
Edge: Milled on all versions

			As-New	Proof
2020	Total sold: 51,055	(33,008 in RM packs)	£13.00	
5,358 of 15,007		Silver 1/2oz (£1) proof		£50.00
5,989 of 7,007		Silver 1oz (£2) proof		£70.00
1,650 of 2,007		Silver 2oz (£5) proof		£110.00
1,007		Gold 1/4oz (£25) proof, price new		£555.00
348		Gold 1oz (£100) proof, price new		£2,250.00
247		Gold 2oz (£200) proof, price new		£4,310.00

COMMEMORATIVE TYPE
MUSIC LEGENDS 2 (of ?)
Standard Fifth portrait of QEII
Design by: Jody Clark
Elton John
Design by: Bradley Morgan Johnson
Edge: (on the 1oz silver proof):
ELTON JOHN

			As-New	Proof
2020	Total sold: 40,5065	(34,756 in RM packs)*	£12.00	
4,094 of 14k		Silver 1/2oz (£1) proof		£45.00
7,494 of 10k		Silver 1oz (£2) proof, with colour details		£80.00
498		Silver 2oz (£5) proof		£90.00
111		Silver 5oz (£10) proof, price new		£525.00
990		Gold 1/4oz (£25) proof		£600.00
249		Gold 1oz (£100) proof, price new		£2,315.00
25		Gold 2oz (£200) proof, price new		£4,370.00

*In addition to the standard BU folder, four other BU folders were sold for £15 each, featuring the artwork of the albums 'Rocket Man', 'Dodgers Stadium', 'Illustration' and 'The Very Best of'. 34,756 total is for all packages combined. 4x gold 1kg coins were also sold.

Note that the precious metal versions of the coins on this page all have different marked face values (indicated in brackets) and that the two smallest silver coins have lower face values than their cupro-nickel BU counterparts.

169

COMMEMORATIVE TYPE
British Red Cross 150th Anniv'
Standard Fifth portrait of QEII
Design by: Jody Clark
British Red Cross
Design by: Henry Gray
Edge (on precious metal proofs):
PER HUMANITATEM AD PACEM

		As-New	Proof
2020 Total sold: 15,1375	(6,500 in RM packs)	£12.00	
1,551 of 4k	.925 sterling silver proof		£50.00
598 of 1,150	.925 sterling silver piedfort proof, price new		£182.50
143 of 250	.917 gold proof, price new		£2,590.00

COMMEMORATIVE TYPE
TOWER 2020 2 (of 4)
Standard Fifth portrait of QEII
Design by: Jody Clark
Royal Menagerie
Design by: Timothy Noad
Edge (on precious metal proofs):
THE ROYAL MENAGERIE

		As-New	Proof
2020 Total sold: 13,996	(9,009 in RM packs)	£13.00	
1,289 of 1,500	.925 sterling silver proof		£70.00
377	.925 sterling silver piedfort proof, price new		£167.50
125	.917 gold proof, price new		£2,590.00

COMMEMORATIVE TYPE
END OF WWII
Standard Fifth portrait of QEII
Design by: Jody Clark
WAR / PEACE
Design by: M Dent & C Davies
Edge (on precious metal proofs):
THROUGH COURAGE AND ENDURANCE

		As-New	Proof
2020 Total sold: 26,475	(9,475 in RM packs)	£13.00	
2,564	.925 sterling silver proof, price new		£90.00
561	.925 sterling silver piedfort proof, price new		£167.50
134 of 275	Silver 5oz (£10) proof, price new		£455.00
225	.917 gold proof, price new		£2,590.00

Other versions of this coin were sold, also some as PNC's, with various replica literature and in NGC 'slabs'.

COMMEMORATIVE TYPE
JAMES BOND 2 (of 3)
Standard Fifth portrait of QEII
Design by: Jody Clark
Underwater Lotus Esprit
Design by: Matt Dent and
Christian Davies
Edge: Milled on all versions

		As-New	Proof
2020 Total sold: 40,564	(25,754 in RM packs)	£13.00	
3,119 of 15,007	Silver 1/2oz (£1) proof		£60.00
4,528 of 7,007	Silver 1oz (£2) proof		£70.00
1,292 of 2,007	Silver 2oz (£5) proof		£110.00
862 of 1,007	Gold 1/4oz (£25) proof, price new		£600.00
346	Gold 1oz (£100) proof, price new		£2,370.00
266 of 250 max??	Gold 2oz (£200) proof, price new		£4,370.00

Note that the precious metal versions all have different marked face values and that the two smallest silver coins have lower face values than their cupro-nickel BU counterparts.

COMMEMORATIVE TYPE
JAMES BOND 3 (of 3)
Standard Fifth portrait of QEII
Design by: Jody Clark
Tuxedo
Design by: Matt Dent and
Christian Davies
Edge: Milled on all versions

		As-New	Proof
2020 Total sold: 32,253	(25,754 in RM packs)	£13.00	
3,062 of 15,007	Silver 1/2oz (£1) proof		£50.00
4,644 of 7,007	Silver 1oz (£2) proof		£60.00
1,200 of 2,007	Silver 2oz (£5) proof		£110.00
857 of 1,007	Gold 1/4oz (£25) proof		£500.00
348	Gold 1oz (£100) proof, price new		£2,370.00
246	Gold 2oz (£200) proof, price new		exists?

Note that the precious metal versions all have different marked face values and that the two smallest silver coins have lower face values than their cupro-nickel BU counterparts.

171

COMMEMORATIVE TYPE TOWER 2020 3 (of 4)

Standard Fifth portrait of QEII
Design by: Jody Clark
The Royal Mint
Design by: Timothy Noad
Edge (on precious metal proofs):
THE ROYAL MINT?

			As-New	Proof
2020	Total sold: 14,262	(9,612 in RM packs)	£13.00	
1,500		.925 sterling silver proof		£70.00
392		.925 sterling silver piedfort proof, price new		£167.50
124		.917 gold proof, price new		exists?

COMMEMORATIVE TYPE MUSIC LEGENDS 3 (of ?)

Standard Fifth portrait of QEII
Design by: Jody Clark
David Bowie
Design by: Jody Clark
Edge: (on the 1oz silver proof):
THE STARS ARE NEVER FAR AWAY

			As-New	Proof
2020	Total sold: 46,715	(39,215 in RM packs)*	£13.00	
5,998		Silver 1/2oz (£1) proof, price new		exists?
7,996		Silver 1oz (£2) proof, with colour details, price new		£97.50
545		Silver 2oz (£5) proof, price new		£195.00
137 of 500		Silver 5oz (£10) proof, price new		£520.00
1,290		Gold 1/4oz (£25) proof, price new		£595.00
349		Gold 1oz (£100) proof, price new		exists?
100		Gold 2oz (£200) proof, price new		£4,370.00
60		Gold 5oz (£500) proof, price new		£10,525.00

*In addition to the standard BU folder, three other BU folders were sold for £15 each, featuring different poster artwork. The 39,215 total is for all four pack variations. 11x gold 1kg coins were also sold.

COMMEMORATIVE TYPE
TOWER 2020 4 (of 4)
Standard Fifth portrait of QEII
Design by: Jody Clark
The Infamous Prison
Design by: Timothy Noad
Edge (on precious metal proofs):
THE INFAMOUS PRISON?

		As-New	Proof
2020 Total sold: 12,980	(9,481 in RM packs)	£13.00	
1,227 of 1,500	.925 sterling silver proof		£70.00
394	.925 sterling silver piedfort proof, price new		£167.50
125	.917 gold proof, price new		exists?

COMMEMORATIVE TYPE
LUNAR YEAR OF THE OX
Standard Fifth portrait of QEII
Design by: Jody Clark
Ox and Chinese symbol
Design by: Harry Brockway
Edge: Milled on all versions.

		As-New	Proof
2021 Total sold: 17,859	(11,859 in RM packs)	£13.00	
2,684	Silver 1oz (£2) proof, price new		£92.50
186	Silver 5oz (£10) proof, price new		£455.00
24	Silver 1kg (£500) proof, price new		£2,270.00
384	Gold 1/4oz (£25) proof, price new		£595.00
850	Gold 1oz (£100) proof, price new		£2,315.00
28	Gold 5oz (£500) proof		no data
8	Gold 1kg proof		no data

38.61 mm • 28.28 grammes • cupro-nickel • various edge

COMMEMORATIVE TYPE
Mr. Men Little Miss, 1 of 3
Standard Fifth portrait of QEII
Design by: Jody Clark
50th Anniversary Mr Men
Design by: Adam Hargreaves
Edge: Milled on all?

			As-New	Proof
2021	Total sold: 18,461	(10,460 in RM packs)	£10.00	
10,182 of 15k		BU version with added colour	£22.50	
1,637 of 9k		Silver 1/2oz (£1) proof, price new	£65.00	
2,944 of 6.5k		Silver 1oz (£2) proof with added colour, price new		£97.50
345 of 750		Gold 1/4oz (£25) proof, price new		£595.00
145 of 275		Gold 1oz (£100) proof, price new		£2,315.00

COMMEMORATIVE TYPE
Mr. Men Little Miss, 2 of 3
Standard Fifth portrait of QEII
Design by: Jody Clark
50th Anniversary Mr Men
Design by: Adam Hargreaves
Edge: Milled on all?

			As-New	Proof
2021	Total sold: 15,946	(8,948 in RM packs)	£8.00	
9,041 of 15k		BU version with added colour	£22.50	
1,223 of 9k		Silver 1/2oz (£1) proof, price new	£65.00	
2,348 of 6.5k		Silver 1oz (£2) proof with added colour, price new		£97.50
107 of 750		Gold 1/4oz (£25) proof, price new		£595.00
52 of 275		Gold 1oz (£100) proof, price new		£2,315.00

COMMEMORATIVE TYPE
ALBERT HALL
Standard Fifth portrait of QEII
Design by: Jody Clark
150th Anniversary
Design by: Anne Desmet RA
Edge (on non-domed precious metal proofs): INSPIRING ARTS AND SCIENCES

2021 Total sold: 16,042	(8,550 in RM packs)	As-New	Proof
		£10.00	
1,544	.925 sterling silver proof, price new		£90.00
850 of 1,000	.925 sterling silver piedfort proof		£135.00
2,035 of 3.5k	.925 sterling silver proof, domed reverse, price new		£120.00
169	.917 gold proof, price new		£2,590.50
199	.917 gold proof, domed reverse, price new		£2,760.00

Note that the domed versions are the same weight as the standard (non piedfort) proof varieties.

COMMEMORATIVE TYPE
Mr. Men Little Miss, 3 of 3
Standard Fifth portrait of QEII
Design by: Jody Clark
50th Anniversary Mr Men
Design by: Adam Hargreaves
Edge: Milled on all?

2021 Total sold: 16,046	(8,796 in RM packs)	As-New	Proof
		£8.00	
8,947 of 15k	BU version with added colour	£22.50	
1,218 of 9k	Silver 1/2oz (£1) proof, price new	£65.00	
2,317 of 6.5k	Silver 1oz (£2) proof with added colour, price new		£97.50
91 of 750	Gold 1/4oz (£25) proof, price new		£595.00
42 of 275	Gold 1oz (£100) proof, price new		£2,315.00

COMMEMORATIVE TYPE
PETER RABBIT
Standard Fifth portrait of QEII
Design by: Jody Clark
Peter Rabbit*
Design by: Ffion Gwillim
Edge: Milled

		As-New	Proof
2021	Total sold: 30,690	(17,243 in RM packs)	£11.00	
4,170 of 5k	Silver 1oz (£2) proof, price new		£90.00
134 of 250	Gold 1oz (£100) proof, price new		£2,315.00

* I don't think this one actually commemorates anything in particular, it's just another Peter Rabbit coin!

COMMEMORATIVE TYPE
MUSIC LEGENDS 4 (of ?)
Standard Fifth portrait of QEII
Design by: Jody Clark
The Who
Design by: Henry Gray
Edge: (on the 1oz silver proof):
PINBALL WIZARD

			As-New	Proof
2021	14,900 Cu-ni £5 FV	(8,400 in RM packs)	£13.00	
5,695 of 10k	£5 FV	BU version with added colour, price new	£22.50	
2,492 of 10k		Silver 1/2oz (£1) proof, price new		£65.00
5,837 of 8,100		Silver 1oz (£2) proof, with colour details, price new		£97.50
536		Silver 2oz (£5) proof with shockwave, price new		£200.00
163 of 500		Silver 5oz (£10) proof with shockwave, price new		£540.00
753 of 1,000		Gold 1/4oz (£25) proof, price new		£595.00
340		Gold 1oz (£100) proof, price new		£2,315.00
129 of 150		Gold 2oz (£200) proof with shockwave, price new		£4,775.00
46 of 64		Gold 5oz (£500) proof with shockwave, price new		£11,835.00
3 of 12		Gold 1kg (£1000) proof with shockwave, price new		£72,295.00

Some versions feature a 'shockwave' effect emanating from the speaker behind 'The Who' logo.

1   2

COMMEMORATIVE TYPE
THE ALICE COLLECTION
(1 & 2)
Standard Fifth portrait of QEII
(as shown opposite)
Design by: Jody Clark
(1) Alice's adventures in Wonderland. (2) Through the Looking Glass
Designs by: Ffion Gwillim
Edge: Milled on all?

Coin 1: Alice's Adventures in Wonderland		As-New	Proof
2021 16,472 Cu-ni £5 FV	(8,976 in RM packs)	£13.00	
9,915 of 15k £5 FV	BU version with added colour, price new £20.00		
1,730 of 5k	Silver 1/2oz (£1) proof, price new		£65.00
3,482	Silver 1oz (£2) proof, with colour details, price new		£100.00
223 of 500	Gold 1/4oz (£25) proof, price new		£650.00
127 of 150	Gold 1oz (£100) proof, price new		£2,440.00

Coin 2: Through the Looking Glass			
2021 14,425 Cu-ni £5 FV	(6,932 in RM packs)	£13.00	
9,242 of 15k £5 FV	BU version with added colour, price new £20.00		
2,840 of 5k	Silver 1/2oz (£1) proof, price new		£65.00
2,840 of 3,500	Silver 1oz (£2) proof, with colour details, price new		£100.00
151 of 500	Gold 1/4oz (£25) proof, price new		£650.00
100 of 150	Gold 1oz (£100) proof, price new		£2,440.00

COMMEMORATIVE TYPE
LUNAR YEAR OF THE TIGER
Standard Fifth portrait of QEII
Design by: Jody Clark
Tiger and Chinese symbol
Design by: David Lawrence
Edge: Milled on all versions.
Available from September 2021

		As-New	Proof
2022 Total sold: 31,396	(22,610 in RM packs)	£14.50	
2,682 of 2,688	Silver 1oz (£2) proof, price new		£95.00
217 of 218	Silver 5oz (£10) proof, price new		£465.00

177

Lunar Year of the Tiger, continued

35 of 38	Silver 1kg (£500) proof, price new	£2,330.00
388	Gold 1/4oz (£25) proof, price new	£650.00
733 of 888	Gold 1oz (£100) proof, price new	£2,440.00
118	Gold 5oz (£500) proof, price new	£11,125.00
8	Gold 1kg (£1,000) proof, price new	a lot!

COMMEMORATIVE TYPE
MAHATMA GANDHI
Standard Fifth portrait of QEII
Design by: Jody Clark
Gandhi commemorative
Design by: Heena Glover
Edge: Milled on all versions.

	As-New	Proof

2021	Total sold: 14,962	(10,064 in RM packs)	£13.00	
2,052 of 2,500	Silver 1oz (£2) proof, price new		£99.50
143 of 175	Gold 1oz (£100) proof, price new		£2,505.00

COMMEMORATIVE TYPE
PETER RABBIT
Standard Fifth portrait of QEII
Design by: Jody Clark
Peter Rabbit 120th Anniversary
Design by: Ffion Gwillim
Edge: Milled on all versions.

	As-New	Proof

2022	Total sold: 27,135	(18,408 in RM packs)	£10.00	
8,659 of 8,600	BU version with added colour		£23.50	
3.495 of 3,500	Silver 1oz (£2) proof with added colour, price new		£105.00
109 of 120	Gold 1oz (£100) proof, price new		£2,725.00

COMMEMORATIVE TYPE
TUTANKHAMUN
Standard Fifth portrait of QEII
Design by: Jody Clark
100th Anniversary of the tomb discovery
Design by: Laura Clancy
Edge: THE VALLEY OF THE KINGS on proofs

	As-New	Proof
2022 Total sold: 25,695 (12,277 in RM packs)	£10.00	
1,892 of 1,922 .925 sterling silver proof, price new		£95.00
778 of 800 .925 sterling silver piedfort proof, price new		£180.00
128 of 200 .917 gold proof, price new		£2,975.00

COMMEMORATIVE TYPE
MUSIC LEGENDS 5 (of ?)
Standard Fifth portrait of QEII
Design by: Jody Clark
The Rolling Stones
Design by: Hannah Phizacklea
Edge: Milled on all versions.

	As-New	Proof
2022 Total sold: 17,596 (13,116 in RM packs)	£11.00	
7,523 of 10k £5 FV BU version with added colour, price new	£23.50	
5,649 of 8k Silver 1oz (£2) proof, with colour details, price new		£105.00
549 of 550 Silver 2oz (£5) proof, price new		£190.00
292 of 600 Silver 5oz (£10) proof, price new		£480.00
631 of 1k Gold 1/4oz (£25) proof, price new		£725.00
240 of 350 Gold 1oz (£100) proof, price new		£2,725.00
84 of 150 Gold 2oz (£200) proof, price new		£5,215.00
21 of 30 Gold 5oz (£500) proof with, price new		£13,500.00

COMMEMORATIVE TYPE
LUNAR YEAR OF THE RABBIT
Standard Fifth portrait of QEII
Design by: Jody Clark
Rabbit and Chinese symbols
Design by: Louie Maryon
Edge: Milled on all versions.

	As-New	Proof
2023 (available from Sep'22) (not issued for circulation)	£16.00	
2,888 max Silver 1oz (£2) proof, price new		£99.50
228 max Silver 5oz (£10) proof, price new		£480.00
50 max Silver 1kg (£500) proof, price new		£2,390.00
388 max Gold 1/4oz (£25) proof, price new		£725.00
888 max Gold 1oz (£100) proof, price new		£2,725.00
128 max Gold 5oz (£500) proof, price new		£12,500.00

COMMEMORATIVE TYPE
KING ARTHUR
Standard portrait of KCIII
Design by: Martin Jennings
Myths & Legends Series
Design by: David Lawrence
Edge: Milled on all versions.

		As-New	Proof
2023	(not issued for circulation)	£15.50	
2,500 max	1oz silver proof (£2), price new		£110.00
600 max	1/4oz gold proof (£25), price new		£799.00
200 max	1oz gold proof (£100), price new		£2,995.00

1oz and 10oz silver bullion versions were also sold, with different wording.

COMMEMORATIVE TYPE
MERLIN
Standard portrait of KCIII
Design by: Martin Jennings
Myths & Legends Series
Design by: David Lawrence
Edge: Milled on all versions.

		As-New	Proof
2023	(not issued for circulation)	£15.50	
2,500 max	1oz silver proof (£2), price new		£110.00
500 max	2oz silver proof (£5), price new		£213.00
600 max	1/4oz gold proof (£25), price new		£799.00
200 max	1oz gold proof (£100), price new		£2,995.00

1oz silver and 1oz gold bullion versions were also sold, with different wording.

COMMEMORATIVE TYPE
PRIDE OF ENGLAND
Standard portrait of KCIII
Design by: Martin Jennings
Dedicated to
England's Lionesses
Design by: Norman Sillman
Edge: Milled on both versions.

		As-New	Proof
2023	(not issued for circulation)	£14.50	
? max	.925 sterling silver proof, price new		£97.50

COMMEMORATIVE TYPE
MUSIC LEGENDS 5 (of ?)
Standard portrait of KCIII
Design by: Martin Jennings
Shirley Bassey
Design by: Sue Aperghis
Edge: Milled on all versions.

			As-New	Proof
2023	Cu-ni £5 FV	(not issued for circulation)	£15.50	
5,000 max	£5 FV	BU version with added colour, price new	£24.50	
2,500 max		Silver 1oz (£2) proof, with colour details, price new		£108.50
350 max		Silver 2oz (£5) proof, price new		£195.00
350 max		Gold 1/4oz (£25) proof, price new		£750.00
150 max		Gold 1oz (£100) proof, price new		£2,770.00
70 max		Gold 2oz (£200) proof, price new		£5,305.00

COMMEMORATIVE TYPE
MUSIC LEGENDS 6 (of ?)
Standard portrait of KCIII
Design by: Martin Jennings
The Police
Design by: Heena Glover
Edge: Milled on all versions.

			As-New	Proof
2023	Cu-ni £5 FV	(not issued for circulation)	£15.50	
7,500 max	£5 FV	BU version with added colour, price new	£24.50	
6,000 max		Silver 1oz (£2) proof, with colour details, price new		£108.50
700 max		Silver 2oz (£5) proof, price new		£213.00
300 max		Silver 5oz (£10) proof, price new		£520.00
500 max		Gold 1/4oz (£25) proof, price new		£799.00
300 max		Gold 1oz (£100) proof, price new		£2,995.00
150 max		Gold 2oz (£200) proof, price new		£5,860.00

38.61 mm • 28.28 grammes • cupro-nickel • various edge

COMMEMORATIVE TYPE
MORGAN LE FAY
Standard portrait of KCIII
Design by: Martin Jennings
Myths & Legends Series
Design by: David Lawrence
Edge: Milled on all versions.

		As-New	Proof
2023	(not issued for circulation)	£15.50	
2,500 max	1oz silver proof (£2), price new		£110.00
500 max	2oz silver proof (£5), price new		£213.00
250 max	1/4oz gold proof (£25), price new		£799.00
200 max	1oz gold proof (£100), price new		£2,995.00

1oz silver and 1oz gold bullion versions were also sold, with different wording.

COMMEMORATIVE TYPE
MARY SEACOLE
Standard portrait of KCIII
Design by: Martin Jennings
Mary Seacole Commemorative
Design by: Sandra Deiana
Edge: THE ONE WHO NURSED
HER SICK on proofs

		As-New	Proof
2023	(not issued for circulation)	£13.00	
1,500 max	.925 sterling silver proof, price new		£82.00
750 max	.925 sterling silver piedfort proof, price new		£135.00
125	.917 gold proof, price new		£3,340.00

COMMEMORATIVE TYPE
LUNAR YEAR OF DRAGON
Standard portrait of KCIII
Design by: Martin Jennings
Dragon and Chinese symbol
Design by: William Webb
Edge: Milled on all versions.

		As-New	Proof
2024 (available from Sep'23)	(not issued for circulation)	£15.50	
3,898 max	Silver 1oz (£2) proof, price new		£103.50
288 max	Silver 5oz (£10) proof, price new		£487.50
50 max	Silver 1kg (£500) proof, price new		£2,716.00
2,888 max	Gold 1/40oz (50p) proof, price new		£99.50
388 max	Gold 1/4oz (£25) proof, price new		£750.00
888 max	Gold 1oz (£100) proof, price new		£2,995.00
128 max	Gold 5oz (£500) proof, price new		£14,190.00

COMMEMORATIVE TYPE
JAMES BOND 1960s (1 of 6)
Standard portrait of KCIII
Design by: Martin Jennings
James Bond Commemorative
Design by: Matt Dent
and Christian Davies
Edge: Milled on all versions.

		As-New	Proof
2024	(not issued for circulation)	£15.50	
4,007 max	Silver 1oz (£2) proof, price new*		£110.00
750 max	Silver 2oz (£5) proof, price new		£213.00
350 max	Silver 5oz (£10) proof, price new		£520.00
650 max	Gold 1/4oz (£25) proof, price new		£799.00
250 max	Gold 1oz (£100) proof, price new*		£2,995.00
100 max	Gold 2oz (£200) proof, price new		£5,890.00

COMMEMORATIVE TYPE
JAMES BOND 1970s (2 of 6)
Standard portrait of KCIII
Design by: Martin Jennings
James Bond Commemorative
Design by: Matt Dent
and Christian Davies
Edge: Milled on all versions.

		As-New	Proof
2024	(not issued for circulation)	£15.50	
4,007 max	Silver 1oz (£2) proof, price new*		£110.00
750 max	Silver 2oz (£5) proof, price new		£213.00
350 max	Silver 5oz (£10) proof, price new		£520.00
650 max	Gold 1/4oz (£25) proof, price new		£799.00
250 max	Gold 1oz (£100) proof, price new*		£2,995.00

*1oz silver and 1oz gold bullion versions were also sold, both with slightly different designs.

183

COMMEMORATIVE TYPE
ROBIN HOOD
Standard portrait of KCIII
Design by: Martin Jennings
Myths & Legends Series
Design by: Jody Clark
Edge: Milled on all versions.

		As-New	Proof
2024	(not issued for circulation)	£15.50	
1,500 max	1oz silver proof (£2), price new		£110.00
500 max	2oz silver proof (£5), price new		£213.00
125 max	1oz gold proof (£100), price new		£2,995 .00

10oz silver bullion versions were also sold, with different wording.

COMMEMORATIV E TYPE
BUCKINGHAM PALACE
Standard portrait of KCIII
Design by: Martin Jennings
Buckingham Palace
Commemorative
Design by: Henry Gray
Edge: Plain Milled on all?

		As-New	Proof
2024	(not issued for circulation, also included in annual sets)	£15.50	£25.00
2,500 max	.925 sterling silver proof, price new		£106.00
800 max	.925 sterling silver piedfort proof, price new		£200.00
2,024 max	Gold 1/40oz (50p) proof, price ne		£99.50
125 max	.917 gold proof, price new		£3,340.00

BU version, standard proof, silver proof and gold £5 version also sold in combination with stamps.

COMMEMORATIVE TYPE
JAMES BOND 1980s (3 of 6)
Standard portrait of KCIII
Design by: Martin Jennings
James Bond Commemorative
Design by: Matt Dent
and Christian Davies
Edge: Milled on all versions.

		As-New	Proof
2024	(not issued for circulation)	£15.50	
4,007 max	Silver 1oz (£2) proof, price new		£110.00
750 max	Silver 2oz (£5) proof, price new		£213.00
350 max	Silver 5oz (£10) proof, price new		£520.00
650 max	Gold 1/4oz (£25) proof, price new		£799.00
250 max	Gold 1oz (£100) proof, price new		£2,995.00

COMMEMORATIVE TYPE
MUSIC LEGENDS 7 (of ?)
Standard portrait of KCIII
Design by: Martin Jennings
George Michael
Design by: Sandra Deiana
Edge: Milled on all versions.

			As-New	Proof
2024	Cu-ni £5 FV	(not issued for circulation)	£15.50	
7,500 max	£5 FV	BU version with added colour, price new	£24.50	
3,500 max		Silver 1oz (£2) proof, with colour details, price new		£108.50
350 max		Silver 2oz (£5) proof, price new		£195.00
175 max		Silver 5oz (£10) proof, price new		£520.00
2,024 max		Gold 1/40oz (50p) proof, price new		£99.50
300 max		Gold 1/4oz (£25) proof, price new		£750.00
150 max		Gold 1oz (£100) proof, price new		£2,770.00

COMMEMORATIVE TYPE
MAID MARIAN
Standard portrait of KCIII
Design by: Martin Jennings
Myths & Legends Series
Design by: Jody Clark
Edge: Milled on all versions.

		As-New	Proof
2024	(not issued for circulation)	£15.50	
1,500 max	1oz silver proof (£2), price new		£110.00
500 max	2oz silver proof (£5), price new		£213.00
125 max	1oz gold proof (£100), price new		£2,995.00

10oz silver bullion versions were also sold, with different wording.

COMMEMORATIVE TYPE
JAMES BOND 1990s (4 of 6)
Standard portrait of KCIII
Design by: Martin Jennings
James Bond Commemorative
Design by: Matt Dent
and Christian Davies
Edge: Milled on all versions.

		As-New	Proof
2024	(not issued for circulation)	£15.50	
4,007 max	Silver 1oz (£2) proof, price new		£110.00
750 max	Silver 2oz (£5) proof, price new		£213.00
250 max	Silver 5oz (£10) proof, price new		£520.00
650 max	Gold 1/4oz (£25) proof, price new		£799.00
250 max	Gold 1oz (£100) proof, price new		£2,995.00
100 max	Gold 2oz (£200) proof, price new		£5,890.00

COMMEMORATIVE TYPE
JAMES BOND 2000s (5 of 6)
Standard portrait of KCIII
Design by: Martin Jennings
James Bond Commemorative
Design by: Matt Dent
and Christian Davies
Edge: Milled on all versions.

		As-New	Proof
2024	(not issued for circulation)	£15.50	
4,007 max	Silver 1oz (£2) proof, price new		£110.00
750 max	Silver 2oz (£5) proof, price new		£213.00
350 max	Silver 5oz (£10) proof, price new		£520.00
650 max	Gold 1/4oz (£25) proof, price new		£799.00
250 max	Gold 1oz (£100) proof, price new		£2,995.00
75 max	Gold 2oz (£200) proof, price new		£5,890.00

COMMEMORATIVE TYPE
JAMES BOND 2010s (6 of 6)
Standard portrait of KCIII
Design by: Martin Jennings
James Bond Commemorative
Design by: Matt Dent
and Christian Davies
Edge: Milled on all versions.

		As-New	Proof
2024	(not issued for circulation)	£15.50	
4,007 max	Silver 1oz (£2) proof, price new		£110.00
750 max	Silver 2oz (£5) proof, price new		£213.00
350 max	Silver 5oz (£10) proof, price new		£520.00
650 max	Gold 1/4oz (£25) proof, price new		£799.00
250 max	Gold 1oz (£100) proof, price new		£2,995.00
75 max	Gold 2oz (£200) proof, price new		£5,890.00

No time or space to add the Myths and Legends series 'Little John' coin, which will no doubt be sold in the same guises as the other Myths and Legends coins.

27.00 mm • 15.71 grammes • .999 Silver • edge: milled

Twenty Pound coins were sold new by the Royal Mint from 2013 to 2020, for £20.00 plus postage. The value of the silver content is currently about £12.25. The coins are not accepted in shops or at any banks or post offices. See also £50 coin on the next page.

OBVERSE 1
Coins 1 - 3

OBVERSE 2, Coins
4 - 8, 10 & 11

5

6, 8, 10 & 11

1

3

Above: 9
(both sides)

2

4

7

* Prices quoted are for coins in original packets.

2013	Coin 1: St. George reverse, 250,000 sold	£16 - £20*
2014	Coin 2: WWI 1914 1918 Britannia reverse	£16 - £20*
2015	Coin 3: Winston Churchill reverse	£16 - £22*
2015	Coin 4: Longest Reign reverse	£18 - £22*
2016	Coin 5: Queen's 90th reverse, 116,354 sold	£17 - £22*
2016	Coin 6: Welsh Dragon reverse (see note, below)	£28.00*
2016	Coin 7: Christmas Nativity scene, 29,929 sold	£24 - £30*
2017	Coin 8: Welsh Dragon (as Coin 6)	£24 - £27*
2017	Coin 9: Royal Wedding, same design as £5, type 45	£17 - £20*
2018	Coin 10: Welsh Dragon (as Coin 6)	£27.00*
2019	Coin 11: Welsh Dragon (as Coin 6, 3,195 sold)	£27.00*
2020	Coin 12: Welsh Dragon (as Coin 6)	£27.00*

The design used on the 2015 Longest Reign coin was also used for a 5oz silver proof (£395.00 price new, 65mm diameter), 1 kilo silver proof (£2000.00 price new, 100mm) and 1 kilo gold proof coins (price new £42,500.00). The 2016 Welsh Dragon coins were sold at the Royal Mint visitor centre in special packaging and later in different, standard packaging. On the Welsh dragon coins the 'TWENTY POUNDS' is incorporated under the dragon and is therefore not included in the wording around the Queen.

The £50 Coin

For a short period the £20 coin appears to have been quite successful for the Royal Mint Ltd, so the marketing department introduced the short-lived £50 coins (and £100 coins, on the next page). The current bullion value of the £50 coin is about £26.50.

A few years ago a gentleman attempted to pay a total of £29,300 worth of Royal Mint £100 coins into his bank account. The bank appear to have contacted the mint, who it seems were getting more of them back than they cared to receive (and once they are out of their packets and have scratches and scrapes they can't sell them again, but still have to recompense the banks), so they issued a memo to the Post Office and to some banks (possibly all banks) in January 2016 telling them not to accept the high value silver (£20, £50 and £100) coins at face value.

This actually had a knock-on effect for other coins deemed as 'commemorative' and as a result it is now practically impossible to redeem standard cu-ni £5 coins at face value and to a lesser degree even the mono-metallic £2 and the older large 50p coins (at least in my experience).

A Royal Mint spokesman says that 'Legal tender allows UK coins to be accepted for payment of debts in court, but only circulating legal tender coins (i.e. the conventional £2 coin and lower values) are designed to be spent and traded at businesses and banks.'

So there is a two-tier legal tender system of circulating coins and non-circulating coins that are legal tender, but aren't really? As far as I'm concerned, with no acceptance at any banks, these coins are all worth whatever the market is willing to pay for them. These were discontinued after 2016, and rightly so!

Britannia Coin   Reverse of Shakespeare Coin

As-New

		As-New
2015	£50 Britannia with lion, in package	£30-£50
2016	£50 Shakespeare theme, in package (14,948 sold)	£40-£60
	Obverse has: ELIZABETH II DG REG FD 50 POUNDS	

189

The £100 Coin

The Royal Mint made and sold its first £100 coin in 2015. 50,000 of them were sold for £100 each. Currently the silver value is about £49.00 and again, I'm not entirely clear on the true legal tender status of these coins (they seem to only be worth £100 when the owner and any potential buyers believe they are, as long as they don't actually try to spend one! See also notes for the silver £50 coins). Late 2015 saw the issue of another £100 coin with the new portrait of the Queen and featuring Buckingham palace on its reverse. The 2016 £100 coin featured Trafalgar Square with the lion in the foreground and Nelson's column in the background. Incidentally, the three designs used for the £100 coins were also used for three coins of the 'Portrait of Britain (2014 and 2016)' series of £5 crown coins. In crown guise they were Tri-Chromatic pad coloured.

The Royal Mint seem to have given up on them now, so I can only assume sales slumped drastically following the revelations that they weren't actually worth what is written on them.

The first £100 Coin (2015)
Standard portrait of Queen Elizabeth II. Design by: Ian Rank-Broadley
The Elizabeth Tower as seen from below. Design by: Glyn Davies and Laura Clancy

The second £100 Coin (2015)
New portrait of QEII with '100 POUNDS 2015'. Design by: Jody Clark
Buckingham Palace with Queen Victoria monument. Design by: Glyn Davies and Laura Clancy

The third and last £100 Coin (2016), Not Illustrated
Portrait of QEII with '100 POUNDS 2015'. Design by: Jody Clark
Trafalgar Square. Design by: Glyn Davies and Laura Clancy

As-New

2015	50,000 max	'Big Ben' tower, specimen in folder	£70-£100
2015	50,000 max	Buckingham Palace, specimen in folder	£70-£100
2016	45,000 max	Trafalgar Square, specimen in folder (14,878 sold)	£75-£100

The Sixpence
Originally a popular 'old school' coin, first made in 1551 as it was conveniently 1/40th of a Pound and people actually used to spend them, until their demonetisation in 1980 (nearly all coin types and denominations were made with the sole intention of being spent in those days - imagine that)! It was re-introduced in 2016 to the same size, weight and silver fineness as the pre 1920 sixpences but is now revalued as six new pence instead of six old pence (which is 2.5p in new pence).

I assume these are aimed at the wedding industry - 'something old, something new and a sixpence in her shoe'? Delightful older sixpence coins in perfect condition are often cheaper and readily available from reputable coin dealers, albeit without the fancy paperwork or packaging.

They were available new for £32.50, in a wedding presentation style box. A Christmas silver sixpence card was available for £22.50. The reverse design was changed in 2023 to feature a CIII monogram and was changed again for the 2024 issue. At the time of writing the 2024 silver sixpence is available in two different types of card packaging for £22.00. The 2016 to 2022 obverse type was the same as the 2015 Britannia £50 coin. 2023 onwards Charles III coins feature the obverse legend CHARLES III DEI GRA REX FID DEF.

A gold version was made in 2021 - Its new-price was £475.00. The 2024 gold version is priced at £590.00

2016 Sixpence -
actual size

Sixpence -
enlarged, reverse
used 2016 - 2022

Introduced as a special optional feature of the Royal Mint Experience tour, the 'Strike Your Own' coins are inexpensive to buy from the source and have proved popular. The exclusivity of the packaging, in that you physically have to be at the Royal Mint premises to get one (even though most of the coins themselves were also made available in some other form of packaging) has caused the odd SYO coin to go a bit potty in terms of resale value. For certain coins, people have travelled to the Royal Mint and gone on many tours over many days and have taken other measures, just to get as many 'Strike Your Own' coins as possible to put straight on to eBay, in order to ride the wave of hype that annoyingly seems to accompany many new coin issues these days. These pages show the standard* SYO coin range so far, with their current market values and other details.

Rumour has it that SYO coins are not quite to the Royal Mint 'Brilliant Uncirculated' standard, as they are not always struck as many times as BU coins. The gate-fold coin cards include some other basic information. The coins themselves are gripped in a plastic holder with a gap at the top to facilitate removal. The cards measure about 12x7cm.

1. 2016 Last Round £1, 18/5/2016 to 31/12/2016.
Heraldic beasts design. None of these coins were made for circulation but they were available in other packs/sets.

2. 2017 New 12-sided £1, 1/1/2017 to 13/10/2017.
Nations of the Crown design. These coins were available in other packs/sets and were also circulated (in standard quality).

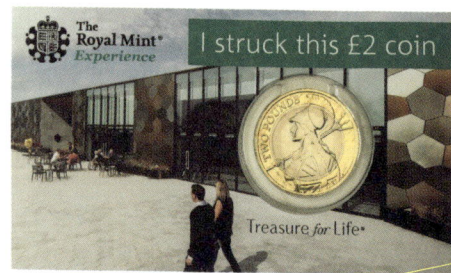

3. 2017 Isaac Newton 50p, 14/10/2017 to 31/12/2017.
4. 2018 Isaac Newton 50p, 1/1/2018 to 18/3/2018.
The 2017 coins were available in other packs/sets and were also circulated (in standard quality). 2018 dated Newton coins were exclusively made available as SYO coins - and as the Royal Mint re-used the cards, they are seen with either 2017 or 2018 printed dates on the back.

5. 2018 Britannia £2, 19/3/2018 to 30/9/2018.
None of these coins were made for circulation but were available in annual BU sets.

*Silver and Gold VIP tour participants can, at a cost of £125.00, strike a silver proof coin which is provided with a COA personally signed by the Queen's assay master.

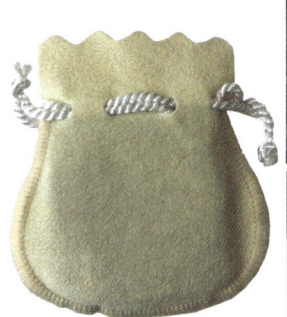

7. 2018 Frankenstein £2, 1/10/2018 to 18/11/2018.
None of these coins were made for circulation but were available in other packs/sets.

6. 2018 Royal Wedding £5, 19 & 20th May 2018.
In a departure from the normal coin-on-a-card format, the Royal Wedding SYO was provided in a plastic capsule, in a drawstring bag accompanied by a 5x5cm printed card. None of these coins were made for circulation but were available in other packs.

8. 2018 Nutcracker £5, 19/11/2018 to 31/12/2018.
The Christmas Nutcracker SYO was provided in a plastic capsule, in the same type of drawstring bag as above right, accompanied by a 5x5cm printed card. None of these coins were made for circulation but were available in other packs.

9. 2019 NEW PENCE 50p, 1/1/2019 to 31/3/2019.
The first SYO of 2019 is the 'NEW PENCE' 50p - the reverse design that was originally used 1969-1981 combined with a 2019 obverse. This coin is also included in proof/silver proof form in special 2019 sets of 50p coins (and may also appear in a BU set).

10. 2019 Britannia £2, 1/4/2019 to 27/6/2019.
Same as No. 5, shown on the previous page. None of these coins were made for circulation but were available in annual BU sets.

11. 2019 Conan Doyle 50p, 28/6/2019 to 23/9/2019.
This coin was also included in annual sets and individual BU packs.

193

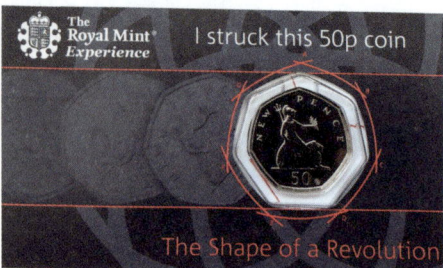

12. 2019 50p with mint mark, 24/9/2019 to 28/10/2019.
This coin was also sold in individual BU packs.

14. 2019 Snowman & Boy 50p, 1/12/2019 to 31/12/2019.
This was the second Snowman themed coin - the first was never offered in SYO guise. This coin was also available in individual BU packs.

15. 2020 Britannia £2, 1/1/2020 to 30/1/2020.
Same as No. 5, shown on the previous page spread. None of these coins were made for circulation but were available in annual BU sets.

13. 2019 Wallace & Gromit 50p, 29/10/2019 to 30/11/2019.
This coin was also sold in individual BU packs.

16. 2020 Brexit on the day, 31/1/2020.
This coin was also sold in individual BU packs and was also circulated in large numbers (in normal circulation quality)

17. 2020 Brexit 50p, 1/2/2020 to 12/2/2020.
For Brexit coins not struck on the day the packaging was very similar (not illustrated) - on the front both references to the 31 January 2020 are omitted and the 'I struck this 50p coin ' has been moved down a line and is also yellow in colour to match the 'A VOTE TO LEAVE AND A NEW ERA' text above the coin.

18. 2020 Megalosaurus 50p, 13/2/2020 to 15/3/2020. This coin was also sold in individual BU packs.

19. 2020 Iguanodon 50p, 16/3/2020 to 17/3/2020 and from 31/7/2020 to 17/9/2020. This coin was also sold in individual BU packs.

20. 2021 50th Anniversary of Decimalisation 50p, 29/5/2021 to 23/9/2021 This coin was also sold in individual BU packs.

21. 2021 Britannia £2 24/9/2021 to 8/11/2021. This coin was also included in annual BU sets.

22. 2021 Snowman & Boy 50p, 19/11/2021 to 3/1/2022. This coin was also sold in individual BU packs.

23. 2022 Platinum Jubilee 50p, 4/1/2022 to 13/3/2022. This coin was also included in annual BU sets.

24. 2022 Platinum Jubilee On-The-Day 50p, 6/2/2022.*

25. 2022 FA Cup £2, 14/3/2022 to 19/6/2022.*

26. 2022 Commonwealth Games 50p, 20/5/2022 to 21/8/2022.*

27. 2022 Pooh & Friends 50p, 22/8/2022 to 27/10/2022.*

28. 2022 QEII Memorial 50p, 28/10/2022 to 20/11/2022.

29. 2022 Harry Potter 50p, 21/11/2022 to 9/12/2022.*

30. 2022 Hogwarts Express 50p, 10/12/2022 to 24/12/2022.*

31. 2023 Edward Jenner £2, 6/1/2023 to 15/2/2023.*

32. 2023 Dumbledore 50p, 16/2/2023 to 26/3/2023.*

33. 2023 Hogwarts School 50p, 27/3/2023 to 5/5/2023.*

34. 2023 Coronation 50p on the day, 6/5/2023.*

36. 2023 J R R Tolkien £2, 21/8/2023 to 15/10/2023.*

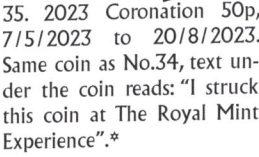

35. 2023 Coronation 50p, 7/5/2023 to 20/8/2023. Same coin as No.34, text under the coin reads: "I struck this coin at The Royal Mint Experience".*

37. Right: 2023 Atlantic Salmon 50p, 16/10/2023 to 5/11/2023.

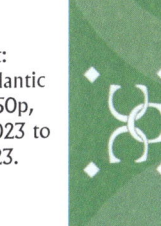

* Coins were also sold in individual BU packs

38. 2023 Snowman 50p, 6/11/2023 to 24/12/2023.*

39. 2024 Bees £1, 2/1/2024 to 31/1/2024. Also in BU sets.

40. 2024 T-Rex 50p, 1/2/2024 to 21/3/2024. *

41. 2024 Stegasaurus 50p, 22/3/2024 to 16/5/2024. *

42. 2024 Diplodocus 50p, 17/5/2024 to 7/7/2024. *

43. 2024 D-Day 50p, 6/6/2024 one day only. *

44. 2024 Team GB 50p, 8/7/2024 to 1/9/2024. *

Strike Your Own (SYO) Coins

Year	Mintage	Coin	Price
2016	40,848	Coin 1, The Last Round Pound	£18
2017	45,726	Coin 2, The New Pound	£15
2017	4,957	Coin 3, Isaac Newton 50p (dated 2017)	£30
2018	20,826	Coin 4, Isaac Newton 50p (dated 2018, exclusively SYO)	£30
2018	19,077	Coin 5, Britannia £2	£25
2018	508	Coin 6, Harry & Meghan £5 (struck on 19 & 20/5/18)	£275*
2018	6,740	Coin 7, Frankenstein £2	£22
2018	3,808	Coin 8, Nutcracker Christmas £5	£28
2019	13,082	Coin 9, NEW PENCE Fifty Pence (exclusively SYO)	£8
2019	9,770	Coin 10, Britannia £2	£20
2019	8,197	Coin 11, Conan Doyle (Sherlock Holmes) 50p	£20
2019	3,428	Coin 12, NEW PENCE 50p with mint-mark	£25
2019	3,429	Coin 13, Wallace & Gromit 50p	£25
2019	877	Coin 14, Snowman & Boy 50p	£70*
2020	2,048	Coin 15, Britannia £2	£25
2020	6,106	Coin 16, Brexit 50p, struck on the day	£10
2020	1,793	Coin 17, Brexit 50p	£15
2020	3,679	Coin 18, Megalosaurus 50p	£21
2020	2,913	Coin 19, Iguanodon 50p	£16
2021	8,167	Coin 20, Decimalisation anniversary 50p	£13
2021	2,971	Coin 21, Britannia £2	£20
2021	3,975	Coin 22, Snowman & Boy 50p	£35
2022		Coin 23, Platinum Jubilee 50p	£15
2022		Coin 24, Platinum Jubilee, on the day 50p	£17
2022		Coin 25, FA Cup £2	£20
2022		Coin 26, Commonwealth Games 50p	£60*
2022		Coin 27, Pooh & Friends 50p	£20
2022	3,995	Coin 28, HM Queen Memorial 50p (Charles III)	£15
2022		Coin 29, Harry Potter 50p	£50
2022		Coin 30, Harry Potter Hogwarts Express 50p	£22
2023		Coin 31, Edward Jenner 50p	£20
2023		Coin 32, Dumbledore 50p	£25
2023		Coin 33, Hogwarts School 50p	£15
2023		Coin 34, Coronation (on day) 50p	£25
2023		Coin 35, Coronation 50p	£18
2023		Coin 36, Tolkien £2	£20
2023		Coin 37, Atlantic Salmon 50p	£35*
2023		Coin 38, Snowman 50p	£17
2024		Coin 39, Bees £1	£20
2024		Coin 40, T-Rex 50p	£20
2024		Coin 41, Stegasaurus 50p	£20
2024		Coin 42, Diplodocus 50p	£20
2024		Coin 43, D-Day 50p	£40
2024		Coin 44, Team GB 50p	£20
2024		Coin 45, RNLI 50p 2/9/24 to 30/9/24 (not shown)	£20
2024		Coin 46, Gruffalo's Child 50p 1/10/24 to date (not shown)	£20

* Prices volatile as not often offered for sale. At least one fake Harry & Meghan card has been seen.

199

From 1971 to 1982, The Royal Mint issued proof coin sets sealed in plastic, enclosed in lightweight card envelopes. The coins within often tone badly over time and the card outer case is sometimes worse for wear. Values at the upper end of the ranges shown below are usually for sets in very good condition. Values fluctuate and sets can often be purchased for less and sometimes they sell for more, especially as gifts for round birthday's, so expect 1978, 1988 and 1998 to potentially climb in value a little during 2018.

Year	No. of Coins.	Price New*	Notes	Value
1971	6	£3.15		£6 - £12
1972	7	£3.25	Inc. Crown	£13 - £20
1973	6	£5.90*		£8 - £12
1974	6	£5.90*		£8 - £12
1975	6	£5.90*		£8 - £12
1976	6	£5.90*		£8 - £12
1977	7	£8.30*	Inc. Crown	£8 - £12
1978	6	£6.40*		£8 - £12
1979	6	£6.40*		£8 - £12
1980	6	£9.00		£8 - £10
1981	6	£9.95		£8 - £12
1982	7	£11.95	20p added	£8 - £12

In 1983, the packaging was changed to a blue leatherette bookshelf type case.

Year	No. of Coins.	Price New*	Notes	Value
1983	8	£17.25	£1 added	£10 - £15
1984	8	£17.95		£10 - £15

From 1985 onward, two types of packaging were offered: The "standard" blue leatherette case, and the "deluxe" red leather case. Values don't tend to be vastly different.

Year	No. of Coins.	Price New*	Notes	Value
1985	7	£18.75 blue / £25.75 red		£10 - £15
1986	8	£21.25 blue / £28.25 red	Inc. commem. £2	£10 - £15
1987	7	£18.95 blue / £25.95 red		£10 - £15
1988	7	£18.95 blue / £25.95 red		£15 - £20
1989	9	£22.95 blue / £29.95 red	Inc. both £2	£35 - £50
1990	8	£21.95 blue / £29.95 red		£12 - £20
1991	7	£22.95 blue / £29.95 red		£12 - £20
1992	9	£27.50 blue / £34.50 red	2x 10p, 2x 50p	£50 - £65
1993	8	£28.75 blue / £35.50 red	Inc. Crown	£15 - £20
1994	8	£24.75 blue / £32.50 red	Inc. commem £2	£15 - £20
1995	8	£26.65 blue / £34.50 red		£15 - £20
1996	9	£29.75 blue / £37.50 red		£20 - £30
1997	10	£32.50 blue / £39.50 red		£20 - £30
1998	10	£32.95 blue / £39.95 red		£30 - £50
1999	9	£33.95 blue / £39.95 red		£40 - £50
2000	10	£29.95 std / £39.95 special		£20 - £30

* The prices marked with an asterisk are what the sets were originally sold for in the USA, converted to GBP at the then exchange rate - source 'Standard Catalog of World Coins' published by KP books.

From 2001 on, it is accepted that all sets will contain the standard 8 pieces: 1p, 2p, 5p, 10p, 20p, 50p, £1, and £2. The Royal Mint, also produced deluxe proof sets and executive proof sets, which all contain the same coins but have better packaging. The deluxe and executive sets are sometimes sold for up to 20% more than the standard sets.

Sets that include currently higher priced coins (e.g. the 2009 set containing the Kew Gardens 50p) are priced higher than others, which is a little odd really, as the numbers of proof sets (and therefore proof coins) made is generally around the same - approximately 35,000 sets were sold in 2009, which is about the same as the number of sets sold in 2008, but just because the 2008 set doesn't include a 'special' coin, it's currently worth well over £100 less! Proof coins are of course very different to their normal circulation counterparts, but in general they don't seem to be viewed as different types of coins by the public, but rather as higher quality versions of the normal coins.

Recently 'Premium' sets have been introduced which include a medallion. In 2013 the Royal Mint made the proof sets available in reduced size 'definitive' form, which include just the standard 1p to £2, a 'commemorative' set which is just the commemorative 50p, £1, £2 and £5 coins and also a complete set (named a 'Collector set') made up of all the coins. I'm starting to lose track, and I honestly don't think the packaging will play much of a roll in the future - the coins are what they are, regardless of the current sales/packaging strategy! Obviously the definitive and commemorative 'short' sets are worth less than the full sets. They now also sell silver proof sets of all of the annual coins, silver proof sets of just the commemorative coins, silver proof piedfort sets of just the commemorative coins and gold proof sets of just the commemorative coins!

If the various types of packaging, alloys and coin configurations weren't confusing enough, the annual proof sets no longer actually contain all of the coins from a given year.

Year	No. of Coins.	Price New (deluxe to 2011)	Value
2001	10	£39.50	£20 - £30
2002	9	£45.50	£20 - £30
2003	11	£46.50	£20 - £30
2004	10	£39.95	£20 - £30
2005	12	£48.50	£40 - £50
2006	13	£49.95	£40 - £50
2007	12	£49.95	£40 - £50
2008	11	£49.95	£40 - £50
2009	12	£49.99	£200 - £250
2010	13	£49.99	£50 - £60
2011	14	£51.25	£180 - £200
2012	10	£75.00 "Collector set"	£60 - £90
2013	15	£110.00 "Collector set"	£130 - £150
2014	14	£110.00 "Collector set"	£170 - £200
2015	13	£110.00 "Collector set"	£100 - £130
2016 (6,919 sold)	16	£145.00 "Collector set"	£170 - £200
2017 & 2018	13	£145.00 "Collector set"	£170-£200
2019 - 2021		£155.00 "Collector set", price new	

In 1982, the Royal Mint introduced Brilliant Uncirculated sets, which contain most of the coins contained in the Proof sets (crowns normally not included). These sets do not have proof-quality striking, and are packaged in a folder style with text to provide historic background information and specifications of the coins.

Year	Pieces	Coins	Notes
1982	7	½p, 1p, 2p, 5p, 10p, 20p, 50p	
1983	8	½p, 1p, 2p, 5p, 10p, 20p, 50p, £1	new £1 added
1984	8	½p, 1p, 2p, 5p, 10p, 20p, 50p, £1	
1985	7	1p, 2p, 5p, 10p, 20p, 50p, £1	½p removed
1986	8	1p, 2p, 5p, 10p, 20p, 50p, £1, £2	Commonwealth Games
1987	7	1p, 2p, 5p, 10p, 20p, 50p, £1	
1988	7	1p, 2p, 5p, 10p, 20p, 50p, £1	
1989	7	1p, 2p, 5p, 10p, 20p, 50p, £1	
1990	8	1p, 2p, 5p, 5p, 10p, 20p, 50p, £1	Large & small 5p
1991	7	1p, 2p, 5p, 10p, 20p, 50p, £1	
1992	9	1p, 2p, 5p, 10p, 10p, 20p, 50p, 50p, £1	lg & sm 10p; EEC 50p
1993	8	1p, 2p, 5p, 10p, 20p, 50p, £1, £5	Coronation Anniversary
1994	8	1p, 2p, 5p, 10p, 20p, 50p, £1, £2	Bank of England
1995	8	1p, 2p, 5p, 10p, 20p, 50p, £1, £2	Dove of Peace
1996	8	1p, 2p, 5p, 10p, 20p, 50p, £1, £2	Football
1997	9	1p, 2p, 5p, 10p, 20p, 50p, 50p, £1, £2	Large & small 50p
1998	9	1p, 2p, 5p, 10p, 20p, 50p, 50p, £1, £2	EU
1999	8	1p, 2p, 5p, 10p, 20p, 50p, £1, £2	Rugby £2 (no normal £2)
2000	9	1p, 2p, 5p, 10p, 20p, 50p, 50p, £1, £2	Public Libraries
2001	9	1p, 2p, 5p, 10p, 20p, 50p, £1, £2, £2	Marconi
2002	8	1p, 2p, 5p, 10p, 20p, 50p, £1, £2	
2003	10	1p, 2p, 5p, 10p, 20p, 50p, 50p, £1, £2, £2	Women's Suffrage, DNA
2004	10	1p, 2p, 5p, 10p, 20p, 50p, 50p, £1, £2, £2	Bannister, Trevithick
2005	10	1p, 2p, 5p, 10p, 20p, 50p, 50p, £1, £2, £2	Dictionary, Guy Fawkes
2006	10	1p, 2p, 5p, 10p, 20p, 50p, 50p, £1, £2, £2	Victoria Cross, Brunel
2007	9	1p, 2p, 5p, 10p, 20p, 50p, £1, £2, £2	Slave trade, Act of Union
2008	7	1p - £1 old designs 'Emblems of Britain'	
2008	7	1p - £1 new designs	
2008	14	1p - £1 both designs	
2008	9	1p, 2p, 5p, 10p, 20p, 50p, £1, £2, £2	Old designs. Olympic £2.
2009	11	1p, 2p, 5p, 10p, 20p, 50p, 50p, £1, £2, £2, £2	Kew, Burns, Darwin.
2010	8	1p, 2p, 5p, 10,p 20p, 50p, £1, £2	
2011	13	1p, 2p, 5p, 10p, 20p, 50p, 50p, £1 x3, £2 x3	

Year	Pieces	Coins	Notes
2011	13	1p, 2p, 5p, 10p, 20p, 50p, 50p, £1 x3, £2 x3	
2012	10	1p, 2p, 5p, 10p, 20p, 50p, £1, £2, £2, £5	
2013	15	1p, 2p, 5p, 10p, 20p, 50p x2, £1 x3, £2 x4, £5	
2014	14	1p, 2p, 5p, 10p, 20p, 50p x2, £1 x3, £2 x3, £5	
2015	13	1p, 2p, 5p, 10p, 20p, 50p x2, £1, £2 x3, £5 x2	
2016	16	1p, 2p, 5p, 10p, 20p, 50p x2, £1 x2, £2 x6, £5	£55 price new
2017/18	13	1p, 2p, 5p, 10p, 20p, 50p x2, £1, £2 x3, £5 x2	£55 price new
2019-2021			£55 price new

The BU sets tend to sell from between 2.5x to 5x the face value of the coins included. Sets in mint condition with absolutely no toning on any of the coins will attract a premium. Some sets are affected by the current higher prices of some of the coins contained within, for example the 2009 set is affected by the current value of the Kew Gardens 50p. See 50p Commemorative Type 13 for further details. 106,332 of the 2009 set were sold.

Recently BU sets of 'definitive' coins have also been sold, which just contain the standard 1p to £2 coins and no commemoratives. Over the years there have also been other packaging options Including a baby theme and wedding theme.

The sets below were specially marketed for commemorative or promotional purposes. Other later sets exist and may be included in a future edition. To be honest though, they aren't really incredibly popular and the total value is usually based strongly on the sum of the value of the coins contained within.

1983	7	½p, 1p, 2p, 5p, 10p, 20p, 50p	
		Specially packaged set for the H J Heinz Company.	
1983	8	½p, 1p, 2p, 5p, 10p, 20p, 50p, £1	
		Specially packaged set for the Martini & Rossi Company.	
1988	7	1p, 2p, 5p, 10p, 20p, 50p, £1	
		Special package celebrating Australia's Bicentennial.	
1996	14 (7+7)	1p, 2p, 5p, 10p, 20p, 50p, £1; pre-decimal 1/2d, 1d, 3d, 6d, 1/, 2/, 2/6d	
		Special package commemorating 25 years of decimalisation.	
2000	9	1p, 2p, 5p, 10p, 20p, 50p, £1, £2, £5 (Millennium)	
		In special "Time Capsule" packaging.	
2004	3	50p (Roger Bannister), £1 (Forth bridge), £2 (Trevithick's Locomotive)	
		"Celebrating Human Achievement"	
2005	3	50p (Johnson's dictionary), £1 (Menai bridge), £2 (Guy Fawkes)	
		new packaging of commemorative issues	

The following are sterling (.925) silver proof sets, designed for various occasions, including the introduction of the coins themselves. These are normally found in hard acrylic capsules, enclosed in a clam-shell case, and with a certificate from the Royal Mint. Some issues post 1998 are included in the main section.

Please note that the coins and sets of coins on the following four pages are not necessarily exhaustive. The pairs and sets of coins in particular have been issued in an almost random fashion over the years and tend to have sold new in fairly low numbers. On the second hand market years later there are very few, if any, that are worth substantially more than the total value of the coins contained within.

Five Pence
1990	35,000	large & small sized pair	£25.00

Ten Pence
1992	35,000	large & small sized pair	£25.00

Fifty Pence
1997	10,304	large & small sized pair	£25.00
1998	22,078	NHS issue and EU issue pair	£55.00
1998		pair, EU silver proof & EU silver Piedfort	£70.00

One Pound
1983 - 88	1,000	set of 6 regional designs, Arms, Shield	£75.00
1984 - 87	50,000	set of 4 regional designs	£90.00
1994 - 97	25,000	set of 4 regional designs	£100.00
1999 - 2002	25,000	set of 4 regional designs	£100.00

Two Pounds
1989	25,000	Bill of Rights & Claim of Rights pair	£60.00
1997	40,000	new bi-metallic circulation issue	£20.00
1998	25,000	new portrait on the circulation issue	£20.00
1997/98		bi-metallic Maklouf & Rank-Broadley pair	£35.00

ALERT

It seems that official Royal Mint cases were once obtainable, and some sets were assembled on the secondary market, with the individual coins and accompanying certificates. Original RM-issued sets usually contain a single certificate, listing each coin in the set.

1981	5,000	set, all issues, 1/2p-50p in base metals, sterling 25p commemorative, 22k gold Sovereign & £5	£700.00
1981		pair, sterling 25p commemorative, 22k gold Sovereign	£250.00
1992	1,000	set, both lg and sm 10p, 50p EEC, and £1	£75.00
1993	1,000	set, 50p EEC, £1, and £5 Coronation commem.	£75.00
1994	2,000	set, 50p D-Day, £1, and £2 Bank of England	£70.00
1995	1,000	silver set, peace £2, UN £2 and £1 coin	£50.00
1996	1,000	silver set, £5, £2 and £1 coins	£50.00
1996		set, all issues, 1p-£1 (25th Anniversary of Decimalisation)	£70.00
	500	pair, 1996 70th Birthday crown & 1997 Royal Wedding Jubilee crown	£60.00
1997		set, 50p, £1, £2, £5 Wedding Jubilee, £2 Britannia	£120.00
1999		set, £5 Millennium, £2 Britannia	£40.00
1999		set, £2 Britannia, £10 stamp	
2000	13,180	set, 1p-£5 Millennium, plus Maundy set (13 pieces)	£200.00
2000		£5 Millennium, plus YR2000 serial numbered £20 note	
		pair, 2002 Silver Jubilee crown & 2003 Coronation Jubilee crown	£60.00
2004		pair, 2004 Entente Cordiale crown & French €1 1/2 commem.	£75.00
2004	750	set, 50p Bannister, £1 Forth Bridge, £2 Trevithick, £5 Entente Cordiale £2 Britannia.	£75.00
-		1999, 2001, 2002, 2003 £2 Britannia uncirculated.	£80.00
2005		Pair of silver proof £5 coins - Nelson and Trafalgar	£65.00
2008		Set of 14 £1 coins, all designs 1983 to 2008. All dated 2008 with gold plated details	£300.00
2015		Silver proof set of definitive coins with the new portrait of the Queen, price new	£240.00
2022		QEII Memorial coin set, 10 coins, each with 26 over 22 mintmark	
		in BU form, price new	£75.00
		in silver proof form (max 1,500), price new	£465.00
		in gold proof form (max 200), price new	£10,715.00
		in platinum proof form (max 96), price new	£13,645.00

The following set was struck in .917 (22K) gold.

2002	2,002	set, 1p-£5 Golden Jubilee, plus Maundy set (13 pieces)	no data

Values of most later sets comprising of various combinations of coins that the Royal Mint offer tend to be worth about the same as the sum of the individual coins they contain.

Piedforts are coins that are double the thickness and weight of the normal version, and are almost always struck in sterling (.925) silver. These are normally found in hard acrylic capsules, enclosed in a clam-shell case, and with a certificate from the Royal Mint. Some of these coins are also listed in the main section of this book.

Five Pence

1990	20,000	.925 sterling silver, small size Piedfort	£20.00

Ten Pence

1992		.925 sterling silver, small size Piedfort	£20.00
1992		.925 sterling silver, pair of both sizes Piedfort	£26.00

Twenty Pence

1982		.925 sterling silver, Piedfort	£25.00

Fifty Pence

1997	7,192	.925 sterling silver, small size Piedfort	£50.00
1998		EEC & NHS pair, Piedfort	£60.00
1992/3 & 1998		.925 sterling silver Piedfort of both EU related coins	£85.00

One Pound

1983 - 88	500	set of 6 regional designs, Arms, Shield, Piedfort	£200.00
1984 - 87	10,000	.925 sterling silver, proof set of 4 Piedfort	£90.00
1994 - 97		.925 sterling silver, proof set of 4 Piedfort	£100.00
1999-2002	10,000	.925 sterling silver, proof set of 4 Piedfort	£100.00
2004-2007	1,400	.925 sterling silver, proof set of 4 Piedfort	£140.00

Two Pounds

1989	10,000	Bill of Rights & Claim of Rights pair, Piedfort	£30.00
1997	10,000	.925 sterling silver, Piedfort	£30.00
1998	10,000	.925 sterling silver, Piedfort	£30.00
1997/98	.10,000	925 sterling silver, Piedfort (pair)	£60.00
1999	10,000	.925 sterling silver, proof Piedfort HOLOGRAM	£100.00

Five Pounds

2005		Nelson & Trafalgar pair, Piedfort	£70.00

Sets

2003		set, 50p WPSU, £1 Royal Arms, £2 DNA Piedfort	£60.00
2004	7500	set, 50p Bannister, £1 Forth Bridge, £2 Trevithick Piedfort	£100.00
2005		set, 50p Johnson's Dictionary, £1 Menai Bridge, £2 Gunpowder Plot, £2 World War II Piedfort	£100.00
2007		£5, both £2 coins, £1 and 50p Piedfort	£150.00
2008		2x £5 coins, £2 and £1 Piedfort	£200.00
2008		The 7 new Dent design coins as silver Piedforts	£300.00
2009		Piedfort gold proof set of 16x difference 50 pence's	£ EXPENSIVE
2010		£5, £2, both £1 coins and the 50p	£200.00

Sets

2010/2011	Capital cities 4x £1 set	£300.00
2013	4x £5 coins, each with different Queen portrait	£335.00
2013	The 5 Commemorative coins + the 2 £1 coins	£560.00 new price
2013	Pair of London Underground £2 coins	£175.00
2014	The 4 Commemorative coins + the 2 £1 coins	£400.00
2015	The 5 Commemorative coins	£300.00

SPECIAL COLLECTOR ISSUES - PATTERNS

Special Collector Issues (Patterns)

A trial bi-metallic piece was issued in 1994 (predecessor to the £2 bi-metallic). The obverse shows a cutty (ship), while the reverse carries the Maklouf portrait of QEII. The ring bears the legend "ROYAL MINT TRIAL PATTERN", and an edge legend of 'ANNO REGNIA XLVI, DECUS ET TUTAMEN". See the £2 section.

Pattern sets issued by the Royal Mint to preview the new issue of "Bridges" £1 coins. All of these coins carry the date of 2003, and rather than having a face value, they are labelled as "PATTERN".

2003	7,500	.925 sterling silver, 7,500 , proof set of 4	£120.00
	3,000	.917 gold proof set of 4	£2,600.00

A continuation of the above set, this set shows the "Beasts" series, which was a runner-up in the design competition for the new £1 coinage. All of these coins carry the date of 2004, and rather than having a face value, they are labelled as "PATTERN". Issued, as listed, in both sterling (.925) silver, and 22k (.917) gold.

2004	5,000	.925 sterling silver, proof set of 4	£120.00
	2,250	.917 gold proof set of 4	£2,600.00

207

Coverage for the bullion issues is deliberately 'bare bones' just in order to give you an idea on the vast range of bullion issues sold by the Royal Mint. There are a lot of them!

The silver Britannia issues began in 1997 with proof-only coins. Commencing in 1998, originally the Royal Mint followed a pattern of using the standard Standing Britannia for every other year (even years), while bringing out new unique designs for the odd years. These coins were struck in Britannia silver (.9584 fine) which I thought was the whole point - coins featuring Britannia made of Britannia standard silver. From 2013 onwards they were struck in .999 silver and the diameter was reduced from 40mm to 38.61mm. Also from 2013 the Royal Mint introduced privy marks (on the edge) and also larger 5oz silver coins, the latter are not included in this book. From 2016 the new Jody Clark bust replaced the Ian Rank-Broadley bust of the queen.

In 2014 the RM introduced the 'Lunar' bullion range of coins, in .999 silver and also in .9999 gold. According to the blurb, they: 'Celebrate Chinese and British heritage with a dynamic design'. The silver 1oz versions are also 38.61mm in diameter.

In 2016 the RM introduced another bullion range of coins called the Queen's Beasts. There are eight different sizes (combined across gold and silver issues), most are available in proof form and some are available as just 'bullion' issues. In 2017 they introduced bullion coins themed as 'Landmarks of Britain' (four different ones so far). It all seems rather complicated and they seem very much aimed at the bullion market and less so for coin collectors. I suspect they are made to compete with other international bullion coin issues.

Bullion Silver (UNC) £2 issues

Year	Mintage	Description	Price
1998	88,909	Standing Britannia (Reverse 2)	£50.00
1999	69,394	Britannia in Chariot (Reverse 1)	£60.00
2000	81,301	Standing Britannia (Reverse 2)	£60.00
2001	44,816	Una & the Lion (Reverse 3)	£70.00
2002	48,215	Standing Britannia (Reverse 2)	£70.00
2003	73,271	Helmeted Britannia facing left (Reverse 4)	£50.00
2004	100,000	Standing Britannia (Reverse 2)	£70.00
2005	100,000	Britannia seated (Reverse 5)	£70.00
2006	100,000	Standing Britannia (Reverse 2)	£40.00
2007	100,000	Britannia seated (Reverse 6)	£50.00
2008	100,000	Standing Britannia (not illustrated)	£50.00
2009	100,000	Britannia in Chariot (Reverse 1)	£50.00
2010	126,367	Bust of Britannia in profile (not illustrated)	£50.00
2011	100,000	Seated Britannia (not illustrated)	£45.00
2012	100,000	Standing Britannia (Reverse 2)	!£40.00
2013		Reverse 2 (exists with snake privy mark#)	£40.00
2014		Reverse 2 (exists with horse privy mark#)	£40.00
2014		Mule error, with Lunar coin obverse (missing edge dentils)*	£100.00
2015		Standing Britannia (Reverse 2)	£40.00
2015		As above, with privy mark#	Scarce
2016		Standing Britannia (Reverse 2)	£35.00

* Not Illustrated. # Snake mintage est. 300,000. Horse est. 1,000,000. Goat est. 200,000

Silver (PROOF) issues (Reverse types from 1998 - 2012 are the same as previous)

1997	£2	4,173	Britannia in Chariot (Reverse 1)	£200.00
	20p	8,686	Both with Raphael Maklouf Bust	£20.00
1998	£2	2,168		£70.00
	20p	2,724		£20.00
2001	£2	3,047		£70.00
	20p	826		£20.00
2003	£2	1,833		£70.00
	20p	1,003		£20.00
2004	£2	5,000		£120.00
2005	£2	2,500		£70.00
2006	£2	2,500	With gold plated details	£130.00
2007	£2	5,147		£70.00
2008	£2	2,500		£70.00
	20p	725		£30.00
2009	£2	6,784		£70.00
	£1	2,500		£30.00
	50p	2,500		£20.00
	20p	3,500		£20.00
2010	£2	6,539		£70.00
	£1	3,497		£20.00
	50p	3,497		£20.00
	20p	4,486		£20.00
2011	£2	4,973		£70.00
	£1	2,483		£20.00
	50p	2,483		£20.00
	20p	2,483		£20.00
2012	£2	2,937		£70.00
2013	£10	4,054	From here on, reverses are not the same as	£300.00+?
	£2	3,468	those used on the bullion series (not illustrated)	£70.00
	20p			£30.00
	10p			£20.00

Britannia
Reverse 1

Britannia
Reverse 2

Britannia
Reverse 3

209

2014	£10		(not illustrated) Price new	£300.00+?
	£2			£70.00
2015	£10	650 max	(not illustrated*) Price new	£395.00
	£2	3000 max		£75.00
2016	£10		(not illustrated) Price new	£300.00+?
	£2	4150 max		£85.00

Britannia - Obverse type used 1998 - 2015

Britannia Reverse 4

Britannia Reverse 5

Britannia Reverse 6

The Lunar series 2014 Horse

Lunar series 2015 Sheep (obverse as 2014 Horse coin)

The Lunar series 2016 Monkey

Special (PROOF) sets

1997	11,832	Set of 4 (£2, £1, 50p, 20p)	£250.00
1998	3,044	Set of 4 (£2, £1, 50p, 20p)	£140.00
2001	4,596	Set of 4 (£2, £1, 50p, 20p)	£140.00
2003	3,623	Set of 4 (£2, £1, 50p, 20p)	£140.00
2005	5,000	Set of 4 (£2, £1, 50p, 20p)	£150.00
2006	-	Set of 5x different £2 with gold plated details	£250.00
2007	2,500	Set of 4 (£2, £1, 50p, 20p)	£140.00
2007		Set of 6 different £1 proofs	£150.00
2008		Set of 4 (£2, £1, 50p, 20p)	£140.00
2009		Set of 4 (£2, £1, 50p, 20p)	£140.00
2010		Set of 4 (£2, £1, 50p, 20p)	£140.00
2011		Set of 4 (£2, £1, 50p, 20p)	£150.00
2012		Set of 4 (£2, £1, 50p, 20p)	£150.00
2013	Now in .999 silver	Set of 5 (£2, £1, 50p, 20p, 10p)	£200.00
		Pair of 20p and 10p	£37.50 new price
2014		Set of 5	£200.00
2015			

Platinum 2007 Coins were issued to mark the 20th Anniversary of the 'Britannia'

2007	£10		1/10 oz Platinum	£200.00
2007	£25		1/4 oz Platinum	£450.00
2007		250	Set of 4 Platinum coins	£3,000.00

Lunar coins, proof issue prices (bullion versions tend to sell for about 2-2.5x bullion value)

2014	Horse design, 1 ounce proof .999 Silver see previous page for picture	£82.50
	Mule error,* with Britannia coin obverse (edge dentils present)	£80.00
	Horse, 5 ounce proof .999 silver	£300.00
	Horse, 1 ounce proof .9999 gold	£1,500.00
2015	Sheep, 1 ounce proof .999 silver	£82.50
	Sheep, Tenth of an ounce proof .9999 gold	£200.00
	Sheep, 1 ounce proof .999 silver (gold plated)	£110.00
	Sheep, 1 ounce proof .9999 gold	£1,950.00
	Sheep, 5 ounce proof .999 silver	£350.00
	Sheep, 5 ounce proof .9999 gold	£7,500.00
2016	Monkey, 1 ounce .999 silver	£82.50
	Monkey, Tenth of an ounce proof .9999 gold	£175.00
	Monkey, 1 ounce proof .9999 gold	£1,450.00
	Monkey, 5 ounce proof .999 Silver	£395.00
	Monkey, 5 ounce proof .9999 gold	£7,500.00
	Monkey, 1kg proof, .999 silver	£2,000.00
	Monkey, 1kg proof, .9999 gold	£42,500.00

All 2014 - 2018 lunar reverse designs are by Wuon-Gean Ho. The 2017 lunar coins featured a rooster, 2018 was a dog, 2019 was a pig by Harry Brockway, for 2020 it was a rat by P J Lynch and 2021 was an ox by Harry Brockway. Both of the recent one were also made available in base metal BU form.   * Est. mintage 33,000.

211

Gold Britannia issues began in 1987, as both bullion issues as well as proof issues. The values of the bullion issues are based on the value of the gold content, which fluctuates daily. The prices for these issues are given only as a guideline.

Bullion .917 Gold (UNC) Issues

£10	tenth ounce	Bullion Value + 30 to 50%
£25	quarter ounce	Bullion Value + 12 to 25%
£50	half ounce	Bullion Value + 8 to 20%
£100	one ounce	Bullion Value + 5 to 15%

The following are 4-piece sets, each coin encapsulated, and housed in a clamshell case,.

Special PROOF sets of 4 coins (for some dates, 3 or 5 coin sets were issued)

1987	10,000	Britannia standing	£4,000.00
1988	3,505	Britannia standing	£4,000.00
1989	2,268	Britannia standing	£4,000.00
1990	527	Britannia standing	£4,100.00
1991	509	Britannia standing	£4,100.00
1992	500	Britannia standing	£4,100.00
1993	462	Britannia standing	£4,200.00
1994	435	Britannia standing	£4,100.00
1995	500	Britannia standing	£4,100.00
1996	483	Britannia standing	£4,100.00
1997	892	Britannia standing	£4,100.00
1998	750	Britannia standing	£4,100.00
1999	750	Britannia standing	£4,100.00
2000	750	Britannia standing	£4,100.00
2001	1,000	Una & the Lion	£4,100.00
2002	945	Britannia standing	£4,100.00
2003	1,250	Britannia with Helmet	£4,100.00
2004	973	Britannia standing	£4,100.00
2005	1,439	Britannia seated	£4,100.00
2006	1,163	Britannia standing	£4,100.00
2007	1,250	Britannia seated	£4,100.00
2008	1,250	Britannia standing	£4,100.00
2009	797 max	Britannia standing in chariot	£4,200.00
2010	867 max	Britannia bust in profile	£4,200.00
2011	698 max	4 coin set	£4,200.00
		3 coin set	£3,200.00
2012	352	Britannia standing 4 coin set	£4,200.00
	99	3 coin set	no data
2013	261	Now .9999 gold	£4,200.00
	136+90 premium	3 coin set	no data
2014		6 coin set	no data
		3 coin set	no data

2015	250 max	6 coin set	no data
	250 max	3 coin set	no data
2016	175 max	6 coin set	no data
	70 max	3 coin premium set	£1,450.00 new price!

Britannia (PROOF) individual cased coins

£100	1997	£3,000.00
£100	Other dates	£2,300.00-£2,500.00
£50	All dates	£1,200.00-£1,400.00
£25	All dates	£600.00-£700.00
£10	All dates	Around £250.00

Britannia (PROOF) platinum cased coins

Values of platinum Britannia coins tend to be as much as 4x the metal value. In comparison to the gold and silver issues, they are not often offered for sale.

The Queen's Beasts

In 2016 the Royal Mint introduced the Queen's Beasts series. There are eight different sizes (combined across gold and silver issues). This book aims to focus on actual coins, rather than the ever diversifying range of gold and silver coins that are not really coins at all in the strictest sense.

Gold Sovereign-based single coins are defined as non-commemorative Five Pounds, Two Pounds, Sovereigns and Half Sovereigns struck to normal or proof standards and sold singularly as gold bullion coins or as proof collectors' coins. The non-proof coins do not have boxes or certificates and are normally just traded as gold. Sovereigns and half sovereigns are 22 carat gold (.917 fine) and weigh 7.98g and 3.97g respectively.

Five Pounds

1984	Cased proof only	£2,500.00
1984	Cased proof only with 'U' in circle next to date	£2,500.00
1985	Cased proof only	£2,500.00
1985	with 'U' in circle next to date	£2,400.00
1986	with 'U' in circle next to date	£2,500.00
1987	with 'U' in circle next to date	£2,500.00
1988	with 'U' in circle next to date	£2,500.00
1989	Sovereign Anniversary type (on it's own, from a set)	£3,100.00
1989	Sovereign Anniversary type, cased proof	£3,200.00
1990	with 'U' in circle next to date	£2,500.00
1991	with 'U' in circle next to date	£2,500.00
1992	with 'U' in circle next to date	£2,500.00
1993	with 'U' in circle next to date	£2,500.00
1994	with 'U' in circle next to date	£2,500.00
1995	with 'U' in circle next to date	£2,500.00
1996	with 'U' in circle next to date	£2,500.00
1997	with 'U' in circle next to date	£2,500.00
1998	New portrait	£2,500.00
1999		£2,500.00
2000		£2,500.00
2000	with 'U' in circle next to date	£2,500.00
2001		£2,500.00
2002	Shield reverse	£2,500.00
2003 to 2010		£2,500.00
2011		£2,500.00
2012		£2,500.00
2013 to 2015		£2,500.00

Two Pounds (double sovereign)

All are cased proofs. The £2 coin has not often been issued on its own.

1987		£1,100.00
1988		£1,100.00
1989	Sovereign Anniversary type	£1,700.00
1990		£1,100.00
1991		£1,100.00
1992		£1,100.00
1993		£1,100.00
1994	(see 1994 error commemorative type 4 £2 coin)	
1996		£1,100.00
2014	In connection with birth of Prince George	£1,100.00

Sovereigns, loose bullion type

Sovereigns of the 1970s and 1980s are generally traded at their bullion value. They contain 7.32 grammes of fine gold. Particularly perfect examples may be worth a slight premium. The dates struck were as follows:

1974, 1976, 1978, 1979, 1980, 1981 and 1982	Bullion Value

Modern bullion type sovereigns, from 2000 to date, tend to sell for a little more than bullion value as follows (very new coins can sell for more):

	£480.00 to £520.00

Sovereigns, cased proof type

1979		£500.00
1980		£500.00
1981		£500.00
1982		£500.00
1983		£500.00
1984		£500.00
1985		£510.00
1986		£500.00
1987		£500.00
1988		£520.00
1989	500th Anniversary of the Sovereign reverse	£1,500.00
1990		£650.00
1991		£650.00
1992		£770.00
1993		£650.00
1994		£650.00
1995		£600.00
1996		£600.00
1997		£600.00
1998		£500.00
1999		£500.00
2000		£500.00
2001		£500.00
2002	Shield reverse	£500.00
2003		£500.00
2004		£500.00
2005 to 2013	(2005 and 2012 had alternate St. George reverses)	£500.00
2014* and 2015		£500.00
2016		£520.00
2017		£520.00

* Also reported with proof reverse and normal BU obverse.

215

Half Sovereigns, loose bullion type

Until recently, the 1982 Half Sovereign was the only non-proof coin and continues to trade at approximately bullion value. In 2000 the Royal Mint started issuing non-proof half sovereigns and have done so each year since. The 2000 to 2007 half sovereigns tend to trade from about £190 to £210 (based on the bullion value at the time of writing). The 1989 and 2002 shield reverse coins and the St. George 2005 coin are the most popular.

Half Sovereigns, cased proof type

Year	Description	Price
1979		£275.00
1980		£275.00
1981		£275.00
1982		£275.00
1983		£275.00
1984		£275.00
1985		£275.00
1986		£275.00
1987		£275.00
1988		£275.00
1989	500th Anniversary of the Sovereign reverse	£550.00
1990		£275.00
1991		£275.00
1992		£275.00
1993		£275.00
1994		£275.00
1995		£275.00
1996		£275.00
1997		£275.00
1998		£275.00
1999		£275.00
2000		£275.00
2001		£300.00
2002	Shield reverse	£300.00
2003		£275.00
2004		£275.00
2005	Alternate St. George reverse	£280.00
2006		£275.00
2007		£275.00
2008 to 2013	(2012 had alternate St George reverse type)	£275.00
2014 and 2015		£280.00
2016 and 2017		£280.00
2017 and 2018		£300.00

Quarter Sovereigns

Introduced in 2009 as a made-up denomination (quarter of a sovereign is a crown, isn't it?) - they seem to sell for £90 - £150, both bullion and proof issue.

1980	10,000	£5, £2, Sovereign (£1), 1/2 Sovereign	£4,200.00
1981	-	Set containing 9 coins including silver Crown	no data
1982	2,500	£5, £2, Sovereign (£1), 1/2 Sovereign	£4,400.00
1983		£2, Sovereign (£1), 1/2 Sovereign	£1,700.00
1984	7,095	£5, Sovereign (£1), 1/2 Sovereign	£2,800.00
1985	5,849	£5, £2, Sovereign (£1), 1/2 Sovereign	£4,200.00
1986	12,000	£2 Commonwealth Games, Sovereign (£1), 1/2 Sovereign	no data
1987	12,500	£2, Sovereign (£1), 1/2 Sovereign	£1,800.00
1988	12,500	£2, Sovereign (£1), 1/2 Sovereign	£1,800.00
1989	5,000	£5, £2, Sovereign (£1), 1/2 Sovereign (Anniversary reverse)	£7,000.00
	7,936	£2, Sovereign (£1), 1/2 Sovereign (Anniversary reverse)	£5,000.00
1990	1,721	£5, £2, Sovereign (£1), 1/2 Sovereign	£4,200.00
	1,937	£2, Sovereign (£1), 1/2 Sovereign	£1,700.00
1991	1,336	£5, £2, Sovereign (£1), 1/2 Sovereign	£4,300.00
	1,152	£2, Sovereign (£1), 1/2 Sovereign	£1,800.00
1992	1,165	£5, £2, Sovereign (£1), 1/2 Sovereign	£4,300.00
	967	£2, Sovereign (£1), 1/2 Sovereign	£1,800.00
1993	1,078	£5, £2, Sovereign (£1), 1/2 Sovereign (Pistrucci medallion)	£4,400.00
	663	£2, Sovereign (£1), 1/2 Sovereign	£1,900.00
1994	918	£5, £2 (Bank of England), Sovereign (£1), 1/2 Sovereign	£4,400.00
	1,249	£2 (Bank of England), Sovereign (£1), 1/2 Sovereign	£1,800.00
1995	718	£5, £2 (Dove of Peace), Sovereign (£1), 1/2 Sovereign	£4,400.00
	1,112	£2 (Dove of Peace), Sovereign (£1), 1/2 Sovereign	£1,800.00
1996	742	£5, £2, Sovereign (£1), 1/2 Sovereign	£4,500.00
	868	£2, Sovereign (£1), 1/2 Sovereign	£1,800.00
1997	860	£5, £2 (bi-metallic), Sovereign (£1), 1/2 Sovereign	£4,300.00
	817	£2 (bi-metallic), Sovereign (£1), 1/2 Sovereign	£1,800.00
1998	789	£5, £2, Sovereign (£1), 1/2 Sovereign	£4,300.00
	560	£2, Sovereign (£1), 1/2 Sovereign	£1,400.00
1999	991	£5, £2 (Rugby World Cup), Sovereign (£1), 1/2 Sovereign	£4,300.00
	912	£2 (Rugby World Cup), Sovereign (£1), 1/2 Sovereign	£1,800.00
2000	1,000	£5, £2, Sovereign (£1), 1/2 Sovereign	£4,300.00
	1,250	£2, Sovereign (£1), 1/2 Sovereign	£1,800.00

2017 Sovereign - a reproduced version of the original
sovereign reverse (1817 - 1820) was used to mark the
200th anniversary of the sovereign.

2001	1,000	£5, £2 (Marconi), Sovereign (£1), 1/2 Sovereign	£4,400.00
	891	£2 (Marconi), Sovereign (£1), 1/2 Sovereign	£1,900.00
2002	3,000	£5, £2, Sovereign (£1), 1/2 Sovereign (Shield reverse)	£4,400.00
	3,947	£2, Sovereign (£1), 1/2 Sovereign.(Shield reverse)	£1,900.00
2003	2,250	£5, £2, Sovereign (£1), 1/2 Sovereign	£4,400.00
	1,717	£2 (DNA), Sovereign (£1), 1/2 Sovereign	£1,900.00
2004	2,250	£5, £2, Sovereign (£1), 1/2 Sovereign	£4,400.00
	2,500	£2, £1 (Forth Bridge), 1/2 Sovereign	£1,900.00
2005	1,500	£5, £2, Sovereign (£1), 1/2 Sovereign	£4,400.00
	2,500	£2, Sovereign (£1), 1/2 Sovereign	£1,900.00
2006	1,750	£5, £2, Sovereign (£1), 1/2 Sovereign	£4,400.00
	1,750	£2, Sovereign (£1), 1/2 Sovereign	£1,900.00
2007		Sovereign, 1/2 Sovereign	£900.00
	700	£2, Sovereign, 1/2 Sovereign	£1,900.00
2008		Sovereign, 1/2 Sovereign	£900.00
		£5, £2, Sovereign, 1/2 Sovereign	£4,400.00
		£2, Sovereign, 1/2 Sovereign	£1,900.00
2009		£5, £2, Sovereign, 1/2 Sovereign and new 1/4 Sovereign	£4,400.00
		£2, Sovereign, 1/2 Sovereign and new 1/4 Sovereign	£1,900.00
2010		£5, £2, Sovereign, 1/2 Sovereign, 1/4 Sovereign	£4,500.00
		Sovereign, 1/2 Sovereign, 1/4 Sovereign	£1,000.00
		'Premium' set, 3 coins as above	£1,200.00

Values of later sets are similar. They are a lot more expensive when bought new.

Based on a tradition dating back to the 12th century, every year on Maundy Thursday (the day before Good Friday), the monarch distributes leather pouches of special coins to selected people in a Royal Ceremony. The number of recipients is equal to the age of the monarch, as is the value of the coins in each pouch.

All Maundy coinage issued under the reign of Queen Elizabeth II carries the same obverse portrait, that of the first bust of the Queen used on coins and designed by Mary Gillick. On decimalisation day in 1971 the Maundy coins were re-valued from old pence to new pence.

Prices listed here are for complete sets in official Royal Mint cases, which became standard in the 1960s. Commencing in 1989, the coins are individually encapsulated within the case.

1971	1,018	Tewkesbury Abbey	£190.00
1972	1,026	York Minster	£200.00
1973	1,004	Westminster Abbey	£190.00
1974	1,042	Salisbury Cathedral	£190.00
1975	1,050	Peterborough Cathedral	£190.00
1976	1,158	Hereford Cathedral	£190.00
1977	1,138	Westminster Abbey	£190.00
1978	1,178	Carlisle Cathedral	£190.00
1979	1,188	Winchester Cathedral	£190.00
1980	1,198	Worcester Cathedral	£190.00
1981	1,178	Westminster Abbey	£190.00
1982	1,218	St. David's Cathedral, Dyfed	£190.00
1983	1,228	Exeter Cathedral	£190.00
1984	1,238	Southwell Minster	£190.00
1985	1,248	Ripon Cathedral	£190.00
1986	1,378	Chichester Cathedral	£150.00
1987	1,390	Ely Cathedral	£140.00
1988	1,402	Lichfield Cathedral	£140.00
1989	1,353	Birmingham Cathedral	£140.00
1990	1,523	Newcastle Cathedral	£140.00
1991	1,384	Westminster Abbey	£140.00
1992	1,424	Chester Cathedral	£140.00
1993	1,440	Wells Cathedral	£140.00
1994	1,433	Truro Cathedral	£140.00
1995	1,466	Coventry Cathedral	£150.00
1996	1,629	Norwich Cathedral	£150.00
1997	1,786	Bradford Cathedral	£150.00
1998	1,654	Portsmouth Cathedral	£150.00
1999	1,676	Bristol Cathedral	£150.00
2000	1,684	Lincoln Cathedral	£150.00
2000	13,180	silver proof set, (also included in the "Millennium Proof Set")	£150.00
2001	1,706	Westminster Abbey	£150.00
2002	1,678	Canterbury Cathedral	£150.00

2002	2,002	gold proof set, taken from special "Golden Jubilee Proof Set".	£1,100.00
2003		Gloucester Cathedral	£150.00
2004		Liverpool (Anglican) Cathedral	£150.00
2005		Wakefield Cathedral	£150.00
2006		Guildford Cathedral	£150.00
2007		Manchester Cathedral	
2008		St. Patrick's Cathedral, Armagh	
2009		St. Edmundsbury Cathedral, Suffolk	
2010		Derby Cathedral	
2011		Westminster Abbey	
2012		York Minster	
2013		Christ Church Cathedral, Oxford	
2014		Blackburn Cathedral	
2015		Sheffield Cathedral, South Yorkshire	
2016		St Georges Chapel, Windsor	
2017		Leicester Cathedral	
2018		St Georges Chapel, Windsor	
2019		St Georges Chapel, Windsor	
2020		Cancelled. Coins were sent out in the post.	
2021		Cancelled. Coins were sent out in the post.	
2022		St Georges Chapel, Windsor (Prince Charles, representing the Queen)	
2023		York Minster (King Charles III)	
2024		Worcester Cathedral (Queen Camilla representing the King)	

ERROR COINS

Error coins have always been very hard to value. It is true for any coin, but is particularly valid for most error coins, in that they really are worth what someone is willing to pay for them, as by their very nature they are often unique. Other error types exist in larger numbers (e.g. the 2008 mule 20p, 1983 NEW PENCE 2p etc) and for those the demand for them sets the value.

See checkyourchange.co.uk for an introduction on error coins, the most comprehensive list of UK decimal error coins (over 400) with many images showing some quite extreme examples.

The Cover.

The cover of this edition shows the King for the first time. The green background colour represents hope and also nature. The coin images are the new Charles III definitives which represent the four nations of the UK and the natural world.